HEADLINE

Dear Damien,

I enclose, as requested, the most recent proof pages complete with my notes and yours. We are very nearly there, I feel, but I would still like you to at least consider (or re-consider) some of my suggestions. I got the impression during our most recent telephone chat that you were a little distressed by some of my thoughts as you said that you found my behaviour 'meddlesome'. Please believe me when I say that I really do not wish to meddle. Anything that I have written in the margin is a suggestion, and not an order. That said, they are not suggestions that I have made 'purely for the sake of it'. I really want this book, as I'm sure that you do, to be the absolute best that it can be. I know it is a cliché, but sometimes less really is more and if you were able to see your way to excising some of those paragraphs that I strongly feel are a little extraneous then I really do feel that the final book would benefit. That said, all of these decisions are of course yours to make. It's your book, it's your life and it's your name on the cover.

May I took this opportunity to say that it's been a real pleasure to work with you on this book. Thank you for being so hard-working, diligent and forthright. It is an experience that I shall never forget. I won't see you at the launch, I'm afraid, as by then I will have commenced my year long sabbatical from the publishing industry, but I hope that it goes very well indeed and that the caterers are able to source those olives that you have so regularly described to our events team.

Best wishes,

Roger Mills

Roger Mills

Headline Publishing Group
020 3122 7222
enquiries@headline.co.uk

Registered
Carmelite House
50 Victoria Embankment
London EC4Y 0DZ
www.headline.co.uk

DAMIEN TRENCH

egg &
soldiers

A childhood memoir

as told to MILES JUPP

HEADLINE

First published in 2017
by HEADLINE PUBLISHING GROUP

1

Cataloguing in Publication Data is available from the British Library

hardback ISBN 9781472239914

Ebook ISBN 9781472239921

Typeset in Palatino by Palimpsest Book Production Limited,
Falkirk, Stirlingshire

Printed and bound in Great Britain by
Clays Ltd, St Ives plc

Headline's policy is to use papers that are natural, renewable and
recyclable products and made from wood grown in sustainable forests.
The logging and manufacturing processes are expected to conform to
the environmental regulations of the country of origin.

HEADLINE PUBLISHING GROUP
An Hachette UK Company
Carmelite House
50 Victoria Embankment
London
EC4Y 0DZ

www.headline.co.uk
www.hachette.co.uk

For my mother

CONTENTS

INTRODUCTION

I am not really sure if I one should think of this book as a *memoir* or rather just as *memories*. Even if a biographical account tells *all* the stories, can it ever tell the *whole* story? I'm not sure that I can say, to be honest. You'd have to ask Ben Pimlott or some such. Peter Ackroyd, perhaps.

I also feel duty-bound at this early juncture to state – utterly categorically – that it was absolutely not my idea to pen this volume. Though I have always been as honest and candid as circumstances and time constraints would allow, a plain speaker if you will, and always been willing to share with my readership certain aspects of my home life and backstory, it would simply never have occurred to me in a million years to think that the reading public would have even the slightest interest in an entirely auto-biographical volume from yours truly. I live a simple and ordinary life, governed by sparseness and sparsity, just quietly getting on with whatever needs to be done and trying to avoid, where possible, fuss of any kind. I always feel deeply uncomfortable when I am the centre of atten-tion. When my book *A Year in the Kitchen* won Book of the Year at the 2011 Culinary Literature Awards (in asso-ciation with BBC Radio 4), I took to the stage at this most lavish of events and found myself standing at the podium unable to say anything at all. So utterly surprised and taken aback was I to be announced as the winner of this most prestigious and highly coveted award that a whole three minutes of wild applause had to pass before I was finally able to humbly assert that the invited audience's standing ovation was completely unnecessary and then begin to read out my prepared speech.

Instead, the initial idea for this book came – as so many of the best ideas I hear of do – from my literary agent, Ian Frobisher. Ian really is everything that you would wish a literary agent to be: kind, thoughtful, encouraging, thankfully no longer drinking and a recent convert to yoga. 'I think you should write about your childhood, Damo,' he told me. 'The people want to know all about you. I know I do.'

'Ian,' I told him, 'I'm really not so sure they do. "The people" want me to tell them what best to do with their apricots. And I am more than happy to oblige.'

'That too, that too. But what about the man underneath all that fruit and stuff? Let him out. I've suggested it to your publisher and they sounded keen as mustard.'

He then *very* briefly outlined some discussions that he had had with them about enormous advances and so forth, but I very rarely pay any heed to that sort of thing so I just listened really intently and let it all wash over me. The gist of what he was saying, I could tell, was that once the publishers had heard the idea, they had started absolutely begging for it. Ian's phone was ringing day and night, he said. Publishers kept sending him bottles of champagne and flowers, and Ian kept having them couriered straight around to my house. We almost had a vase crisis. The only way to stop these overtures, it seemed, was just to admit defeat, sit down and write the ruddy thing. This, then, is precisely why we find ourselves where we are. The publishers have spoken. We must not ignore the will of the publishers.

It is, of course, a terribly humbling thing to be asked to open up about one's early life like this. I am not, by nature, especially self-reflective and nor do I have any particular penchant for dwelling on the past. Thus I have spent the past few months while I have been writing this in a state that psychologists would describe as 'completely out of my comfort zone'. The journey that I have been on in that time has been not a little nerve-wracking. Writing autobiography is a massive responsibility. Almost but not quite, in fact, a burden. But please, I beg of you, spare me your sympathies and suspend your critical faculties. I am a cookery writer, not a biographer, and so hope not to be judged by such standards. I like to imagine that if Antonia Fraser suddenly decided to write a book about aubergines and the many wonderful things that you can do with and indeed to them, that you'd be kind enough to give her a gentle ride. I hope, therefore, that you could see your way to giving me one.

What I have attempted to do is to lay down not just those stories that are, to me at least, the most vivid of my early years, but also those that I feel have had – and in some cases continue to have – the most profound effect on me. It would be lovely to say that writing a book like this is easy, but actually it isn't. It's agony at times. It's extraordinary too not only what the mind has allowed itself to forget but also what it has forced itself to remember. It is also amazing how different some of my recollections are to those of my friends and family. My mother, for example, insists that she taught me to make a roux. I do not have the skill to persuade her otherwise, but the truth as I recall it is that I learnt it from a book. If I'd only ever learnt to make a roux from my mother then I wouldn't have ever learnt that the flour really has to be cooked, and thus my sauce (like, I am sad to relate, so many of my dear mother's) would never have held. That's not a criticism of my mother, by the way. It is an observation of her cooking style and reportage of a difference of opinion. Of which we have several. She uses supermarkets, for instance, and resolutely refuses to use a Bag for Life. (I looked behind her fridge the other day. It was like a landfill site.) She has also described self-checkouts as 'a good thing', which despite being unusually open-minded of her, strikes me as being completely unconscious of the wider economic impacts of their emergence, and unsympathetic to the inevitably damaged morale of the supermarket workforce, but there we are. I doubt very much that she would like to be given a health check-up by a robot, so I am not at all sure why she is happy to have her courgettes weighed by one.

This book has been written, it goes almost but not quite

without saying, for YOU. I have always valued my readers, and I hope I always will. I know that this book is about ME, but it is YOU who I have been thinking of when I have been writing it. It is YOU who I am seeking to inform, to surprise, for whom I seek to elucidate. It is YOU with whom I am sharing the good and the bad, the highs and the lows, the delicious and the rather less so. It is YOU in whom I am confiding. When I have been sitting slumped and weary in front of my laptop, so whacked out by it all that I have barely been able to put finger to button to continue, it is only by thinking about YOU that I have been able to pick up my sword and soldier on with the text. When I have been lying awake at night unable to sleep it is YOU who I have been thinking of. When I have stepped into the shower every morning it is YOU I think of first. (The same thing happens in the bath of an evening too, by the way.) It is YOU I was thinking about only the other morning when my partner Anthony and I were waiting at some traffic lights and he asked me what it was I was ruminating about. 'THEM,' I told him. By which I meant 'YOU'. It is, after all, YOU who I ultimately wish to please.

But though I have been thinking about YOU, and writing this book I hope entirely for YOUR benefit, I have also undoubtedly benefited myself. I have had to revisit parts of my life that I haven't thought about for years. I've thought about things that I didn't even know I remembered. I've remembered things that I didn't even know that I knew. Some things that I thought I knew, it turned out that I didn't. And some things that I only *thought* I knew, I now know I really did know. Which was a bit of a relief.

Undoubtedly, I have been able to lay a certain number of childhood traumas to rest.

'Has it been cathartic?' Ian asked when I handed him the first draft.

'Unbelievably so,' I replied. 'And I've learnt so much.'

'What about?' he asked.

'Me,' I said.

And I have. But, just to be clear, I've done it for YOU.

Damien Trench, Queen's Park, 2017

Chapter 1
THE BEGINNING

Damien, do you think we should call this bit THE BEGINNING? Because I'm not sure that it really is.

I'm clearing my throat. Easing them in. Don't rush me. Or I shall panic. I've thought of a very clever way to make it clear when I'm really beginning.

So then. Where to start? No place like the present, as far as I'm concerned. And I have just had one of those absolutely mad mornings when you pop out of the house only intending to have a quick perusal of some clay tagines, and somehow end up coming home a full two hours later with nothing to show for your travels and indeed travails but a brand new gas ring expander. I think I was probably as surprised as anybody. But then sometimes life is just like that, isn't it? We are none of us truly in control of our destiny and I considered it in no way a wasted morning.

Inspiration really can strike at the most unexpected moments. I once dashed out of a Franco Zeffirelli retrospective at our really rather excellent local independent arts cinema and made kulebyaka for eight. If you can find rhyme or reason in such an action then you are, I think it is only fair to say, a far better man than I. It was, by the way, delicious. If I made it again – and I quite seriously think that I might – then I would consider adding very slightly more dill and I would perhaps go out of my way to find a bigger onion. It would also be sensible to cook such a thing at a time when there were seven other people about to help me eat it. But despite these findings, I was perfectly happy with the results. I may have to wait for another day to see *Young Toscanini* on a big screen, but at least I know that I have it in me to produce a seriously good Russian pie on a whim.

It is so vitally important to listen to one's instincts, I always think. I once asked our builder Mr Mullaney if he wouldn't mind painting our downstairs loo for us. Mr Mullaney has often insisted, modestly, that interior decorating and building really are completely different skillsets and that both jobs are best left to their respective specialists, and I can see where he's coming from – up to a point – but I've noticed many times over the years that painting walls is actually something that the man has a real flair for, and that he owes it to himself – if no one else – to be more confident in that regard. He has a wonderful, gentle touch, is equally impressive with either brush or roller, and is (without wishing to smother him with praise) perfectly capable of painting one's smaller rooms.[1]

Anyway, I made him an espresso, begged him a little, and dangled the possibility of a mid-to-late-afternoon dark chocolate and spelt flour brownie in front of him (the poor – and indeed Irish, have I mentioned this? – man is a coeliac; an affliction that he bears with considerable – and indeed I would quite honestly go so far as to say *characteristic* – fortitude). The end result was that he very graciously accepted the brief, and agreed to put his excellent brush skills to use. I chose a rather vivid electric blue

1 He's also a very good plasterer – something often considered a bit of a 'dark art' by those in the know.

that had absolutely leapt out at me in a chalk paint shop that had recently opened in our area, and the good man set to work. When it had dried, I took one look at it and realised – instinctively – that I in fact preferred it the way it had been before, several shades lighter. Mr Mullaney painted it again, and life went on.

The point is, I had listened to and obeyed my instincts, and I haven't once regretted the entire episode for even an instant. My partner Anthony came home later that evening and wouldn't have even guessed, until I told him, that our downstairs lavatory had been out of action owing to works for much of the day. He couldn't even smell the fresh paint. But then again, how could he have? The whole house, downstairs lavatory included, was absolutely filled with the scent of my jumbo batch of dark chocolate, spelt-flour brownies. Sadly, Mr Mullaney didn't ultimately have a chance to sample them, as he left slightly earlier than usual as the result of a headache – provenance unknown. So yes, instinct: a wonderful tool that we would all be, I am quite convinced, absolutely lost without and some-thing that one should always rely on, quite irrespective of its outcome. If I hadn't thought that the downstairs lavatory might benefit from being a different colour then I would never have made the brownies, and they put Anthony, I can tell you, into a rather wonderful mood.

Anyway, it'll soon be time to prepare lunch, and so I had better put down my pen, don my apron and do something semi-daring with some tomatoes.

Chapter 2

THE REAL BEGINNING

So when was I born? And where? To *whom* was I born, and was I a natural birth or did I emerge as the result of a caesarean? Let us leave those questions for the moment, and think instead about the sort of world that I was born into.

I have lived in fascinating times. That much is for sure. I have not, however, always necessarily been aware of the times at the time, if that makes sense. And I think it does. Because we are all of us aware of the same things in different ways. Some of us see the big picture, others only see things close up. I tend to focus on those things in the margins, to seek comfort in the peripheries. For instance, I recall the day that Mrs Thatcher resigned chiefly because I attempted to make a tiramisu that didn't set. In my naivety and innocence I simply hadn't beaten the yolks and sugar anything like hard enough, and thus in a way my tiramisu was as much doomed in the beginning as Mrs Thatcher was in the end.

I was very upset about the tiramisu, and cried for some time. My mother was also in tears, but in her case the tears were for the end of the reign of Britain's first female Prime Minister, and not because I had wasted so many eggs and sponge fingers. I can remember her standing by the oven in our kitchen surrounded by our chipped blue Formica units dabbing the corners of her eyes with a tea towel advertising Bushell's Blue Label. Through the window behind her I could see my father outside on the patio performing a sort of dance, somewhere between a jig and lindy hop. I can remember those details, but I couldn't tell you the date. Not without looking it up. (It turns out it was 22 November 1990 that Mrs Thatcher resigned. If it was November that means it would have been dark by the time I was back from school and cooking. I only remember now that the reason that I could see my father out in the garden at all was that he was lighting fireworks.)

I can picture that kitchen in Willesden, north-west London, so very clearly. The aforementioned cupboards, the dining table that was slightly too big, the built-in oven (Hitachi). There was a boiler in what should have been a fireplace with a chrome pipe coming out of it, that a plastic bag had melted against long ago and which drove my mother and me wild. Nothing would shift it. We tried pretty much every commercial multi-surface cleaner on the market, and all to no effect. We tried paint stripper. Even bleach. My sister, not untypically, thought that the problem might be solved by taking a hammer to it. It could not.

I have always been fascinated by my surroundings – the sights, the smells, the sounds, the tastes. Sitting at my antique desk for the first time, for instance, I could only begin to write once I had taken the time to study its surface, to take in its colour. What had been the causes behind the scratches and lines upon it; what stories did they tell? Who had sat there before me? Did they perhaps write novels or love letters upon this desk? Or had they simply taken the opportunity to crack on with a bit of light admin? Who can say? All I know is that my attention to detail when it comes to my immediate surroundings means that the bigger picture has sometimes escaped my attention. In my life there has been the fall of the Berlin Wall, the Beirut hostage crisis, the assassination of the Ceausescus, the 9/11 attacks, the break-up of the Soviet Union – and I have to say I can't really remember a great deal about them, other perhaps than what I was doing at the time. Probably cooking. Or reading. Or writing. Or just having a bit of a think, which is no bad thing. Unless one's thoughts turn dark. And then the next thing you know you're staring at a blank wall, or the sea, or a disused railway line and there's an empty bottle and a half-eaten simnel cake beside you and some pages that have been torn from a diary and ripped up. But that sort of thing is very rare. Thankfully.

I was born in the 1970s. I would love to be more specific than that, but I am afraid that my alert consciousness of the ever-burgeoning threat of identity theft prohibits me from so doing. The last thing I want to do is to commit private details to print and then find that my identity is being used by somebody else to do online shopping[1] or

1 I hate online shopping partly because of the enormous – possibly irreparable – damage that it has done to small, local traders and also because I find it simply impossible to

perhaps even help them spy for an enemy power. I'm actually pretty aghast at the thought of being dragged into some sort of international espionage scandal. I am, of course, completely aware that the security and intelligence services of all nations feel that they have a job to do (with, I must say, wildly varying degrees of justification) but I would rather that they got on with it without my involvement. Frankly I would much rather be kept in the dark about such things anyway so that I can get on with more important matters such as working out what on earth to do with a cabbage glut.[2]

---

remember passwords. My partner Anthony very kindly remembers them for me, although he did once change all of them to 'forgetfulcookerywriter', which I thought was brutal and unnecessary. He does goad me sometimes.

2 I was inspired to tackle this cabbage conundrum head on as a result of a large number of my friends getting in touch with me over the winter period to tell me that they kept being given cabbages in their vegetable boxes, and were unsure what on earth to do with the things. Cabbages are very much the iceberg lettuce of the vegetable world; the sort of thing that one sometimes can't help look at with anything other than a sense of impending doom. I know a lot of people who just put them, untouched, straight into their compost bins and I can see why. But there are alternatives. Cabbage leaves fried in butter are absolutely delicious, and I know that it's not everybody's cup of tea but you can do a lot worse than making sauerkraut. All you need is a jar, some caraway seeds and black peppercorns – perhaps even an onion if you're so minded – and then a spare four weeks in which to allow it to ferment. If you like eating smoked sausages with mustard (and, frankly, who doesn't?), then I can assure you that your digestive system will be extremely grateful for the addition of this sort of roughage. Or, if you've not got four weeks to spare, shred the cabbage as finely as

Nevertheless, I wouldn't want you to come away from this book with the idea that I'm paranoid, so I'm also happy to say that I was born nearer to the end of the seventies than their beginning. That's your lot, I'm afraid.

I was born (via natural birth) in the maternity wing of a hospital in Dollis Hill, north-west London that has long since been turned into luxury flats. It happened, I am told, in the middle of a most blustery night after a fourteen-hour labour. My mother, Janet, resisted all drugs and probably even all advice but out I eventually slid and, by all accounts, took to the breast *immediately*. My father, Sam, was there and my sister, Angela, was at home being watched over by a friend of my parents. She took, as older siblings used to being the centre of attention often do, an instant dislike to me almost as soon as I was brought home from hospital and commenced a campaign of violence against me that lasted for many years and resulted in countless visits to doctors and, on one occasion, a child psychologist. A few years later, I had a baby brother, Ralph, and he too was, completely unprovoked, extremely aggressive towards me. His behaviour was somewhat less nuanced than my sister's, whose behaviour, though cruel, was admirably creative.

My earliest memory is of standing on a little stool in

---

you dare and then sauté it in white wine and oil with a few raisins in and possibly some seeds of your choice. Might I humbly suggest fennel? Lovely with a bit of pork and a glass of white wine chilled to the point of being glacial. Hope that helps.

my bedroom. I had a decorative plate on the wall – some sort of agricultural scene if I recall correctly, hay thrashing possibly. The plate was held up by a wire hanger, and hanging by a loop of ribbon from one of the little arms that protruded from underneath it was a birthday card cut in the shape of the number two. I was reaching up and tugging at the little card when my sister appeared from nowhere and shoved me extremely hard. I teetered for what seemed like an age and then, grabbing hold of the card in an attempt to steady my fall, I pulled it and the plate off the wall and fell down off the stool. As a result of my sister's version of events – I was, on account of my age and my injuries, completely incoherent – my parents held me responsible for what happened.

With hindsight I do not blame my sister for this. She saw an opportunity to get away with something and so she took it. But possibly as a result of this I have always been incredibly sensitive to any false accusations. A few years ago a lady sent me a very angry letter indeed about a recipe of mine in a newspaper. Despite it being a Southern Indian dish (involving lamb shanks), I had – possibly a little unconventionally – advocated the inclusion of a couple of spoons of harissa paste which is, of course, North African. For reasons I have never fully understood, newspaper sub-editors have a tendency to edit recipes that I submit rather heavily, cutting out what they wrongly suppose to be extraneous information or anecdote. In this instance 'a couple of spoons from a tube of harissa paste' had been shortened to 'a couple of tubes of harissa paste'.

This furious lady had, as a result of this act of journalistic vandalism, been on the receiving end of an absolutely appalling and at times savage digestive experience. So too, it transpired, had several of her guests, many of whom – including some prominent members of her local council's planning committee and somebody involved in storylining the once popular television soap *Brookside* – had continued to suffer from agitated bowels for several days after, as she went on to explain in somewhat graphic detail.

I could understand her anger, but I certainly could not fully understand why she was directing it at me. Surely people occasionally taste as they go when they are cooking to ensure that things haven't become tangy to the point of being unpalatable? I couldn't believe that at some point in the five-hour cooking process she wouldn't have had a little taste of the stuff just out of idle curiosity. She might not have been able to save the dish, but she would certainly have been able to save her guests from the distressing litany of cramps and convulsions with which they were all racked for what sounded like the best part of a working week.

Nor could I understand why, given that the dish must have been impossibly hot, they had contrived to polish off the entire thing. Was it bravado? Stupidity? Perhaps it was simply good manners. I suppose we have all been in the position of not wanting to offend a dinner party host who we know to have been slaving over a hot stove for hours, occasionally claiming to have a migraine so that we can excuse ourselves instantly, or pretending to be a social smoker so that we can nip out to the garden and have a quiet retch.

Anyway, I replied to the lady and told her that although I had every sympathy with her situation it was, alas, not I who was at fault, but the sub-editor responsible for maiming my copy. This did nothing to quell her anger. So a few days later the sub-editor and I found ourselves on a train heading for Humberside where I had agreed to cook for the lady in question by way of an apology. The sub-editor was an apologetic enough fellow, but by no means a serviceable sous-chef. I had assumed that the lady in question would ask us to dine with her, but in fact she made us stay in the kitchen and treated us as staff while she and her friends ate in the dining room, a most unsatisfactory arrangement. I imagined that she might at some point acknowledge that I was not at fault, whilst still accepting our apologies. In fact, as soon as we'd finished the washing up we were ushered out of the house with the words 'I hope you've learnt your lesson' and forced to trudge off despairingly in the direction of the Ibis. The newspaper in question had to pick up the tab for the whole thing, and is now in serious financial trouble. I cannot pretend that I wasn't irked by the experience at the time, but thankfully I am completely and utterly over it now.

At the time of my birth, my mother worked for various charity groups and my father was a structural engineer, but they rarely spoke about work when they were at home. Besides, I was a baby, so even if they had spoken about it, I imagine that I would have understood very little. (Not that I understood little for long, you understand. My verbal skills came along at an absolute pace and I had, almost from the off, a very advanced reading age. I read Olivia Manning's *Balkan Trilogy* at the age of seven. Loved it.) Still, I think they both found what they did rewarding; the mortgage was paid, and there was always meat in the refrigerator. And sometimes the freezer too, which I am not keen on. If I knew then what I knew now – and had been able to articulate it – I would have tried to convey to them that freezing meat is not remotely sensible behaviour and as well as limiting the flavour does irreparable harm to the texture. It's to do with enzymes. But then, isn't everything?

My parents, both originally from the north – my father from Yorkshire and my mother from Northumbria – met as students at the University of Bangor, where the 1960s seemed to pass them by completely. They were, however, contemporaries of Roger Whittaker, and my father has an awful lot of anecdotes about his whistling. Nevertheless, it sounded as if they had been very happy there, and regularly took the opportunity to explore the country and the coastline in an Austin 1100 that my father had spent all his savings on. They got engaged on the promenade at Llanfairfechan on a hot day in 1963 and celebrated with ice creams.

These days my mother avoids dairy altogether. Something to do with her bowels.

Chapter 3

AN EDUCATION

I started going to a nursery school at the age of three. Or possibly two. Four perhaps? Isn't it funny how it can sometimes be so very difficult to remember these sort of details, and yet so incredibly easy to recall others? (Maybe it isn't at all funny. Maybe it's infuriating and indicative of some sort of degenerative condition from which I am suffering. Perhaps it's age?)*

So though I cannot remember my exact age when I started going to nursery school, I could easily describe to you in great detail every single garment I was wearing, including briefs. But just because I can remember such details, it doesn't mean that I am compelled to prove it to you by sharing such details. My briefs are my business and mine alone.[1]

* Damien, I wonder if it might be better just thinking about these sorts of things rather than actually writing them down?

I'm giving a voice to my fears. Is that wrong? You do remind me though: I probably ought to start taking a cod liver oil supplement.

1 Well, apart from my partner Anthony, obviously. And a girl called Jennifer who occasionally irons for us. Not that she irons my underwear – that would be an extraordinary pernickety activity. Not that they would be complex articles to iron in any way whatsoever – they aren't pleated or brocaded or anything like that. I simply mean that the ironing of underwear – be they briefs or trunks (and as I say I reserve the right to hold such information back from you. Although I certainly don't mind telling you that they are definitely not Y-fronts – if they're even a single size too snug, you can find

19

What I am more than happy to share with you, however, is the sort of shoes I was wearing: Start-rite sandals were practically *de rigeur* in those days, certainly in the circles in which I moved. I've always found there to be something very cheery about the Start-rite logo – that of two children, dressed for winter, walking not so much hand-in-hand as arm-in-arm. It's a boy on the left, and a girl on the right. I've always assumed – and I dare say that I am by no means alone in this – that they are supposed to be brother and sister, but they could just be good friends. Or cousins, perhaps. I used to find it a rather aspirational image, but when we were young, my sister would never take my hand. She doesn't take it now, either, come to think of it, but then she has rather less cause to. I could never under-stand why she had this attitude, but my mother said it was something to do with an incident on an ice-rink that my sister has never forgiven me for. Certainly, I've never had particularly good balance, so it's not impossible that on such an outing I might have reached out to her as I was falling and taken her down with me.

These Start-rite sandals were cherry red, with a simple design on the toe that looked as if it had been composed

---

yourself constantly being seized by involuntary grimaces when you're in the process of sitting or standing. If they're too loose, they have a quite dreadful tendency to wrap them-selves around various parts of you, leading to discomfort – possibly even rashes – through overheating, which is abso-lutely not my idea of fun and frankly I'd be rather amazed to hear that it was yours) – as I say, the ironing of underwear is, in my opinion, really quite unnecessary.

by spirograph. They had proper, hand-stitched soles, and each had, on a narrow strap, a single, brass-effect buckle with a circular, shiny (chape)* and a rather delicate prong.

As with much of what I wore, they were hand-me-downs from my sister and I loved them. I wish I could say that they eventually wore out, but the sad truth is that the leather on the strap snapped just below the buckle when I got my left foot stuck whilst attempting to clamber (irreverently in retrospect) on the cannon outside the front of the Imperial War Museum. People who saw me blubbing around the museum that afternoon must have assumed that it was for our war dead that I wept (and of course I sometimes do) but on that occasion it was all about the demise of those beautiful Start-rites.

'Tiny Steps' Nursery was an absolutely wonderful place. It was a very large building, taking up three Queen Anne-style villas, about two-thirds of the way up Throckton Avenue, an incredibly steep road in that little bit of north-west London that is never quite sure if it's Barnet or Brent and which had a gradient of about one in three. I had cause to walk up it recently en route to a Moroccan wholesaler that a friend of mine had been (quite rightly) raving about (I just resisted the urge to pick up a *couscoussier* on impulse. Had I known they sold cookware, I'd have brought a second Bag for Life. I've already made plans to return to buy myself a *gsaa* and a scented water dispenser, but I think I'll make the trip in a taxi). I couldn't believe that my three-, or two-, or four-year-old legs had been able to carry me up that hill all those years ago. I

* 'Chape'? Is this a spelling mistake?

The chape is part of a buckle. Have it independently verified if you don't believe me.

So it is. Apologies.

Accepted.

21

do a lot of walking these days, but I had to stop twice on the way up and I had stiff calves for days.

Throckton Avenue was, like all the best avenues I often think, tree-lined, and for several months of the year, those trees produced a wonderful pink blossom.

'Pink ice cream!' I used to point at it and say.

'No,' my mother would reply. 'Blossom.'

And on we'd walk, my sister stomping ahead and moaning about us having to drop me off at nursery before we'd dropped her off at school. Actually, it wasn't always my mother who would take us to school; she and my father would usually take it in turns. Very occasionally indeed both parents would take us, which sounds like the most unimaginable fun, doesn't it? But somehow it never was.

You see, my parents walk at very different paces because, despite being of a similar height, they have very different lengths of stride. My father's legs seem to make up nearly half of his total height, whereas my mother's legs somehow make up less than a third. I know this to be the case because she forced us to measure them once during an argument that she and my father were having on the very subject while I was trying to help them pack up some things for a picnic in Gladstone Park. Quite how she compensates for the shortness of her legs over the rest of her height I'm not in a position to say. Her neck is certainly long, but in an elegant rather than freakish manner, so it can't be that. I can only conclude that she must have rather a deceptively long torso, as if she had a particularly extended head I'm sure I would have noticed by now.

The result of all this is that my parents both naturally walk at a pace that the other finds completely dementing. My father struts about like a boy scout on the rampage, whereas my mother moves as if she is being driven by an early prototype for a piston engine, albeit a serene one. If my father walks slowly enough for my mother to keep pace with him he always complains that he feels as if he's going backwards. He pleads with her to walk a little faster but she simply refuses to, as she puts it, 'bustle'. 'Bustling', she has always maintained, 'is ungainly and unnecessary.' So on those rare occasions that both of my parents accompanied us on the walk to our respective schools my father and sister – after bickering and losing patience with us – would be marching furiously ahead whilst my mother and I attempted to keep our cool and glide along at our own happy speed. When my little brother Ralph came along he would run up any hill as a matter of principle, and then wait at the top in order to throw things at us.

My parents have been married for an incredibly long time, but have sadly never managed to reconcile their different rates of ambulatory progress and thus almost never walk anywhere together if it can at all be helped. Sometimes they arrange to meet somewhere at a particular time and walk there separately. Otherwise they go by car, or by bus, or rather less frequently but by no means so rarely that it isn't worth mentioning, by barge. I relate this only because my partner Anthony and I also suffer

Damien, I'm not entirely sure that all of this stuff about walking and legs isn't a little bit de trop?

How so?

It just seems, if you'll forgive me, a little bit extraneous or at least tangential. One minute you're writing about attending nursery school – an account I'm absolutely certain that the readers are desperate to bury themselves in – and the next you're discussing the length of your partner's legs.

Well, I am sorry that you feel that this is extraneous. Anthony's legs are very much a feature of my daily life. As indeed is the rest of him.

Perhaps it could be a footnote?

'Footnote'? Is that a joke?

No. And my point is that whilst the stuff about your parents' legs is, one might argue, part of the childhood narrative here, the discussion of yours and Anthony's adult legs, beautiful a picture as it is, is somewhat less so.

from a considerable stride differential, and yet we have managed to embrace each other's leg lengths very happily. Despite our differences, we have successfully settled on a pace at which we can both walk comfortably side by side, without the need arising for either party to make insulting remarks about the other's suitability for circus work. Admittedly, if Anthony is walking alone then he absolutely powers along, positively tearing up the place, whereas if I am alone I perhaps take the opportunity to have a bit of a potter. A gentle lollop, you might say, but only if you meant it kindly. I don't know why it is that we've been able – perfectly easily and with the minimum of fuss – to arrive at a walking pace that satisfies us both while my parents who have been together four times as long have never managed to. Perhaps we're just the lucky ones, and should take more chances to count our several, if not many, blessings.

I think what I used to find so wonderful about Tiny Steps Nursery was the opportunities that it provided to use one's imagination, and to engage in one's hobbies and interests in an environment that was in no way judge-mental. How unlike, to pluck a completely random example from the ether, modern society. When I first started there, the days were given over almost entirely to play. There was paper, there were crayons, there were musical instruments, there was a beautifully diverse array of dressing-up costumes (my favourite was either the policeman, the auxiliary nurse or, and this might surprise you, the builder. Some days I'd wear all three!) and there

All I can say is, and I'm not sure if you mean to be, that I find this stance somewhat passive-aggressive. But fine. Have it your way. Actually, no. Let's leave it as it is.

were more toys than I had ever seen: cars, dolls, dinosaurs, teddy bears. It was heaven.

As I write I am almost welling up as I vividly recall one particular piece of what modern parlance doubtless describes as 'play equipment'. In my second year at Tiny Steps – perhaps I was four? – I was in a class called 'Parrots'.[2] The classroom for Parrots was at the back of the building, on the first floor. It would once have been a quite fabulous sitting or family room when the building was in its original incarnation as a house, before it required fire doors and a sink in each room and lots of tiny toilets and so forth. It was a very high-ceilinged room as I recall, although it's not absolutely impossible that my memory is playing its usual tricks on me. I was, after all, only perhaps four years old, and thus what I thought of as being high-ceilinged may very well have been quite simply normal-ceilinged. Perhaps it wasn't even normal-ceilinged. Perhaps the ceilings were abnormally low, and I just didn't realise. Perhaps it was a room in which all normal-sized adults were required to stoop just to be able to fit inside, and thus what seemed at the time to be caring and attentive behaviour from the staff was merely necessitated by the room's dimensions. Your guess is as good as mine. It was probably, it being an old house, and all

2 All the classes at Tiny Steps were named after animals, although 'Parrots' is the only one that I can in fact recall. There may well have been one called 'Monkeys', but I'm fairly sure that there wasn't one called 'Badgers'. It just seems very unlikely.

things being considered, somewhere between normal- and high-ceilinged.* But I remember it, as I say, as being high-ceilinged. I do hope that I am painting a clear enough picture for you.

* Damien, are you absolutely wedded to the ceiling stuff? It is perhaps a smidgeon discursive.

I intend it as an extremely honest reflection on the frailties of the human memory, and it absolutely holds its own as a piece of prose on those grounds.

As you wish.

The rooms at the front of the building looked out, as is so often the case, over the street. But the rooms at the back looked out over the garden. Well, over what once would have been a garden, but was now quite definitely a playground. Where once there would have been vege-table and salad patches, there were now patio slabs. Where once there would have been lawn, there was tarmac. Where once there would have been traditional garden furniture, perhaps even a love swing, there were now toys suitable for children – little carts, giant chess, hula hoops.[3]

It wasn't totally without greenery, however. There were

3 I never got the hang of hula hooping. I'm not quite sure why. My hips are, and indeed have always been, perfectly decent ones and I'm capable of moving them in time with most rhythms, even the Latin ones. I love to dance, actually, although Anthony is somewhat less keen. If I'm ever at a wedding and struggling to find him, then I know not to even check the dance floor. Instead, I scan the seating laid out around the dance floor or, if the food's been a bit on the rich side, the lavatories, where he likes to sit in the privacy of the cubicle and read newspaper articles on his phone. He's often content to while away hours in this manner. I am not of this disposition, but then I have always found hand dryers too loud. Anyway, I am yet to master hula hooping and I don't think mastery of it is especially likely to make it on to my bucket list. Unlike, for instance, sharing a pot of tea with the actor James Wilby (star of, amongst others, *Regeneration* and *Gosford Park*. And *Maurice*, lest we forget), which is unques-tionably in my top three.

some tall, splendid trees at the far end, largely of the non-deciduous variety. Personally I prefer my trees deciduous, as I find not being able to follow the passing of the seasons plays absolute havoc with my body clock, but I can understand the need for privacy that such trees allow. There was a set of very small raised beds where pupils were permitted to try their hands at growing carrots and the like, but they always looked a little sandy and dry to me, as if they'd been salted by an invading force. I'm making it sound a little sad and gloomy, this playground, but really it wasn't at all. It was a place of great jolliness, filled with the sounds of play and laughter and abandon. In winter we'd all have to line up in our coats and gloves and hats before we were allowed out there. In spring a jumper would suffice. In summer, if it was incredibly hot, we wouldn't wear clothes out there at all. They'd just put the sprinklers on and we'd all sprint about the place naked, chasing after each other and playing games, blissfully unaware that such behaviour would seem an ethical and pastoral anathema within less than a generation.

We had a fabulous view of the playground in the Parrot Class, as there was the most enormous bay window. When I first arrived in the Parrots, I could barely see over the ledge, but I must have grown an inch or two that winter – maybe I was three, come to think of it? Would that be a sensible age to shoot up two inches over the course of a single season? – because by spring I could definitely see right over it and across the whole playground. And the views of the skies were incredible. There were very few high-rise buildings in that part of London in those days, and you could stand looking out of that window at such an angle as to not be able to see any other buildings at all, just vast expanses of London sky without, seemingly, any London beneath it. I used to love a cloudy day with a definite, but slow, breeze, so that I could stand at the bay window, choose a cloud, and just watch it make its slow progress from one end of the window to the other. Sometimes I used to wish that the wind would suddenly change direction, just so that I could watch the same cloud float back the other way again, but of course it never did. And just as well really, looking back, because in purely meteorological terms such an occurrence would have had unthinkable consequences.

But there were days when I didn't look out over the playground, or up at the skies, or even out of the window at all. Because one day there suddenly arrived – without any great fanfare it must be said, it was just plonked there, and no actual attention was drawn to it – a brand new wooden kitchen set. In a way, I'm probably lucky that the presence of this new playset wasn't trumpeted more, or there would have been an absolute mad rush on the thing, and I would probably not even have had so much as a look-in.[4] But, as it stood, no other child paid the new

4 It is one of the most certain facts of my life that if there is a queue for anything, I will somehow always contrive to find myself at the very back of it. Some people always seem comfortable in a mad scramble, always knowing exactly where to head and making a dash for the appropriate place. Personally I cannot move until a mêlée has evolved into some

wooden kitchen set even the slightest attention. I had the

---

kind of order. That is to say, I cannot conceive of joining a queue until one has actually formed. Order, and I hope I don't sound like a member of the Third Reich when I write this, is actually rather necessary. If anarchy were as good an idea as some like to make out, then I like to think that the movement would probably have got off the ground rather more than it appears to have done. The same is also true, in the West at least, of Communism. And perhaps, even, of what might be termed 'hard-leftism'. That said, I would cheerfully vote for anyone (anyone *at all*) who stood on a platform of renationalisation of the railways. Of all public transport, actually. We simply have to invest more in infrastructure, or Project Great Britain is almost certainly doomed to failure, as I recently somewhat unsuccessfully attempted to explain to a ticket collector who was somewhat unsuccessfully attempting to explain to me the difference between 'off-peak' and 'super off-peak' times. When Christiaan Huygens invented the pendulum clock, there was no mention of such times in the day, so why modern train companies think that they have the right to impose such nonsense upon a system that has worked *perfectly well* for so long I have frankly no answer. And nor, it must be said, did the ticket collector. If one finds oneself in that most wretched and upsetting of situations, that of waiting at a train station when they do not publicly advertise the platform from which one's chosen service is leaving until the very last minute (and why is that I wonder? Do they not know? Or are they keeping it from us? Are they perhaps forcing us to riot as a means of suppressing us? Who's to say?), then I am nearly always the last to board the train and, invariably, find myself without a seat, and thus have to spend the entire journey standing in a vestibule (where one is generally in the way of people needing the lavatory) or perched upon the edge of a luggage rack (which are generally made of metal, and thus one has to contend with a cold bottom). My need for order is one of the very few reasons why I am still prepared to love the post office. I know that some people think that it is the most almighty faff to be told by an automated voice which window thing, gloriously, all to myself. It was a thing of absolute beauty. I did not have the necessary expertise at the time to tell if it had been machine-made or hand-turned, but to me the wood was delightfully smooth and soft to the touch. It was varnished, but only lightly, so as not to seem heavy or hard or sticky. There was a small basin with taps that you could turn. No water came out of them, obviously, as

---

they are to present themselves at, but personally I find it a very useful system. And the machine says 'please'. Despite my fears about robots taking jobs I would far rather be directed by an automated voice than eventually get to the front of the queue, be unsure of where to go, and then have to suffer the indignity of desperately trying to work out for myself which window I should present myself at while a member of staff waves ineffectively at one, and people behind make sarcastic remarks. This is why I am only too happy to still visit post offices rather than – as my partner Anthony has – getting hold of my own franking software and printing out the labels myself. (Anthony did in fact try to demonstrate to me how to operate the system myself, but I didn't think it was anything like as straightforward a thing to do as he did, and before we knew where we were, words were being exchanged, the lid of his laptop had been snapped shut, and we had recommenced an old argument that we'd been keeping on ice since a visit to a temple at Segesta in 2004.) Speaking for myself, I am only too happy to keep using the post office. (Although I shan't be using their passport 'Check and Send' service again, good as it is, as a result of some extremely upsetting remarks made by other customers about the amount of time I was taking up when I was attempting to renew Anthony and my passports in the Salusbury Road branch one lunchtime during the passport backlog crisis of 2014. As I finally left, one elderly lady said 'good riddance' *extremely* loudly, in exactly the same tone of voice one imagines that people might have used when commenting on the fall of Mussolini.)

it had not been plumbed in, but I knew from watching my parents wash up which direction it was necessary to turn a tap in order to open it, and also in which direction to turn a tap in order to close it. I gleefully provided my own sound effects and that little kitchen had excellent water pressure, let me tell you. There was a small drying rack next to the sink, into which you could slot the beautiful little plates that one had pretended to wash and rinse, and a small jar into which you could place utensils to dry. There was a surprisingly generous amount of worktop space for preparation, and a four-ring gas burner (again, and for rather more obvious reasons it must be said, not plumbed in). There was also an oven underneath it into which you could slide roasting tins or baking trays, and which had a beautiful little mechanism which meant that the door closed gently and never slammed. But better than of all this, to my mind, was the food; exquisite wooden representations of all manner of victual, and all so very satisfying to the touch. Vegetables that one might expect to be hard, such as marrows, were wooden. Food that one might expect to be softer, such as broccoli, were rendered in shaped foam. Some items were pre-sliced and then stuck together with little bits of Velcro that came apart easily when any force was placed upon them, so that one could actually experience the sensation of chopping courgettes. It really was the most miraculous bit of kit.

Wonderful as it was to the touch, however, for the eyes it constituted a veritable feast. I had until that point in my life never known that food could have such colours.

The carrots were bright orange, the cucumbers were a rich green. This was all new to me as, for some reason, there was almost no foodstuff that we ate at home that couldn't, in the cooking or preparation process, somehow be turned the colour of hummus. I can't think how this can have been. Perhaps everything was boiled, and for too long. Perhaps the hostess trolley in which everything we eventually ate sat for such long hours had some sort of depigmenting effect. Perhaps we only ever ate chickpeas. Or perhaps, in the words of Paul Simon, 'It's not that the colours weren't there, it's just imagination they lack.'

That kitchen set changed my life. Here were cooking utensils and ingredients presented to me in a way that I found addictive. I couldn't wait for a period of free play to be announced so that I could rush over to that window and get roasting or simmering or browning or steeping. It just goes to demonstrate the value of play. And I hope it's no insult to my parents to say that I was set upon the path of gastronomy not by anything they ever cooked at home but by some pieces of coloured wood.

'Are you sure you wouldn't like to go outside and play with the others, Damien?' the teacher would ask, during break times, as she pulled up the adjacent window to lean out and have a cigarette.

'I'm fine, Miss,' I would say. 'I'm cooking.'

I had no game plan in those days. I suspect none of the children did. Everything I did, I did simply on instinct alone. And I loved it. One day, I remember taking one of the little wooden onions and some of the foam mushrooms and throwing them into the pan. I tossed them about in the manner in which I must have often seen my mother do. I then threw in the chicken and left it there for a while. There were clear plastic tumblers with perforated lids that were there, I suppose, to represent herbs and seasoning, and so after a while I pretended to scatter some of their contents over the pan. I didn't know it at the time, but I was fricasséeing.

Chicken Fricassée

My first attempts at fricassée, though inadvertent, were steps in the right direction. It seems like a very old-fashioned dish these days, and you don't see it on menus all that often. Personally, I think that is a bloody shame, because chicken fricassée is a jolly important part of French cuisine. Versions of fricassée can be dated back as far as 1300 during the reign of Philip IV. One feature that I rather love about it is that it has the taste of something that has been slow-cooked – and I am mad about slow cooking. Love it – but actually it doesn't take all that long at all. Not that I'm saying it's cheating. It palpably isn't. Food done well just takes as long as it takes.

So although this might not be a fashionable dish, that doesn't matter very much to me. Because it has an enduring appeal that transcends fashion. It is at once simple *and* complex, ancient and modern, sauté and stew. At a rough estimate I've probably eaten something in excess of 370 chicken fricassées over the years, but the best one I ever had was in a little tiny pensione in the Dordogne where Anthony and I once went to escape all the English in the larger restaurants. A charming old lady served us up an absolutely massive pot of the stuff in her very simply appointed and really rather small front room. It was so comforting that we both practically passed out, and I had no room for pudding. The plan was to drive back to our rented villa – we'd not had anything much to drink – but no sooner had we got into our rented car outside her house, Anthony, once he was done with the fuss of contorting himself into position behind the wheel, immediately fell into a deep and stubborn sleep from which I was utterly incapable of rousing him and we ended up there for the whole night. Anthony slept and snored right through until eight in the morning. I had a rather more fitful night. It became surprisingly cold, and I was convinced that I could hear wolves. Nevertheless, a superb fricassée, irrespective of the unsatisfactory back-pain-inducing slumber that followed it. And indeed the screaming row that followed that. And then the silent breakfast that followed that. Hey ho.

Pour une fricassée très spéciale et délicieuse you will need ...

An entire chicken – big as you fancy as long as it's free-range, organic, corn-fed and has lived a life of absolute bliss in a caring and trusting environment. Ask your butcher to chop up and bone the thing for you. I always do, despite the fact that I am more than capable of cutting up a chicken by myself, because my butcher is such an absolute artist, and it's a pleasure to watch him at work. (It's well worth learning to carve and chop meat, by the way. There are courses, both day and residential, and you will learn so much about meat, knives and indeed yourself. Anthony and I went on a course at Kate Humble's farm in Wales and we found it to be both informative and exceedingly emotional. There's something about standing side by side and carving away at mighty joints of meat that really brings people together.)

Butter, 5 oz of. Also – and you don't hear me say this very often *at all* – it needs to be unsalted. I know. I know. *I know*. But all rules have their exceptions and this happens to be butter's.

Extra-extra virgin oil, 1 tbsp thereof. There are so many types, but I've recently been using a Portuguese oil called Esplendido Douro (it's won prizes and everything!) that I was given as a present by a dear friend of mine to make up for a small misunderstanding. The people who press it pride themselves on just how balanced its flavour is, and they are not in any way daft to do so. I could drink it by the glass, quite frankly. You can use whatsoever brand you choose, of course. But just make sure that it is as cold-pressed and extra virginal as possible.

Some salt. Maldon. Of course.

Some pepper. You choose.

A lovely carrot, peeled and diced. I don't like to do my dicing square, if you get my meaning. I prefer it a little more rectangular. I mean cub*oid* rather than cub*id*.

Celery, 1 stalk of. Sliced neatly. I like to slice my stalks at intervals of about three quarters of a centimetre, but I'm all too aware that opinions vary on the subject and I'm not about to get into an argument over it.

A lovely little onion, peeled and indeed diced. Always do this on a separate, designated chopping board. You can never banish the smell of onions from anything that they've been chopped on. Goodness, the arguments we've had about that over the years. I've had to label the chopping boards, which I'd sworn I'd never do.

Mushrooms, 9 oz thereof. Button will do, but if you're feeling flush you can opt for cremini; they are a little more flavoursome and indeed have a slightly browner colour, which is rather thrilling. Rub a little of the skin off the mushrooms' caps using your thumb and then quarter them. Actually, quarters are perhaps a little too big, I sometimes feel. Could you manage fifths? Worth the effort, I'd say.

Plain flour, 2 tbsp of. I'm not one of those people who say that 'flour is flour', but I certainly wouldn't push you in the direction of any one brand over another. (That said, Shipton Mill flour really is something. Or the flour from Talgarth Mill, should you find yourself at a loose end in the Brecons.)

White wine, 1 small glass of. Always the good stuff, mind. There is no such thing as cooking wine. 175 ml is all you need, but why not pour a 250 ml glass and take a few sips for yourself? (No one will know.)

Some chicken stock, your own preferably, or that made by your own butcher or butcher's wife or husband. You want it to be as thick as is humanly possible. Broth-like. I've made my own for years and I've never once regretted it. You'll need a little under 1 litre, but why not measure out a whole litre and take a few sips for yourself? (No one will ever know.)

Fresh parsley, the flat-leaf variety (I hardly ever use the other sort these days. I've gone right off it for some reason). A pair of sprigs.

The same amount again of fresh thyme.

A bay leaf. Not nice to look at, I know, but they somehow hold their own.

Eggs, 2, yolks of. Ideally these will be as large as you can find. Crack them open as soon as you can so that they can be at room temperature.

Double cream, about 3 tbsp of would be my preference, but you must do what you think is right. Not everybody is as daft about the stuff as I am.

The juice of 1 lemon, big as you can find without the involvement of pesticides.

Fresh tarragon, 2 mighty handfuls of, given a proper chopping in the mezzaluna.

First you must season your chicken. Do not skimp on this. Place the pieces in a bowl, scatter a lot of salt and perhaps half as much pepper again all over it and then rub it all in by hand. Then let the chicken pieces sit in the seasoning for a moment or two while you pop off and get your absolutely biggest and heaviest pot down from the shelf. Put the pot on a steady heat, not too much mind, and add two thirds of your butter and a lot of olive oil. Watch the butter melt (always a lovely sight) and then once it has done so completely, you may add your chicken. This does not have to be done in one batch, so only put in as much as there is room for. Every piece of chicken needs its own space in the pan, so spread them out evenly as if you were organising the participants in a yoga class. The chicken should commence its browning skin down first, and then once you're happy with its colour, turn it over and do the other side. Then put the browned chicken to one side in a dish, and commence the next batch until you have browned it all. Congratulations. Your fricassée is *en cours*.

You should still have a nice hot pot on the stove containing lots of butter and oil and hopefully by now a few extra bits and pieces that will only serve to add more flavour. Lower the heat, and when you feel ready please add your diced carrot, your sliced celery and your chopped onion to the pot. Don't stir it relentlessly, but do be attentive. I like to do this with a sauté paddle, but a wooden spoon works almost but not quite as well. Pay close attention to any chicken residue burning itself on to the pan. Not only will this keep it as part of the mix, but it will also save you some valuable minutes when it comes to doing your washing up later. Washing up can be great fun, of course, but you don't want to spend longer doing it than is absolutely necessary. Not when you can be delicately arranging yourself on a sofa in front of *The Crown*. (Isn't it marvellous?)

It might take as many as ten minutes for the carrots, onions and celery to go brown. Really the onion should be your guide. If you manage to turn carrots brown in that time then there's something up with your stove. Only when you are completely happy with the colour of your onions should you add your fifthed mushrooms. These, with a minimal of prompting, should soon begin to give forth some extra moisture, as well as taking on a darker hue and becoming nicely shiny. When your mushrooms have achieved this state it is time to add your flour. This needs to be mixed pretty thoroughly – if you have been using a sauté paddle up until this point, now is the time to put it with the washing-up things and switch over to a wooden spoon. I've got a lovely battered old one in the farmhouse style which I've been using very cheerfully for years and hope to be for many more to come. I may well be buried with it.[5]

Do not allow yourself to be distracted at this point. If anyone comes into the kitchen now you have my permission to scream at them. 'GET OUT!' you should bellow. 'LEAVE THIS PLACE.' (This might sound a tad over-dramatic, but trust me: it works.) The flour will disappear into the liquid extremely quickly, and as soon as it does that is the moment to pour in the wine and stir it until the mixture thickens, which again happens far quicker than you might expect. Once it's thickened, in goes the stock, which you must pour in gradually while stirring gently but rhythmically.

When the stock has all been added you may put your chicken back into the pot, ideally with the skin facing upwards although this isn't absolutely essential. Now you need to add your parsley, thyme and the bay leaf. Some would suggest binding them together with kitchen twine, and I certainly used to do that until an incredibly thoughtful friend gave me a set of washable cotton spice bags. Absolute life-changer. Such good cotton, in fact, that I sought out the spice bag's manufacturer's cotton supplier (an

5 This is meant only as a figure of speech. I intend to be cremated and scattered somewhere quiet. Although perhaps my wooden spoon could be cremated with me. Useful bit of kindling, actually.

ethical company in Jodhpur) and had some pillow cases made up.

Turn up the heat a little and bring the pot to the boil. Having done so, reduce the heat so that it might simmer. Balance the pot's lid half on, and then dance a little jig because you've earned yourself half an hour at the kitchen table with a magazine and a cup of something hot.

When this blissful half hour is up, take the lid off completely, remove the chicken with your slatted spoon and put it on a fresh plate. Then allow the now chicken-less mixture to simmer all by itself for a further five minutes and then fish out your herbs and remove the pot from the heat.

Now you have to take on the rather fun job of indulging in a spot of sauce thickening. To do this, you must pop the egg yolks into a nice little mixing bowl, pour in the cream and then using your miniature whisk (I like to use the seven-inch one for this), whisk the mixture very thoroughly. Just this alone would make your sauce very thick indeed, and so you need to quieten its power a little. You do this by taking a large wine glass of sauce from the pot, and ever so slowly and delicately pouring it into the bowl while whisking *relentlessly*. When all the sauce has taken, you can pour this little lot back into the pot and stir it in. Then return the chicken to the pot, and add the lemon juice, the tarragon and the remaining third of the butter. Put the pot back on the heat and bring it to a simmer. Give it one brief stir, and then it is ready to serve. Some like to have it with rice, but Julia Child was always an evangelist for serving it with mashed potatoes. And who, frankly, are any of us to argue?

I have such amazingly happy memories of my time at Tiny Steps, but it is no longer operating, I'm sad to relate. It somehow managed to lose its charitable status, and Brent Council were forced to intervene. But whatever the eventual shortcomings of the institution might have been (I think it might have had something to do with safe-guarding), I shall always be grateful for the time that I spent there, for without it my life could well have taken a completely different path. If I had not attended Tiny Steps, then perhaps I would not have encountered a delightful kitchen playset at such an impressionable age and had my head and heart so thrillingly gripped and turned in this manner. It was that beautiful and brightly coloured plaything that set me upon this highway, after all. You could call it Providence, or you could call it Fate. Whatever it was called, from the moment that I first encountered that kitchen playset, the fact that I would make my life all about food had an inescapableness to it, for which I shall be indebted for ever more.

What if I'd gone to another nursery school where there was no such playset? What and where would I be now? Perhaps I might instead have becoming obsessed with a puppet theatre, and I would these days spend my time parading about the stages of a variety of publicly funded provincial playhouses giving my Hamlet or Caliban. I might even be in Hollywood, being an all-action hero and only daring to consume one small meal and a smoothie a day for fear that I'd look unflattering in my superhero Lycra.

I could equally have been captivated by a fire station playset, and now spend my days as a much valued member of the emergency services, a real-life fireman. I'm not awfully good with heights, so I'd probably be given some sort of job on the ground, such as connecting the big hose to the water outlet. Or just folding everybody's trousers up for them at the end of each shift.

It could all so easily have been otherwise.

Chapter 4

A CHILD CALLED DAMIEN

So what was the infant Damien Trench actually like? At Tiny Steps I was a contented little fellow who spent his days blissfully imagining that he was a cook and occasionally dressing up as a nurse. But at home things were very different. My mother ruled the kitchen in those days, and I was considered too young to be of much help in that area. How I longed to be allowed to don a pair of oven gloves and to slide a prepped, plump chicken into the oven to roast. How I dreamt of being allowed to use the sharp little knife to slice carrots into batons. I would even have happily have done the washing up, but that was my father's role, and he required no assistance at all, thank you very much. We don't want children dropping things, now, do we?

My father was, now I look back on it, rather a grumpy man. These days, happily retired and not having to share his home with children, he is a more measured and mellow fellow. My mother used to like being in charge very much, and would as a result frequently become a little flustered. All my father wanted, on the other hand, was, just once in a while, to be *listened to*. My parents have always insisted that my sister, my brother and I were all planned pregnancies, but nevertheless I still got the impression that we were a shock to my father. He likes the time and the space to think a little, and he also relishes silence. 'The noise,' he used to frequently opine, 'the NOISE!'

We were, I am afraid, not a quiet household. My sister and my brother were both rambunctious, and if I ever felt things were becoming a little unfair then I used to scream. They would throw things, and call each other names, and valuable objects were smashed and shattered with a shameful regularity. My mother, who has always liked things to be extremely orderly, despaired of this sort of behaviour and would bellow at us if we upset the neatness that she liked to impose. She had astonishingly good eyesight and hearing. If we had moved something that we shouldn't have, she would always spot it. 'If I'd worked in film, I'd have been the continuity girl,' she often told us. If someone was planning some naughtiness, she would hear it. What she didn't seem to have, however, was a sense of smell. Combined with the fact that she seemed completely incapable of mastering how to work her cooking clock, this meant that many of the meals she slaved over would be ruined. 'Something's burning!' my father would bellow, suddenly sprinting through from the sitting room where he was attempting to read, and throwing open the oven door only to disappear into a cloud of thick smoke. 'Jesus Christ!' he would howl, while flapping his arms wildly in an attempt to clear the air enough for him to be able to see.

'What on earth are you doing?' my mother would ask when she came into the kitchen.

'I'm trying to prevent a house fire,' he would shout.

I'm not sure what it was that my mother used to try and cook, but an awful lot of afternoons concluded with someone having to nip out to a shop and buy some fish fingers. 'Why don't we just agree to have fish fingers in the first place?' my father would say. 'Even *I* can cook fish fingers. Then you wouldn't have to cope with the guilt of nearly setting fire to the place the whole time.'

My mother did not enjoy my father saying this, but eventually succumbed to his pleading and just let him cook the fish fingers. My sister and my brother loved them. I thought rather less of them, but then perhaps it was inevitable that we should have such differences.

I have told you a little of my sister and my brother, but let me handle each of them in more detail in turn. I shall start with my brother, and come to my sister later. If necessary. It may well be that enough of her personality will come across from these pages, without me having to make a specific detour. She, as you will see, was the one who I saw far more of as I grew up.

My younger brother Ralph (pronounced Ralph) and I – I don't think he'll even slightly mind me saying this – are not particularly alike. In fact, I hardly need worry what I say or write about him because he is extremely unlikely to read this volume. As far as I am aware, he has not ever read a single thing that I have ever written,[1] and is extremely unlikely to start now.

His big interest is, and always has been, sport. He plays it, he watches it, he talks about it, he reads about it. His job even involves sport, although I'm a little scant on the details. It is, I think, something to do with corporate hospitality at sporting events.[2] He still plays a bit of sport for

1 He calls me 'Chef', despite the fact that I make it extremely clear in as much of my writing as possibly that I simply do not see myself as a 'chef'. I see myself very much as a 'writer' and 'cook' or, if I may be so bold, as a 'cookery writer'. A chef is someone who works in a professional kitchen. I do a lot of work *in* my kitchen, but it is not a professional one. It is a perfectly normal, albeit generously proportioned, domestic kitchen. And when I write – in my perfectly normal, albeit not all that generously proportioned, study – I am writing as a domestic cook. And I think that that is actually incredibly important. Because, for the most part, the people I write for are also purely domestic cooks. Inevitably some professional cooks *do* read my books; Simon Hopkinson once told me that he always keeps one of my books in his lavatory and makes a point of reading random extracts from it if he's ever feeling frustrated in there, and I have to say that I find that extremely flattering. It's not, in its own way, all that different from me taking Madhur Jaffrey into the bath with me. The point is, if you cook professionally in a kitchen, then your writing is, and I don't mean this to be in any way disrespectful, not accessible to normal people. Is a normal person going to cook roast pollock frumenty? No. Is Heston Blumenthal (and I count myself as a fan) going to cook toad in the hole? Almost certainly not. Unless it contains actual toads.* And even then they'd probably have to be freeze-dried and then injected with stock made from the vital organs of unlikely animals.

2 He has, on a couple of occasions, very kindly invited Anthony and me to attend some sports events that he has

This seems unlike your usual tone, Damien. Is the toad thing a joke?

It does read like one, doesn't it? Sometimes, if I'm writing late into the night, then it's not impossible that wine has been taken. Perhaps it should be cut.

Not all jokes are bad things, Damien.

Personally, I dislike them intensely.

It suddenly occurs to me that there could be room for one here about Heston Blumethal's frighteningly realistic spotted dick?

I strongly feel otherwise.

Apologies

47

fun these days, but as a child he seemed to be engaged in some sort of sporting pursuit pretty much all the time. I felt, as a young man, that the amount of time he spent in such pursuits was having a very negative impact on his academic studies. As an adult, though, I realise that he didn't actually have, shall we say, any great aptitude in that direction. Thus any pursuits that kept him out of the classroom were probably a very good idea.

In retrospect I don't think it's unfair to say that in much

---

been working on at Twickenham, but we have always had to decline. Anthony, who I think I may have mentioned is really quite a big fellow, used to play rugby for his public school. It was very much against his will, and he was always painfully aware that he was being selected not so much for his skills as for his heft. People were quite shouty, apparently, and there was always rather a lot of shoving. After one rather vigorous encounter he was forced to wear a neck brace for six months, and the experience has left him with a deep-seated hatred of both the game, and indeed the people who play it. Once, while changing trains en route to visiting friends in Mortlake for tea and a stroll, we encountered some rugby fans making their way home from a game at Twickenham. The platforms were incredibly crowded and some songs were being sung. There was – quite rightly, in my view – a police presence. Anthony had gone very quiet and nervous-looking, and I could tell that he found being in the company of this sort of people very upsetting. 'Will you be OK?' I asked. He nodded, wordlessly, but then suddenly dashed off and was violently sick into a (regrettably) see-through bin. A police officer then asked him if he'd had too much too drink, and we ended up in a rather lengthy conversation about social responsibilities. It seemed easier to go along with it rather than kick up a further fuss. Not least because Anthony, once he starts to be sick, rarely lets up any time soon. He was still going when the policeman wandered off, telling me to 'look after him, mate'.

the same way that I always felt rather cruelly exposed on, for instance, a football pitch, whenever Ralph was sitting at a desk and attempting to learn something, he felt woefully and pathetically out of his depth. A lot more, of course, is known these days about learning difficulties. But even if as much had been known about them then as is now, it would have made no difference to poor Ralph, who is genuinely just not that bright. I hope that does not sound as if I am being unkind. It's not intended as a criticism; I offer it merely as fact. My intention, as ever, is just to be honest. Throughout my career as a writer I have always believed that honesty must be at the heart of what I do. If I started telling people that courgettes come into season in March just because it suited me, then I would be being dishonest. And if I – or indeed any other cookery writer – was found to be peddling this sort of information in print or, heaven forfend, online then I would rightly deserve to suffer death by lethal injection or, worse, to be drummed out of the Food Writers' Guild.[3]

3 There is, of course, no such thing as the Food Writers' Guild. And if you were to encounter such an organisation, then I am afraid to tell you that they are charlatans whose work I absolutely will not endorse. I made the name up simply to make a point. There is, however, something called The Guild of Food Writers, and I have no hesitation in telling you that it is a simply marvellous organisation. Their awards bash, a rare exception in these sorts of events, is a genuine hoot. I went to one two years ago and Jay Rayner, unusually for him, told a most amusing story from the lectern about fettuccine that kept me chuckling for some hours. I cannot remember what it was, but my goodness did I laugh. Tears streaming down my cheeks and everything. Anthony was worried that my drink might have been spiked.

Anyway, I don't feel at all guilty commenting on Ralph's intelligence (or lack of it), because it has never once held him back – either in his work on sports events and hospitality or during his time at the University Of Durham.

We didn't play together all that much when we were little, and nor do we socialise all that much together now. It wasn't so much the age difference but rather the extreme differences in our personalities and levels of hand-eye co-ordination. I enjoyed things like reading, thinking and listening to classical music. I enjoyed making pencil sketches, and painting in ink wash. I cooked whenever I could. Ralph, who was already much bigger than me by the time I was five, enjoyed shoulder-barging me and stealing any personal items that I particularly cherished. He once grabbed hold of my (heavily annotated) copy of *The New Junior Cookbook* and hurled it from my bedroom window out into the garden where it landed in our fishpond. (The fishpond contained no fish – my sister had killed them.)

I used to enjoy sitting at the desk under my cabin bed doing little jottings or writing a diary with my headphones on (I was given a Sony Walkman for my birthday in 1986), listening to a tape I had of Daniel Barenboim playing Chopin. Ralph would creep up behind me without my noticing, remove my headphones and bellow, 'Let's wrestle!' into my ear at a most unsettling volume. The next thing I knew I would have been thrown across the room, and Ralph would then land heavily on me and put me in a headlock. On several occasions I blacked out, and goodness only knows how many of my pencils got broken. I never fought back; I just didn't see the point. If I ever struck him, he only hit me harder. Besides, it wasn't really the punches that hurt me the most. It was the big, silly grin on his big, silly face, and the way that when it was all over he would get up and laugh and ruffle my hair as if I'd enjoyed the experience as much as he had. I also suspect, although he's never once admitted to this, that he used to steal my rechargeable batteries so that I couldn't listen to my Walkman. I tried not to make a big fuss about this, and just hum to myself instead, but it was never really the same. And though I hesitate to offer up such a gobbet in print – but again, my total commitment to honesty compels me – I must add that one particularly foul habit of Ralph's was to walk into my room, break wind and leave. Oh, how he'd laugh. But oh, how I would suffer. I used to have to beg for pot pourri for birthdays and Christmas.

He then won, at the age of eight, a sports scholarship to a boarding preparatory school. This came, I must tell you, as a blessed relief. He would be away at school for the duration of every term, and most of his holidays were taken up with residential sports camps, or indeed going on tours. My parents missed him dreadfully, and I think my sister was also sorry he went away because she saw him as a worthy combatant. This all said, I did and continue to love him very much, we maintain an extremely civil relationship (helped, I suppose, by his relentlessly outgoing nature and optimism) and I wouldn't have had it any other way. I do wish he wouldn't call me 'Chef' though.

Fresh Salmon Fishcakes

We were served fish fingers so often as a child that I can no longer stomach so much as the thought of them. I can perfectly understand *why* we had them so often. They're certainly convenient, and they're certainly tasty. They're also reliable and infinitely preferable to something that's just been burnt. But to my mind they are perhaps a little *too* convenient. Yes, we can all get tired after a hard day at the coalface, and so I can all too well understand the temptation to just fling something into the oven, and then twelve minutes later, perhaps having turned them once at some point in the middle, pull out a tray of something pretty edible, and a rather pleasing burnished orange that goes down jolly well with some mash and peas. However – and I do not intend this to be in any way a criticism of my parents – I am really not sure that it is genuinely advisable to set children the example so early in their lives of a reliance on frozen foods. The frozen food aisle in a supermarket, or even the freezer cabinet within your local convenience store, is, simply, an area to be avoided at all costs.

As I believe that I have written elsewhere, I do not visit or use supermarkets myself. I can understand, however, that some people genuinely believe that they have no time or options to do their shopping elsewhere. I can understand their point of view (I am, after all, nothing if not empathetic), but I don't really believe that these people are being completely honest with themselves. I'm absolutely rushed off my feet from dawn till dusk most days (by way of example I plumped cushions for twenty-five minutes this morning, something that I could well have done without, but my partner Anthony briefly and unthinkingly sat down rather heavily on one of the sofas after breakfast, and so I was simply left with no option), and yet I somehow find the time to visit a vast array of independent shops every single day. People who claim that they don't have time to shop anywhere other than supermarkets simply need to set aside a little bit of time every day, and then have a ruddy stern word with themselves. Please shop local, and please buy fresh. Rant over.

Here then, is what I believe that people should cook instead of fish fingers. They are twice as nice, and three times as hearty. And probably about eight times the price, but it simply doesn't do to dwell on the negatives.

For these you will need …

Potatoes, approximately 1½ lbs of, and they need to be *floury*. (Practically everybody uses Maris Piper almost by default, but lately I've been experimenting with Estima or Desiree, sometimes doing half and half, and I have to say that I've found the results to be never less than thrilling.)

Fresh salmon, around about 20 oz thereof. Which is probably the equivalent of about five fillets. I know that you can buy salmon fillets from a supermarket, but what have we just been talking about? Exactly. Go to a fishmonger, and they will have a whole fish and will be more than happy to do whatever you ask with it. It will, what is more, quite definitely be fresher. You need to ask for wild salmon, by the way, not farmed. Wild salmon get lots and lots of exercise, and their flesh is consequently firmer and leaner and more flavoursome. Farmed salmon look to me as if they've been sat on their backsides all day waiting for death. And perhaps they have been.

The zest of 1 lemon, unwaxed of course. Never buy waxed lemons, because you can't take the zest off them without having to scrub thoroughly first, rendering the whole waxing process utterly needless. Perhaps it's injecting money into an economy somewhere, but otherwise it's hard to see the point. You should always use the zest. If I see that I'm about to throw half a juiced lemon into the waste bin and it hasn't had its zest removed, I instantly take it off and find a way of using it – perhaps some biscuits or a quick pan sauce. Once you've zested the lemon, do hold on to the wedges.

Dill, fresh

Parsley, likewise (a good handful of each by the way)

Ketchup, tomato. (Seriously, you'll thank me. I would never advocate the use of ketchup unless it was absolutely necessary. And remember, there are many different makes of ketchup, not just you know who. Stokes and Tiptree's Wilkin & Sons both do good ones, to name but two.)

Mustard, English

Plain flour, organic, 4 very heaped tbsp of (and I mean *very* heaped)

Eggs, free range, 2

Breadcrumbs, 5 oz of. Irrespective of everything that I have said above about freshness, your bread for breadcrumbs does not actually *need* to be completely fresh. Something very slightly less than fresh will do, because the key thing here is that the bread must be dry. I like to take some fresh bread, slice it and then bake it for a few minutes until it is dry. Then I put it in the food processor and give it a decent blitzing. Not too decent though. We want to use these crumbs to achieve some crunch, not just make a fine flour or then where would we be?

Some sunflower oil (again, *I know*, but trust me on this)

Start by peeling your potatoes, giving them a bit of a slice, although you can afford to leave them in fairly sizeable chunks. Having done so, then pop your peeled potatoes into a pan with a little bit of salt and a decent amount of water (you'll know how much, I'm sure) and then bring to the boil on your gas ring or equivalent.

Once you've got the pan of potatoes up and running, season your salmon fillets fairly generously, and then place them under the grill. (The grill needs to be on, by the way. Sounds patronising to say, but it's such an easy mistake to make. 'Gosh, these chicken breasts seem to be taking a long time,' you might think to yourself while preparing a Caesar salad in advance of a small and indeed informal picnic. 'What the dickens is going on up there?' 'Are you sure you've turned the grill on, Damien?' 'Yes, of course I've turned the ... oh. Well, that's the problem isn't it? Thank you, Anthony. You have averted a CRISIS.') The grill doesn't need to be on all that high, because you're only trying to *just* cook the salmon, but give the fillets about three minutes on each side. The potatoes will probably need about thirteen or fourteen minutes to become tender, so you've probably got the time to allow the salmon to cool a little. Once the fillets have cooled sufficiently you need to break them up into flakes. You can do this using a fork or your fingers, but personally I like to do it with my fingers. Something about the touch, I think.

By the time you've finished this delightful duty, your potatoes will still not be *quite* tender, so you've got a little free time. Perhaps enough to double-check you have all the other ingredients lined up, or maybe you could just stare out of the window. (Personally I never think of time spent staring out of the window as wasted. Unless it's dark, and you really can't see anything. Or if you're on a train and you're stuck in a tunnel. Happened to me recently just past Swindon. Ninety minutes of sheer hell, since you ask.) Once the potatoes are tender, drain them, let them rest for a little while, and then set about them with the masher. Personally I absolutely love mashing, and I very much doubt I'm alone in this regard.

Once you achieved a pleasurable mash – one that feels both cloud-like and robust, both fluffy and also heavy – you can mix in the zest, the herbs, a little bit of salt and pepper and the ketchup and mustard. Just how much mustard and ketchup you add is really at your discretion. Personally I think a little bit of mustard gives a surprising kick, whereas a lot is just too shocking for some palates. Ketchup you can be less nervous about. It's all about piquancy, but don't forget that it actually has a very strong flavour. We want to enhance the flavour of the salmon, not mask it. Mix in the salmon last, and do it with real care please, as you probably instinctively broke it down to exactly the right-sized chunks the first time around. Again, this is a job that you could do with your hands rather than a utensil to make absolutely sure. They're about to get dirty anyway, as your next job is to shape the mixture into cakes. There is enough mixture here to make six jolly big ones, but if you prefer the idea of making a greater number of smaller ones then I, for one, wouldn't hold it against you. It's your life, after all.

Put the cakes to one side. (It seems somehow silly writing the word 'cakes' at this point in the process. They're patties, really. But then 'patty' has meaty connotations, doesn't it? As ever, there is simply so much to think about.)

The next bit is rather fun. Lay out three dishes in a row. Into the first place your flour, into the second your two eggs, lightly beaten, and into the third the breadcrumbs that you so perfectly blitzed not long ago. Then take each patty and in turn dip them (both sides and edges) into the flour (a little shake afterwards is very much required), then the egg and finally the breadcrumbs. You really do want them to be properly covered in each.

Then get a lovely thick-bottomed frying pan, pour the sunflower oil in, and get it on a medium heat. (If you're unused to using sunflower oil, then I must warn you that it gets hot *very* quickly, so be prepared to turn it down.) The fishcakes/patties will need about three and a half minutes on each side, but you should judge it by sight alone. If you keep a close eye on them, you will suddenly be aware that they have become the most *perfect* colour. Serve them immediately. And remember the wedges that I politely asked you to hold on to? This is what you need them for. You can never squeeze too much lemon on to a fishcake. Trust me. I've tried it. Damn nearly turned my fingers into ceviche, but by crikey it was worth the agony. As is so often the case, what was hell on the fingers was heavenly on the tongue.

(If you make these and find that you don't enjoy them as much as fish fingers, then I think it best you see a doctor. It could well be symptomatic of a serious problem, not just of personal taste, but of your olfactory system as a whole.[4])

4 This is, in retrospect, a rather flippant remark. Please don't waste the time of any NHS workers. Ever. They have quite hard enough a time of things as it is. And they have my total support.

Chapter 5

A SICKLY, SICKLY CHILD

I do, these days, consider myself to be a reasonably robust and rather healthy gentleman.[1] I do have what might best be termed a considerable appetite, it is true,[2] but then I like to temper that affliction by eating dishes that are made

1 Some may, I dare say, take issue with my use of the word 'gentleman', but I hope that I am. I really do make an effort to be polite at all times, and only very occasionally do I snap and just hurl foul abuse in the direction of another person. I *hope* that when I do, the circumstances are mitigating. Only a fortnight ago, I'm afraid, I was in discussion with a man from Open Reach about what might be best termed the 'intermittent' internet coverage in the area. I think it took until his third successive shrug for me to decide that enough was enough, but my goodness I made my point. I used – to my shame – several words that I wouldn't normally and the phrase 'over a ruddy barrel' was also deployed.
2 Not, it must be said, as considerable as that of my partner Anthony, who really does have to be watched. You wouldn't believe the quantities of things I have seen suddenly disappear inside that man. 'Charcuterie board for two, please.' 'I'm not actually in a charcuterie mood today, Anthony, if you don't mind.' 'It's just for me,' etc. etc. It's terrifying to watch sometimes. No one, I'm afraid, ought really to eat meats in the volumes that he does, or it can make night time an absolute hell. I struggle to persuade him of this fact, but then I suppose you just have to pick your battles sometimes, don't you? His kidneys will have a word with him one day, and then he'll *have* to listen.

with the best ingredients available. (Generally speaking, therefore, that means that I am also often eating dishes made with the *healthiest* ingredients available. This is not a universal truth, it must be said – I do not think, for example, and I am choosing an example completely at random here, that one can derive anything like as much pleasure on the palate from lean ground beef as one can derive from those versions which come with rather more fat on them – not too much, mind – but nevertheless it remains *generally* to be the case. I must confess that I am struggling a little here to quantify *exactly* the perfect amount of fat that the best beef mince ought rightly to contain. I have been visiting the same marvellous butcher for years and he knows exactly how I like it. Like the best butchers, he works more on instinct than anything else. I am actually rather envious of his extraordinary ability to judge the properties of meat so acutely by sight alone. He can look at any cut of meat and instantly and instinctively give you an exact roasting time for it to a discrepancy within under three minutes. He is also quite the best person in this corner of the world to talk to about marbling. I am not above – if I'm wandering past his shop and it looks quiet enough and I don't have a deadline looming over me – popping in to have a bit of a general natter and just seeing where it takes us. On one occasion he made us both an actually rather nice cup of coffee, described to me his rather forthright position on the monarchy and we then managed three quarters of an hour on brisket. Not a wasted morning.)

Additionally, I also take rather a lot of exercise. I do not mean by this that I am a regular gym goer. If anything I am an irregular gym goer. My partner Anthony goes through phases where he suddenly gets very into weight-lifting, but I can't really see the point myself. There's a limit, I think, to how pleasurable bulk is. And besides, I get quite enough of an upper body workout in the kitchen; stirring and whisking, obviously, but also baking. (I was told that following Richard Bertinet's method for working enough dough to make two substantial loaves is an equiv-alent workout to half an hour of Israeli martial arts, and I'm perfectly happy to believe it.) I find it hard to motivate myself to do gym work alone. People say, 'Well, you should listen to music or the radio,' but it's never worked for me. I did once experiment with using a running machine while listening to BBC Radio 4's *The Today Programme* but it's hard to regulate your breathing when you're screaming the words, 'Oh for Christ's sake, let her speak!' every forty-five seconds.

For this reason I do so much prefer to attend classes. I'll just turn up at my local council-run leisure centre[3] whenever I fancy and will very happily take part in pretty

3 Always checking first, of course, that it's *actually still there* and hasn't been summarily closed in order to cover the cost of the banking crisis. Perhaps one day I shall ring up and find that it's been merged, like every other council facility, with the library. I'm sure I shall turn up to the library one day and there'll be a small section for books in one corner, a 'one-stop shop' in another and exercise equipment in another, the whole place divided up into zones like on that *Crystal Maze* programme I used to rather enjoy.

much whatever they have going on at the time. This results in a wonderfully varied array of exercise; I've tried Body Pump (enjoyed the workout, but not the music), spinning (the faster I cycled, the more I somehow felt disassociated from my own legs, a sensation that strangely made me panic about my self-worth and contributed to my being sick in the changing room; otherwise fun though), Aqua Zumba (better than I thought it would be, although the chlorine levels in the pool are not good for my skin, particularly my upper arms), something called 'power-bagging' (complete disaster) and once, because there was nothing else on, I even joined a post-natal yoga group (absolutely loved it. Very supportive ladies. I would have signed on for a whole course if the instructor hadn't advised strongly against my doing so. Shame).

But my main form of exercise is actually incidental; I walk a frankly huge amount, often whilst carrying things. If we were in one of those absolutely crazy households who insist on doing a weekly shop by car I wouldn't get half as much walking done. But as I like to do a daily shop, sometimes twice daily, in order to cook with the freshest ingredients possible, I actually manage to achieve quite a bit of wear and tear on the old shoe leather.

Walking is also a great way of clearing the head and mulling over one's thoughts, and personally I consider it to be absolutely fundamental to the writing process. To walk is to simultaneously unblock – and indeed unlock – oneself, to free the mind, and to get the creative juices flowing. I was once commissioned to write a 500-word piece about the calabash tree for the now sadly – and indeed inexplicably – defunct *Veg* magazine (a sort of fanzine for vegetable enthusiasts, set up by the late Felix Dennis. It was a wonderful, absolute superb and really quite cutting-edge publication in its day, but for reasons I've never quite understood, they struggled to sell advertising space). I set off in typically breezy fashion, my fingers dancing across the keyboard, and ideas pouring out of me like water from a drainpipe in the middle of a monsoon, but 200 words in, disaster struck: for the first and thankfully so far only time in my career I suddenly seemed completely incapable of adequately describing gourds in a way that I really felt did justice to their white, spongy flesh. It was frightening actually. I tried everything: a cup of coffee, some light stretches, looking out of the window for a bit, rebooting my laptop. Nothing worked, and I became, I'm afraid and embarrassed to relate, uncharacteristically short-tempered. All seemed lost until Anthony very constructively – and indeed forcefully – suggested that it might be rather a good idea for me to get out of the house for a spell. So I pulled on a coat and went for a calming stomp around the park. Seven laps of hard thinking later I had completely unbunged myself, and I practically ran home and then dashed off another 600 words without drawing breath. I was absolutely delighted with the results, and so too was the editor. (I later discovered that he had moved abroad soon after the magazine's demise and had set himself up hosting architectural tours of the Alhambra. I wish him well.)

I also eat a *lot* of roughage. Seriously.

So all this being the case it's rather funny to think that as a child I was actually really somewhat sickly. Who can say why? Nature? Nurture? Naughtiness?

Well, we can rule the last of those possibilities out *instantly*. Of all the issues that I faced in my childhood, naughtiness was absolutely, positively, not one of them. Ralph and Angela were complete tearaways, but I quite simply wasn't. I was actually very helpful: washing up, hanging out laundry, ironing. I certainly did a vast amount of hoovering, and I loved every minute of it. I needed a little help at first, of course, but once my father had shown me how to change the bag, I was up and away. Had they been able to speak, I am quite sure that our carpets would have thanked me profusely for the care and attention I lavished on them. 'Have you been a good boy this year?' Father Christmas would always ask me at the grotto set up at our church's Christmas Bazaar. 'I have been *extremely* good,' I would tell him. 'As I am every year.' I would then reel off a healthy quantity of anecdotal evidence in support of this claim before listing, by way of contrast, some of the recent rather less decent behaviour of my brother and sister, so as to demonstrate that if any member of our family was worthy of receiving a gift then it was almost certainly – as any judge in the land worth their salt and reviewing the evidence in front of them would undoubtedly attest – me.

'Yes, yes,' Father Christmas would always say when I had finished my speech. 'There's a queue, you know.'

Then he would give me exactly the same gift – usually some cheap, mass-produced chocolate produced in the West Midlands (I'm sure you know to what I refer) – that he gave my brother and sister anyway. This was, quite clearly, an injustice. When I later learned that Father Christmas was not in fact real, all I felt was a great sense of relief that such a poor arbiter of morality, so frail a judge of right and wrong, did not exist. And nor, as far as I could see, did he deserve to.

All I know is that by the age of eight I had somehow contrived to contract pretty much everything that could conceivably have come my way. Mumps struck me down when I was just a tender four-year-old. My mother and father and sister and brother and I* had been visiting relatives in the north of Scotland, not all that far from Inverness, having driven up in the family Vauxhall. I'm afraid I couldn't even hazard a guess as to the model; such things have never really held my interest. All I could tell you for certain was that it was a sort of yellowish colour (dandelion? sandstorm?) and the seats were upholstered with plastic, meaning that in the summer months, when the weather was hot and my sister and my brother and I* were *forced* (I wish that was too strong a word to use, but it isn't) to wear shorts, during journeys of over an hour our bare legs would stick to the seats, and when we eventually arrived at our destination – or stopped to relieve ourselves – we had to be practically peeled out of the car, like strips of bacon that had been left neglected for far too long in a non-non-stick frying pan on a medium

Could you just say 'my family' here?

I'm trying to paint a picture.

'My siblings and I'?

Just don't like the word. Try saying it out loud. See? It's ugly.

heat. In fact I briefly attempted to get 'the non-non-stick frying pan' to catch on as a nickname for our car with my brother and sister, but they were having absolutely none if it. Which hurt as much, if I'm honest, as the regular pinches and punches that they meted out. Vicious little creatures that they were.

But the Vauxhall, whatever model or shade of yellow it was, did not last the holiday. Driving back from a day trip to Ullapool (where I'm 95 per cent certain that I saw a man feeding chips to a seal), fumes started being emitted from parts of the car that are simply not supposed to emit fumes. As I recall it, in the chaos my father opened the glove box and there were fumes in that too. If my mother was driving, then it must have been night, as my father lacked the confidence in his eyes to perform to a similar standard once the sun had set. Who knows why this was? Ageing? Some sort of trauma? Perhaps it was a lie, and he just fancied snoozing. I'm not sure I would have blamed him. I've never learned to drive myself for a wide variety of extremely valid and considered reasons, and consequently am always driven by others – usually my partner Anthony – and I have to say I really do find it extremely agreeable. It's rather nice to be free of responsibility every once in a while. Especially when your life is as hectic as mine.

The AA man or the RAC man or whoever it might have been[4] was duly summoned, examined the vehicle and,

---

4 I have sat here at my desk for nearly twenty minutes trying to remember which vehicle recovery service my parents were members of at the time, and I'm sad to relate that I simply

*Please think about using 'siblings'. It's making sentences needlessly long. NO.

whilst my sister and my brother and I sat in the back seats * eating the last remaining egg rolls from a picnic that had sadly had to be abruptly curtailed earlier in the day as a result of the inclemency of the weather, informed my parents that the Vauxhall had reached the end of its natural life. 'We are each of us allotted a number of years upon this earth,' I imagine he said. 'And we are but slaves to forces too magnificent and mysterious for us mere mortals to comprehend,' he doubtless continued. 'Our role upon this planet we call home is not to question or query, to regret or to repent, merely to be gracious and grateful for such mercy, compassion and clemency as we have been shown,' he very probably concluded. I think it was the RAC.

We were thus left without a vehicle to call our own for the remainder of our holiday, and therefore my parents were forced to book tickets – doubtless at considerable expense – on the sleeper train for our eventual return south. We had adjoining cabins, with an open door between them, and my sister and my brother and I quar-relled viciously about who should get which bunk, as we

---

cannot recall. They were members of both over the course of my childhood (one of them was abandoned in favour of the other at some stage, partly on grounds of cost and also as the result of surliness shown to my mother by a mechanic who had been called out for reasons that he considered to be somewhat extraneous. 'Women like you …' he had begun to say, and my father interjected not to defend her but in fact to say, 'There are no other women like her') and this fact may have clouded my recollections somewhat. Sorry not to be more help.

all wanted a top bunk, but only two were available. Eventually, after several coins had been tossed and we had played a number of eliminator rounds of paper, scissors, stone, my sister and I emerged victorious and I was helped up into one of the top bunks. The height was too great for me, however, and I felt instantly sick, and thus ended up on the bottom bunk anyway.

I can remember as if it were only yesterday the little hand basin and the slightly stiff sheeting; the tartan blanket and a complimentary soap. I am also certain that was the first time my sister and my brother and I ever experienced the phenomenon of bottled water. It seems ridiculous to think of it now, but at the time it was a source of great excitement and perhaps even incredulity. I imagine it's how children feel today the first time they ever see a set of quintuple-bladed herb scissors.

And it was on that bottom bunk, as our train thundered through the bleak yet beautiful, strident yet stunning landscape of the Scottish Highlands (none of which I could actually see at the time because the blind was down and it was the middle of the night and thus dark anyway) that I first began to experience what I later discovered to be the initial symptoms of the mumps infection. Oh, the itching. The restlessness. The being bed-ridden and thus not able to get out and change the world-ness of it all.

'There's something wrong with me,' I said.

'We know,' my brother and sister chorused.

'Seriously, though, my body is covered in little ... bumps.'

'Sounds as if you've found your nipples,' my sister said.

'Not them. Other bumps. And they're itchy. They're really itchy. They're ... AAAAAARGH.'

'Go and find Mum and Dad.'

And so I got out of bed and went into the corridor, and then opened the door to the compartment that my parents were sleeping in. My mother was making a noise that I'd never heard her make before, and they seemed to have left the top bunk free, rendering the earlier arguments between my sister and my brother and I completely redundant.

'Hello?' my dad shouted, and I heard the noise of sheets being hurriedly rearranged.

'It's Damien,' I said. 'What are you doing?'

'We're *trying*,' my father said, 'to enjoy the last night of our holiday.'

'I'm covered in bumps.'

'You can't be,' my mother said, finally emerging from the opposite end of the bed to my father.

'I am.'

'It'll just be midge bites,' my father said. 'The best thing for those is sleep. Go back to sleep. Your mother and I are desperate to ... sleep too.'

I do hope, in retrospect, that I hadn't interrupted my parents doing what it appears that they might have been doing. It's possible, in purely practical terms, but I don't think making love on a train would be their style. And if it was their style, it's not a predilection that I have inherited. Not on British trains, at any rate. European sleepers are far roomier. And so back I trotted to our compartment, and spent the rest of the night scratching myself daft. By the time we arrived in London I was half demented. My parents took one look at me and dragged me straight off to the doctor. And mumps it was. By the close of play that night both of my (siblings) had contracted it too, and were blaming me for it.

And yet you use it here?

Somehow it just works here.

In fact, I was curiously susceptible to infections and fevers for much of my childhood, really running the whole gamut, as my mother would put it. My sister and my brother had the most extraordinary resilience, still do in fact; it is my sister's pain threshold that is actually staggering, though. I don't think I've seen her so much as wince. Even the time she got a tent peg embedded in her temple as a result of an accident she had with a catapult when trying to stun a heron. I, however, have always been lot more vulnerable and in a number of ways. But I was struck down with mumps, chicken pox, measles, whooping cough, German measles, slapped cheek disease (or parvovirus) and – far later than should have been physically possible – nappy rash.

Any malady that contracted used to result – in addition to all the other symptoms – in a high fever, which in turn usually resulted in hallucinatory episodes. According to my mother, my parents would often be awakened at night by the sound of my screaming and run into my bedroom to find me howling at thin air.

71

'What is it now, Damien?' they would ask.

'It's the Nazis!' I'd shout. 'They've come for us!'

It wasn't always the Nazis, of course. Sometimes it was aliens. Sometimes it was medieval soldiers. Sometimes it was trolls. Occasionally it was wolves. On one occasion I was utterly insistent that the cast of *Rainbow* were looting the house while Grotbags (who wasn't even *in Rainbow*, and thus had no business being there), made foul smells in the bathroom.

Sometimes I'd get up and wander about when I was hallucinating. I'd kick open the door to my parents' bedroom, and march about the room screaming, 'Give it back!'

'Give what back, Damien?'

'The things that you have taken, you unutterable bandits! I shall avenge your crimes!'

Then I'd be administered some Calpol or Gripe Water (yummy, genuinely) and led gently back to my bedroom to sleep off my visions.

Our family GP, Dr Hardy, was never the most sympathetic ear when we described my symptoms to him. We'd sit in front of him in his brown little office with its discoloured charts and diagrams on the wall and he would roll his eyes and yawn whenever I attempted to explain exactly how I felt.

'Is there nothing this child is incapable of catching?' he would ask.

'He can't catch a ball,' my father would say.

'You do not surprise me,' Dr Hardy would reply.

'And this man has sworn the Hippocratic Oath,' I used to think to myself. 'What a dog he is.'

Iced Buns

Is there anything – truly – more comforting than an iced bun? Well, it depends on the time of the day, really. First thing in the morning? Not the right thing really. Too sweet for first thing. You'd feel guilty sinking your teeth into something that sweet and soft the first moment you wake up. And breakfast isn't the right time for sweet things either. Panettone or brioche (lightly toasted) are strange exceptions to this rule, but iced buns – for reasons best known only to themselves – aren't. But nor are they an evening snack. Their time has gone by then. That's when you need something more akin to a brownie, something that if served hot could be accompanied with a scoop of ice cream and be a perfectly acceptable pudding. If you see anybody eating iced buns first thing in the morning or last thing at night then I'm afraid you've met someone who is either extremely silly or is some sort of dangerous maverick who has so little regard for the rules of social order that they are best steered well clear of. That said, my partner Anthony would happily eat iced buns at any time of the day, but then he is utterly incorrigible. He would unrepentantly eat curry at any hour if unmonitored. I once saw him rise from the breakfast table and take a packet of pork scratchings from the larder, which he then proceeded to eat whilst standing. It's a wonder we can cohabit sometimes. The right time to eat an iced bun is either bang slap in the middle of the morning or bang slap in the middle of the afternoon. Those are your options and you can frankly like it or lump it.

As a child I was delighted to discover that I could make my own iced buns. I was walking past a window of a café with my mother and I spotted some on the counter underneath a glass bell. I began to drool wildly.

'Look, Mother! Iced buns! Do you think we might …?' I slavered.

'No, Damien. I do not. If you want to eat an iced bun, you can make one yourself.'

I genuinely believe that she thought that would be the end of the matter. But she was wrong. The moment we got home I looked up the recipe in one of her cookbooks, and got baking. I consumed eight of the things that afternoon, and later that evening I was extremely sick. But I had made my point. (In addition to a small stain on the carpet at the foot of our stairs.)

If you're feeling glum, then for goodness sake eat an iced bun. (I honestly think I'm a loss to the advertising industry sometimes.)

For the bun bit, you will need …
>   Plain flour, 1 lb of
>   Salt, approximately 1 thimbleful of

Caster sugar, 3 oz of

Salted butter, 2 oz of and in as softened a state as you can achieve legally but not a liquid one

Fresh yeast, just under 1 oz of

A pair of eggs

Some milk, ideally full fat, a smidgeon over ⅓ of a pint

The zest of 1 lemon

For the iced bit, you will need …

Icing sugar, 6 oz of

Lemon juice, some

Water, a little

Start by putting your oven on a low temperature and get out a lovely big bowl and lovely big sieve (a lot of people only have one sieve, I recently discovered. I was shocked. Anyway, if you've only got one, that'll have to be the one that you use – but don't be afraid to consider getting another) and sift all of the flour and salt through one and into the other (I shouldn't have to tell you which). Then put the bowl into the oven and allow the flour and salt, and indeed the bowl, to warm. Remove it from the oven and add the sugar, the butter and the yeast, which you must crumble in gently. Mix it all together manually, by which I mean with your actual hands. It's nice to get dirty once in a while, isn't it? Then give your hands a little wipe with something appropriate and beat the eggs, milk and lemon zest together in another nice bowl, a small one this time. Manually create a hole in the middle of the flour and butter *et al* and pour the milk and egg *et al* into it.

Now you must work it for a good while, again manually. After some minutes everything will have combined to form a fairly viscous batter, which requires you to beat it. You can of course do this with your Magimix or KitchenAid or similar, but I find that bashing away furiously with both hands is a lovely way to pass some time when one is alone in the house. You will eventually produce what is undoubtedly dough, which you must then cover with a tea towel or some cling film and allow to rise in a warm place. This is why it was so important to choose a lovely big bowl, because it needs to have enough capacity for the dough to double in size. Who knows how long this might take? An hour and a quarter at the very least, I would have thought, but do watch over it closely.

When your dough has doubled in size, turn it out on to your work surface, which you have lightly floured especially for the occasion. Divide the dough into a dozen identically sized pieces, and then work each one either into a nice round shape or an oblong one. It doesn't matter which shape you choose, but it does matter that you take some time over it so as to ensure that the dough is properly kneaded. Then arrange them all neatly on a buttered baking tray, and drape some lightly oiled cling film over the top of them all. Again, leave them to rise. They'll need about half an hour so that leaves you plenty of time to run around once with the Hoover or watch an old episode of *The Golden Girls*.

Get your giggles out of the way and get back to the kitchen in good time to set your oven to gas mark 7 so that it's at the right temperature for you to slide the buns in and give them a right good baking for precisely ten whole minutes. Amazing how it's ten minutes precisely, isn't it? Not nine. Or eleven. Or forty-seven. Precisely ten. It's just one of those mathematical laws that holds true wherever you are in the universe. You then need to turn the temperature down to gas 5 and give them another couple. Take them out of the oven and you will see that they have risen considerably. Separate them out, taking care not to burn your precious fingers, and then put them aside to cool.

Once the buns have completely cooled, and having washed out your only sieve or picked up one of your back-up ones, sift the icing sugar thoroughly into a clean bowl. And then slowly, gradually, stir in both the lemon juice and water. Take almighty care over this, watching the mixture change until you have achieved your dream consistency. Then take a spoonful of the icing mixture and pour it slowly over each and every one of the buns and watched it harden and take on a beautiful sheen.

There. They are ready. If a home-made ice bun doesn't raise your spirits, then you must somehow have been possessed by the spirit of a nineteenth-century Russian novelist and you probably need to get yourself looked at. They're dreadfully moreish though, the buns, so do watch out.

Chapter 6

GOOD PEOPLE AND BAD PEOPLE

I cried the day that I left Tiny Steps for the last time. I had missed many days of school owing to sickness, but the time I had spent there I valued enormously. The thought that I was never going to see that marvellous wooden kitchen playset left me deeply depressed. I had made some wonderful friends in my time there, and been invited to so many exciting parties by the other children. We'd play musical statues and musical chairs and 'What's the Time, Mister Wolf?' Then we'd eat enormous quantities of crisps and sweets and jelly. Goodness only knows the damage we must have been doing to ourselves and to our digestive systems. I nearly always went home with a headache, and to this day the sight or thought of party food of this sort makes me feel completely nauseous. Sometimes there'd be a clown called Smarty Arty or Johnny something and we'd all laugh and scream and shout as they performed tricks and juggled. The first time I saw a rabbit appear from a magician's hat I passed clean out. A lot of people are sneery about smelling salts, but as a child I never went anywhere without them.

The teachers we had at Tiny Steps were wonderful too. Kind people.

I am quite convinced that teaching really must be one of the very hardest jobs in the world, and I doubt very much indeed that I am alone in thinking this. (Who knows? Maybe I am alone in thinking this. There's simply no way of knowing. I'm not a mind reader, now am I?[1]) What greater responsibility could any adult have than to stand up, lesson after lesson, day after day, in front of class after class, and be responsible for shaping the way that these young people develop? To try to get them to show an interest in mathematics or to understand the wider ramifications of Henry VIII's Act for the Dissolution of the Greater Monasteries (1539)? Well, let me tell you: nothing. There *is* no greater responsibility. Other jobs may run teachers close when it comes to stress levels – kitchen work, perhaps, or some areas of the military – but when it comes to *responsibility*, there is none greater. All that being said, however, I think that it is also fair to say that being given that level of responsibility is also quite the most enormous privilege. Which is why I personally think it's a shame that so many of them just aren't up to it.

There was a rather excellent commercial that they showed in the cinema some years ago that was part of a drive to recruit more people to train as student teachers. It was, like so many of the best ideas, rather simple. We,

---

1   Just done a quick Google. Turns out that I am quite definitely *not* alone in thinking this. It's a very commonly held view indeed. Which gives, if anything, more weight to my argument. Not that I've made one yet. But I soon shall be. All being well.

the viewer, would see a variety of popular celebrities of the time (New Labour faces such as Tony Blair and Eddie Izzard and so forth) filmed so as to appear in their place of work or enjoying some doubtless much-deserved leisure time, looking down the lens and saying a person's name. When the last of the celebrities had looked down the lens and uttered a name (it was Blair himself who spoke last, as I recall: top billing for The Man, as the excellent diarist Chris Mullin always referred to him), the screen went momentarily blank, and then across it in white lettering appeared the words YOU NEVER FORGET YOUR FAVOURITE TEACHER. I think they then gave the address of a website, or a number you should call or something, but the point had already been made. Brilliantly.

'What a simple but brilliant idea,' I remember whispering to my partner Anthony.

'Shush,' said somebody in the row behind, rather sharply.

I turned round and apologised to the aggrieved party, but they just shushed me again, and so I gave up. I tried to enjoy the film, but it was hopeless. This touchy zealot had ruined the evening for me, and there was simply no way back. Anthony, as is so often his habit, fell asleep moments into the film and dozed throughout. At one point, as is also so often his habit, he began to snore at a volume that was, if not deafening, then rather greater than that at which I had earlier whispered. I turned round to see if the person who had been so offended by my (quiet by comparison) utterances was going to shush Anthony for his respiratory rumblings but they too were also sound asleep. Goodness knows what this film was but the evidence so far suggests that it was very likely to have had Orlando Bloom in a prominent role. (Nothing against the man personally. I'm sure he's tidy, conscientious and good to his mother but, as far as I'm concerned, he's no Dennis Price.)

I still can't remember the film, but I shall never forget the commercial. Because it's true: you never do forget your favourite teacher. But nor, crucially, do you forget your *least* favourite teacher. The one who was most unpleasant, or uncaring, or who lacked basic niceties, or who joined in with name-calling. Or who, repeatedly, found ways to humiliate you.

One such lady was a Miss Proctor. After leaving Tiny Steps I was sent for a small time, and much to my shame, to a small private preparatory day school in north London. I wish I could say that my parents eventually withdrew me from it for ideological reasons, but actually it was a combination of a long and wretched drive in the morning rush hour[2] and the fact that I had reached the age at which one is legally required to leave such a school.*

2 Driving in heavy but slow-moving traffic has always left me feeling somewhat sickly. I think my brain must find it hard to reconcile the constant throbbing of the engine with the dispiriting lack of progress. Anthony and I were once stuck in a tailback near the Hammersmith Flyover that we found so vexatious that we actually pulled over and booked into the Novotel for a night. Not an experience I wish to repeat.

Does this make any sense?

I think so.

Well, it's left me baffled. Were you removed from the school or did you just leave when you were supposed to?

The point I'm trying to make is that I wish that I had been removed on ideological grounds, but unfortunately I wasn't. And the drive was such a faff that it didn't make sense for me to go on to the senior school there. Please don't ask these sorts of questions. I'm trying to write a book. You might imagine that these sorts of interjections are helpful but they're actually dispiriting and hurtful.

Sorry.

Thank you. Apology accepted. Only constructive notes from now on, if you please.

As soon as I walked into the place on my first day, I knew there was something wrong. The atmosphere seemed to me to completely unconducive to offering what might be termed a rounded education. There was a trophy cupboard up on the wall in the entranceway full of shiny cups and shields and the odd cap, all of them celebrating sporting achievements. The place was noisy, and everyone, staff and pupils alike, travelled about the place unnecessarily fast. This did not seem like my sort of place at all. My mother had also told me, ominously, that they didn't teach cookery.

As these sort of schools go[3] it was really not all that impressive, but it fancied itself as being rather smart. In truth it was not a big-hitter academically, and actually the

---

3 North London seems at times to be absolutely crammed to bursting with self-satisfied little establishments of this sort, blond boys in blazers being collected in 4×4s driven by ladies who dress as if they're straight out of a hot yoga class and who seem to think that double yellow lines and zig zags are painted on the streets by the council as a way of indicating where to park if you're nipping into Starbucks. Where I live now I am actually frightened to leave the house between half past three and half past four because I know these people will have taken over the streets like an invading force, and are generally in a mood to take no prisoners. I have seen parking wardens reduced to tears by their antics. On another occasion I found myself writing the words 'YOU ARE A DISGRACE' on a piece of card, and popping it under someone's windscreen wiper so that they would see the words when they climbed into the car. I watched from a safe distance as the mother in question tore up the card and threw the pieces into the gutter. Honestly, it's so hard to love this country sometimes. Still, I hope it made her think.

sports results were, from everything I could gather from the boys who were actually chosen to represent the school in competitive sports, really nothing to write home about.[4] There were some music lessons on offer, but these were largely taught by people who, looking back at them from the perspective of an adult, were clearly angry depressives. A man called Mr Timothy who taught strings was rumoured to have hit a boy with a cello once, and he was considered one of the more sensitive members of the department. The whole place could have done with a lick of paint, to be honest, which was ironic because the best person in the whole place by a country mile was the art teacher, Mrs Kensham. More of whom later.

Miss Proctor became my form teacher when I was seven, which any child psychologist worth their salt would tell you is an absolutely *crucial* stage in one's development. There are things that you can shrug off with the absolute minimum of fuss at the ages of six or eight and leave no trace of behind, but which can absolutely floor you at

4 I never really felt that my own preferred sport, badminton, was something that the school took particularly seriously. Certainly they never went so far as to actually arrange any competitive fixtures with other local schools. It was just myself and a boy called, I think, Gareth gently knocking the shuttlecock back and forth in short and undemanding rallies in a rather tattered gymnasium that contained no line markings for badminton or indeed a net. But we were happy. Well, not happy exactly. We didn't actually have anything in common apart from a fear and hatred of the contact sports on offer and consequently barely spoke to each other. But we were content and, crucially, safe.

seven and leave a scar that can never be healed solely by the passing of time. In this sort of school, your form teacher is the single member of staff with whom one has the most contact, so of course it is absolutely vital that you are able to rub along free of friction and are capable of understanding each other.

My partner Anthony occasionally likes to get involved in amateur dramatics and has explained to me that the dynamic between teacher and pupil in such a scenario is very similar to that between actor and director. He was once playing a vital role in a three-night production of what I think was Noël Coward's _Present Laughter_* (although it could just as easily have been something else) and working under a director with whom I think it is fair to say that he did not see eye to eye. She was, as I'm sure all directors worth their salt must surely be, extremely thorough and well prepared. But she also had a personality that for some reason – possibly chemical – did not gel well with Anthony's. He is a much gentler soul than people might initially presume for a man of his height. He is also not especially flexible in the physical sense and his habit of spending a lot of time making himself comfortable (not unlike the manner in which a sleepy dog likes to walk in a few circles, as if flattening the ground, immediately prior to settling down for a nap) can sometimes make people think that he must be lethargic.

He also gets very stressed about 'props'. Despite seemingly being able to operate his ruddy and beloved iPad with his eyes shut, he is not necessarily all that adept with

* Damien, is this sort of detail really necessary, esp. if it turns out that it's not correct?

Who can say?

his hands in other areas of life. In the olden days he would probably have been referred to as 'clumsy', but hopefully we have moved on as a species since those dark days. I remember that in the run-up to the play's opening night he was terribly fraught about all of the props that he was expected to handle in the course of carrying out his role to the best of his abilities – particularly, as I recall, some sort of business involving a candlestick – and used to come home from rehearsals late at night and sit on the sofa with his head in his hands and repeat the phrase, 'Why the bloody hell do I get involved in this sort of nonsense? I simply cannot cope' over and over again. He also, I should add, has a rather quiet natural speaking voice, and so throughout rehearsals the director used to bellow 'WHAT?' at him almost every time he spoke, which had an appalling effect on his nervous system and made him even jumpier than normal.

In the run-up to the performances this doubtless gifted woman made my poor Anthony so stressed that life in our normally tranquil and (I like to think) extremely well-run house became utterly unbearable. Anthony has a very high threshold when it comes to stress and is most adept at keeping it at bay. But when it eventually crashes through his defences ... well, my goodness. He once came home from rehearsals and ate an entire loaf of shop-bought white bread in the downstairs lavatory. I was, quite justifiably, livid. Shop-bought bread is disgusting. Then he would lie awake long into the night, moaning almost continually and, eventually, began to suffer (at least he *claimed*) from heart palpitations. When he did finally get off to sleep cold sweat would literally pour off his vast frame and it was even less pleasant than you might imagine. The whole thing was easily as stressful for me as it was for him, if not more. I was simply incapable of getting off next to a man who was muttering about suspected cardiac irregularities. I don't mean this to sound in any way 'New Age', but once your circadian rhythms are out of whack, you've little chance of achieving anything meaningful with your day. (Housework: perhaps. Bottling: potentially. Writing: absolutely not. Impossible.[5]) When the play was all over (I rather enjoyed it actually, he's got a lovely speaking voice), we celebrated by practically skipping to our local branch of the White Company and splashing out on some fresh bedding.

Now, I'm sure you think that my describing this behaviour by Anthony's director is simply a way of me seizing the opportunity to get a few things off my chest, and to carry out some sort of bitter personal vendetta by criti-

---

5 If someone asks me to write something after a restless night, then frankly they can whistle Dixie for it unless they're prepared to be sympathetic about my sleeplessness. But how many commissioning editors ring one up and begin proceedings by asking how one has slept these days? Very few indeed. No wonder print journalism's in crisis if there's so little thoughtfulness going on. Or perhaps this decline in manners and caring is a symptom of this decline in newspaper circulation rather than the cause of it. One wonders what the answer could possibly be. It's chicken and egg stuff, isn't it? Undoubtedly the answer must lie somewhere between the two.*

* It's because of the internet, Damien. Which reminds me: answer your emails.

Please keep your notes on-topic, else I shall be distracted. Not at all helpful, do please desist.

cising this dreadful-sounding woman in print. Let me assure you that it is not. It is because when I watched the way that the ghastly behaviour of this absolutely unbearable creature made my poor partner Anthony feel, I could empathise with him. The panic, the night sweats, the comfort-eating and the heart palpitations; this was how my fear of Miss Proctor used to manifest itself when I was just a meek seven-year-old child, in desperate need of approval, encouragement and the right kind of attention. I dreaded going to school every single day for that whole academic year. The very mention of Miss Proctor's name often brought on panic attacks not unlike the ones to which I am still, ever so occasionally, susceptible.

It is even now, after all these years, not immediately obvious why she should have taken such a serious dislike of me. I have always been a conscientious student, and used to make a point of asking as many questions in classes as ever I possibly could. Or simply putting up my hand and making helpful statements. Usually they were related to the matter in hand, but if I felt there was something from outside Miss Proctor's sphere of knowledge that I thought might be of interest to her and the class then I felt duty bound to share it. It can't possibly have been this that upset her, so what could it have been? Perhaps it was merely a matter of her own insecurity, which was dazzlingly apparent almost whenever she spoke. Whatever it was, her upset evidenced itself clearly by her taking any opportunity that she could to humiliate and belittle me.

Sometimes when handing back a piece of work of mine that she had marked (she used to reach out towards me and then let go of the piece of paper or exercise book ever so slightly out of my reach so that it would fall to the floor and she could chastise me further), she would draw attention to any mistakes I had made in a voice that was definitely far louder than that she used when pointing out small errors to the other pupils.

Once she told me that a story I had written was 'wildy unbelievable'. 'It's important to be creative, Damien, but at the same time I can't help feeling that your stories would benefit from being both shorter and more credible.' I took (and indeed still take) issue with her advice. For one, it wasn't a made-up story: it was a factual account of the time that I was violently sick in an old lead mine during a family trip to the Heights of Abraham in Derbyshire. And also, I had edited it as carefully as I possibly could, stripping out all details that would neither entertain, inform nor act as precautionary advice to the reader. (Which is, as it happens, how I still approach my work today.) I had even omitted from my account the precise wording of the extremely graphic tale that my sister had told and what it was that she was doing to me during the telling that had triggered this wave of sudden nausea.

And she, just as Anthony's director had done to him all those years later, claimed that I mumbled. Which I definitely didn't. (Anthony *is* a bit quiet. In my own instance it was a total fabrication. The importance of clear enunciation was absolutely drilled into me at home from a young age. Anthony's background is Scottish Presbyterian, and thus silence was encouraged where possible.) She would frequently shout 'WHAT?!' after I had spoken. To this day, I cannot hear or read or even write the word 'what' without feeling shame and humiliation. (So that's two waves of shame and humiliation in this paragraph alone; no one ever said that writing wasn't meant to be painful.)

One incident sticks out above all the many, many others. As I said, the school[6] was not endowed with many facilities, and thus inevitably had no swimming pool. In fact I'd say that building a swimming pool probably ranked fairly low down the list of potential improvements that the school might have thought about making. Personally, I'd have started with lavatory doors that could actually be locked. Then some windows in those lavatories that could actually be *unlocked*. Then some raised beds for pupils interested in learning how to grow vegetables and salad etc.

But swimming, all prospective parents of pupils were

6 I am not going to name it here, and it no longer exists. The building (which was, apart from the art teacher, its best asset) is still there, but like everything else, it has become flats. We drove past it the other day, in fact. Lord alone knows how but they even acquired planning permission to have those sort of pretend two-dimensional balconies screwed on to the front, meaning that even if you live on the third floor you can have a French window in your sitting room. Absolutely daft. They don't add charm, but they do add value, apparently. What a world.

* Damien, why do you keep putting so many words and phrases in italics?

It's so that I know where to do the emphases when I do the audiobook.

We were thinking of asking Martin Jarvis.

I would be honoured. Absolutely the right choice. Such a sensitive voice. Very versatile. No complaints here whatsoever. If, however, by any chance he is not able or willing to do it, then I would very much like to.

We've asked him. He's available and willing.

Are you absolutely sure he's the right choice? Perhaps I ought to do it.

We all think Martin would be perfect. He's very experienced and very quick. Which would help claw back some of the time that we've lost.

If you say so. All I ask is that I sit in on all the recordings. That way I could give him a gentle nudge if there's any nuances I feel he's missed.

I'll ask.

Super.

told, was an important part of the syllabus, and thus swimming had to be done. There was a council pool, rather a nice one actually, only twelve minutes' walk from the school. Every Wednesday afternoon, all of the pupils in Miss Proctor's class would line up in pairs at the top of the steps outside the school's rather grand entrance, and march in procession through the streets to the swimming pool. It was all very strictly timetabled, as school life tended to be. (Why is there no room in school life for spontaneity* for heaven's sake? What sort of people are we trying to produce? Automatons? The sort of people who think that there is one right answer to every question and no possible room for a bit of intellectual wriggle? Small wonder that almost everyone from this school that I ever meet has grown up to become a sneery management consultant.)

Other schools used to book the pool as well, so the whole arrangement was monstrously tight. Twelve minutes' walk to the pool. Five minutes to change. Twenty-five minutes' instruction. Five minutes of 'free time' – which I could personally have done without, consisting as it did of everybody fighting to get on to one of the big floats while hitting each other with the little floats – then a whistle. Five minutes to get showered, dried and changed back into school uniform again, before another school arrived to use the changing room. Twelve minutes walk back to the school. Done. Whole operation pulled off in a smidgeon over an hour.

This might seem, to the reader, like efficiency. But as

far as I was concerned, the whole thing was flawed. Five minutes for getting out of school uniform and into one's swimming costume is ample. But five minutes to shower, dry and get dressed again is anything but. There was only one hair dryer for a start, and even that worked intermittently. I would never think of myself as a time waster or dawdler. I am one of life's active participants, not a spectator. I like to be thrown into the deep end and just get on with it. (Except when swimming. I prefer to use the steps.)*

Extraneous. Disagree, I'm afraid. Vital.

But even with that being the case, I do not feel that getting changed after swimming is something that can ever be *rushed*. Not least because I sometimes have homeostatic issues triggered by tight deadlines. Something about showering and drying at speed after swimming used to bring me out in a sweat, which sometimes necessitated a further shower, putting greater pressure on the available time and thus commencing a vicious cycle. Rare was the week when I wasn't the last to be changed, and even though I soon gave up even trying to be dry before I put my uniform on, I would often still be struggling to get my shoes on[7] when Miss Proctor would burst through the

7 I briefly considered experimenting with wearing slip-on shoes as a way of hastening the process, despite the fact that I am against them on principle. Anthony has a pair and I forbid him to wear them when I am in his company. We have reached a compromise whereby he is allowed to wear them if he is out socialising with some of his friends from the banking world. I insist, though, that he has to put them on and remove them on the outside step. My hope, strictly between ourselves, is that one night he will come back the

changing room door (inappropriate, I always felt) and tell me to 'just get a ruddy move on'.

'Everybody is waiting for you, Damien,' she would always say. 'What's wrong with you?'

'I really am going as fast as my body and the available facilities will allow,' I would reply, and she'd storm out again, making unkind remarks about me at a volume that carried into the changing room. 'Little arse,' I remember her saying one time. 'Miniature Liberace,' she said on another occasion, which I must say made no sense whatsoever.

These weekly trips to the swimming pool began to play absolute havoc with me. I was desperate not to go, but my parents were not the sort to dash off sick notes willy nilly.

'I feel too ill to swim,' I'd say at breakfast.

'You should swim *because* you're feeling ill,' my mother would say. 'Swimming is good for you.'

'He doesn't have to go swimming if he's not feeling himself, does he?' my father would say.

'Are you a doctor all of a sudden?' my mother would ask.

'No,' he'd say. 'Are you?'

'That is completely irrelevant,' my mother would say. And off I'd go to school with my swimming things and without a sick note. My sister never had that sort of problem. Quite the reverse, in fact. At one point she and some of her contemporaries were actually banned from

---

worse for wear, accidentally leave them out on the step and a fox takes them. A man can dream.

every council swimming pool in Brent for a period of eighteen months. I was never told what she'd done, but I can remember when it happened. I was sent out of the kitchen at suppertime and there was the most blazing row.

'I didn't do anything,' I could hear my sister bellowing. 'None of us did.'

'Then why did the man from the council say you'd left the place looking like a cell in the Maze Prison?' my father asked in a harrowed voice.

It was all too much for my young ears, and so I pootled off to my bedroom.

My confidence suffered, and so did my swimming. I could hardly concentrate on backstroke or the like whilst all my thoughts were consumed with the prospect of getting changed again afterwards quickly enough to escape the ire of Miss Proctor.

Things came to a head the week we did life-saving. Everybody else was utterly thrilled about the prospect of jumping into the pool wearing their pyjamas, but I was rather less keen, rubber bricks or no rubber bricks. It had taken me rather a long time to get out of the habit of getting my pyjamas wet accidentally, and the thought of doing it deliberately seemed to me an all-too-painful reminder of those days. In addition, my pyjamas were hand-me-downs from my sister. Personally I rather liked the pattern on them, and found them to be extremely comfortable, but they were reviewed unfavourably by my classmates and the Scottish swimming instructor. They were also a heavy cotton, and consequently rather weighty when saturated, and thus my bottoms kept falling down whenever I dared to remove my grip on their waistband. For twenty-five minutes I exposed myself almost continually.

Inevitably they were removed from me by wags the moment that the whistle for free time was sounded, and then passed around the class. They were even more popular than the big floats all of a sudden. I could have had a big float to myself if I'd been interested, and indeed been prepared to climb on to one whilst naked from the waist down. Instead, I spent the entire allotted five minutes desperately and vainly trying to get them back. It was only when the whistle sounded again that I could ascertain their whereabouts – hanging from the end of the high diving board. As my classmates sprinted back to the changing room, it was left to the swimming instructor to try and get them down off the high board using one of his big long poles with a hook on the end that they use to help people in dire straits.

And in dire straits I certainly was. The pole wasn't long enough to reach the top of the diving board from the edge of the pool and the instructor told me that he wasn't going up there. 'Sorry pal, I don't do heights.' I am no fan of heights either, but there was absolutely no way I was going to abandon a pair of perfectly decent, if somewhat sodden, pyjama bottoms.

'Fine,' I said. 'I shall have to go up there myself.'

I climbed out of the pool. The instructor looked aghast.

'Oh God,' he said, and threw a float at me. 'Use that to cover yourself up. Why didn't you have your swimming trunks on underneath?'

'I don't think the letter about life-saving made it particularly clear that that was what was intended,' I said, covering my offending area with the float.

'Well, everybody else understood,' he said.

'I know,' I said. 'I know.'

'You just go up there, and I'll look the other way. Where's your teacher? This sort of thing absolutely shouldn't happen. I get told this again and again.'

I climbed up the ladder with one hand, using the other to preserve what little modesty I had left.

'Use both hands!' boomed the instructor. And began blowing his whistle to get some attention.

I didn't know if he meant to climb with, or to protect my nether regions.

'CAN ANOTHER ADULT PLEASE COME AND ASSIST ME?' he began to shout. I could hear the panic rising in his voice.

It was nothing as to the panic I felt having climbed to the top of the ladder, and stood up to my full height. It really was horribly high. I began to tremble, but couldn't stick my arms out to balance myself, without further compromising the poor instructor who was now in a complete state himself.

'Oh God! My bloody job's on the line here,' he kept saying. 'CAN SOMEBODY *PLEASE* COME AND HELP US!'

I inched forward slowly.

'This goes against all the training,' the instructor was saying. 'Where the hell is your teacher?'

'I don't know,' I said. 'Probably getting something out of the vending machine.'

He blew his whistle again, and hollered for further assistance. There was a handrail on the high diving board, but only, for reasons best known to the health and safety department of Brent Council, running along the middle third of one side of its length. After a few ungainly shuffles I had managed to reach it, but my pyjama bottoms were still some distance from me. I edged further along the board until there was no handrail left to support me. I took a tentative step forward, looked down and then completely froze. Becoming all too aware of the considerable height, the idea occurred to me that perhaps the safest way for me to convey myself to the end of the diving board would be upon all fours. I gingerly lowered myself on to my knees, and began to slowly head off in the direction that would enable me to be reunited with my clothing.

'Whatever you do, do NOT fall!' shouted the swimming instructor.

There is probably something even more stupid that he could have shouted in the circumstances, but it's hard to imagine what on earth it might be.

'I'm trying really rather hard not to,' I assured him.

'I really shouldn't have let you go up there like that,' he lamented. 'Not on your own. And certainly not naked from the waist down. There's too many bloody rules in these places and I'm managing to break them all at once. I keep having to move jobs because of shite like this. Other people's stupidity ends up looking like *my* fault.'

It was rather hard for me to see things from his perspective at this precise moment, as I was in the business of seeing things all too vividly from my own. I could see my hands, I could see the narrow diving board, and I could see occasional glimpses of my knees and then all I could see was the drop[8] and the chlorinated water beyond it. From this height the distance between the water's surface and the square tiles that indicated the bottom of the pool looked too close together to be actually safe, were I to lose my footing and topple off the high board.

'It must just be a foreshortening effect, it must just be a foreshortening effect,' I repeated over and over to myself in an attempt to remain calm. It wasn't a particularly successful attempt, it must be said. But I reckoned it made for a better use of my time than me just pounding away at the board with my fists and wishing damnation upon whoever it was that had flung my pyjama bottoms (and I had my suspicions) into this most unhelpful of places in the first place.

Looking down at the drop had put me into such a panic

---

8   I've just used Google to try to work out the likely dimensions of the diving board, in order to ascertain the likely height of the drop. I have found the figure, but I cannot actually bear to write it down because even the thought of it is quite sickening.

that I could no longer bear to keep my eyes open, and so I screwed them tightly shut and began feeling my way forward blindly, like a hill walker searching for the top of a cliff in a heavy mist.

'Am I nearly there?' I called to the swimming instructor.

'I don't know,' he called back. 'I've shut my eyes. I can't bear to look.'

'We can't both have our eyes closed,' I said. 'One of us has to be able to see.'

'You open yours,' he said. 'You're the one that's not properly dressed.'

'Through no fault of my own,' I reminded him. And continued my journey into the unseen.

I could hear the swimming instructor appeal, in a more feverish voice, for help. But there was neither sign nor sound of assistance.

'Maybe you should just come down?' he called to me.

But at that moment, I felt wet cloth and knew that I could only have finally reached my sodden pyjama bottoms. I opened my eyes to confirm that this was the case and tried to lift them, but they were snagged on something on the underside of the board. I put a hand underneath the board and felt slowly around for the offending cause of the snag. A small section of the elastic waistband[9] or some such had become wrapped around a bolt, and it was hard to pull the pyjama bottoms free without making the board bounce precariously. The only

9 I prefer a drawstring on my pyjama trousers these days, and I doubt it's unrelated.

thing for it would be to get right to the end of the board, and then lean forward and down until I was in a position to see the underside of the board and ascertain the exact source of my present difficulties. I somehow managed to achieve this fairly quickly and to resolve the problem, despite my ears being filled with the voice of the swimming instructor shouting 'I can't look, I just can't look!' over and over again, when I heard a sudden noise from the other end of the pool. A door had been kicked open and I heard the unmistakeable bellow of Miss Proctor.

'DAMIEN TRENCH! WHAT IN HELL'S NAME DO YOU THINK YOU'RE DOING?' she shouted up at me. At least I assume that's how the sentence ended. Because once I heard the word 'hell' I could only hear the sound of rushing air. The unthinking Miss Proctor had distracted me at the vital moment, I'd looked back in her direction, lost balance, and tumbled forward off the diving board.

I performed a number of completely inadvertent somersaults, and hit the water feet first still clutching the pyjama bottoms. Down to the bottom of the pool I sank, my eyes and ears and nose all wide open – presumably – in shock. All I could see, smell and hear was bubbling, chlorinated water, and lots of it. I slowly returned to the surface, gasping for air, my eyes and lungs burning.

'I told him not to go up there, but he just wouldn't listen,' I heard the instructor saying. 'If this goes to tribunal I need you to take my side.'

I was in no position to offer up an alternative view of events because I was too traumatised by my discovery that in the process of pulling my pyjama bottoms free they had been badly ripped, right down the back. The discovery of this damage had left me *incandescent*. The fact that my parents were sending me to a fee-paying school at which the atmosphere was so unsettling and riddled with so much injustice and ambivalence towards the needs and comforts of others that circumstances could arise leading to the damage of another person's pyjamas was, I felt, symptomatic of even worse societal problems at large.

As I tried to climb the ladder from the pool, my path was blocked by Miss Proctor, who was standing with hands on hips, looking down at me as if I were something upsetting that she had found on the heel of her shoe and was simply incapable of removing.

'What do you think you're doing?' she asked in a clipped whisper that chilled me to my very core.[10]

10 It does to this day, in all honesty. I went to a home interiors shop a few months ago to. To browse, really, but I ended up deciding, as one occasionally does, to buy a brand-new free-standing bath because I thought that its feet went rather better with the feet of our bathroom armchairs than the feet of our current bath. If you follow me. I was just explaining this to the sales lady, when she said, 'And what sort of bath do you have at the moment?' in a voice so cold and reminiscent of Miss Proctor's that her questioning instantly reduced me to jelly. Cold sweat began to cover my temples. One of my knees buckled and the other locked. It was as if Miss Proctor herself were admonishing me for already possessing a freestanding bath and a pair of armchairs whose feet didn't quite match, which did sound (in this moment of self-examination, the sort which Miss Proctor's behaviour often triggered) a bit silly.

'My pyjama bottoms were in need of rescue,' I informed her. 'I – and indeed my pyjama bottoms – have fallen victim to a most unfortunate set of circumstances.'

There was something about the way Miss Proctor used to inquisition me that always made me speak in somewhat archaic language.

'What a *stupid* thing to do,' she said.

'It was most foul of the perpetrators, this plot,' I said, still speaking as if the pair of us were actors in a costume drama.[11]

I froze and so the sales girl repeated the question. '*What sort of bath do you have at the moment?*' she said, carefully stressing every word and using the tone of voice that one might more readily associate with enquiring of elderly relatives if they have remembered to make use of the lavatory facilities, and if not, might it not be a good idea before we all get in the car? Her question left me glued to the spot. 'I'm so sorry,' I eventually muttered. 'I've made the most terrible mistake.' I attempted to turn and flee from the shop, but had momentarily forgotten that I had one wobbly knee and one locked one, and was consequently unable to flee in anything even approaching a straight line. Instead I lurched left, and then right, and then left again before finally tripping over a set of fireplace tools (that had earlier caught my eye until I noticed that they were reproduction) and landing face first in a pile of decorative pine cones. Thank God they were there, in fact, or else I would have landed face down on a cast-iron fire grate that I noticed, as I was helped to my feet, was genuinely antique and not in the least bit reproduction.

'Do you need us to call someone?' the lady who by this time might as well have been Miss Proctor asked me. 'I want for nothing,' I replied with as much confidence as I could, in the circumstances, muster. As I limped from the shop I had the distinct impression that people were staring at me.

11 A quite ludicrous thought, actually. I would probably be just

'Stupid of *you*, you idiot,' she said.

'*Me*?' I stammered. 'Miss Proctor, am I really likely to have stolen my own pyjama bottoms?'

'I wouldn't put anything past you, you attention-seeking dolt.[12] Now get out of the pool,' she added, whilst finally stepping out of my path. 'You're making us all late. The whole class will have to wait for you. There's no time to shower, just get yourself dried and dressed and stop eating into the timetable. We'll all be waiting outside.'

And with that she flounced off. I climbed out of the pool and eyed the swimming instructor, who was standing there looking sheepish, and not without justification.

'See you next week,' he said. 'If I'm still here.'

I did not answer him. Instead I made my way to the changing room, which was now full of children from another school who had almost as little sympathy with my predicament as Miss Proctor had, blocking the path to my locker and making a series of extremely unhelpful and hurtful remarks. I couldn't really get dressed until the changing room had emptied again, and thus was feeling extremely flustered by the time I was able to join my own classmates in the corridor.

---

about able to pull it off but Miss Proctor would be appalling casting in any costume drama, requiring as they do a certain degree of finesse and a lightness of touch. Miss Proctor's best chance of appearing onscreen would be in one of those documentary reconstructions that the natural history department make – possibly one about the discovery of fire.

12 Dolt. Standard dictionary definition: 'a stupid person, nincompoop or clown'. Completely unjustifiable label. She marked my work every week for heaven's sake.

'Would you like to apologise to the class for keeping everybody waiting?' Miss Proctor asked.

'I offer my most sincere apologies to all concerned,' I muttered and everybody laughed at me.

'Right then. Can we finally leave, or is there any other way you'd like to hold us all up?'

'No, no,' I said. 'You may proceed.'

And off we went.

I wish that was the end of the story, but sadly it wasn't. This episode has a conclusion, but it is not one that I feel able to tell just yet, because it is simply more pain than I can cope with all at once. We shall return to her. For the moment, though, let us leave all thoughts of Miss Proctor to one side.

Chapter 7

THE SAINT

I mentioned earlier that the best person in the whole place was the art teacher, Mrs Kensham. The school was absurdly, ludicrously, fortunate to have her in their employ and if the rest of staff room didn't realise it then they were a pack of bloody fools. She was genuinely the only person in the building who seemed to understand what pastoral care actually was. If ever I had a problem – and I'll be honest, I had many – it was to Mrs Kensham's art room that I would take myself and let it all just pour out of me. She was a wonderful listener, and also had the biggest box of tissues that I've ever seen.

Technically, if one had a problem one was supposed to go and speak to one's form teacher. As I hope I've already made clear, this was not an avenue I was very likely to pursue. For reasons that I could never understand, the school did not see fit to appoint Mrs Kensham a form teacher. I suspect, although I have no proof of this, that this is because of an institutionalised distrust of people who expressed any sort of interest in the arts. Music was encouraged to an extent, but sadly that extent being that everybody was forced to learn violin via the Suzuki method.[1]

So it was left to Mrs Kensham to fly the flag for the real arts. Her lessons were the things that I looked forward to most at that school. Other people yearned for break time, and the chance to play football in the playground.

1 Shinichi Suzuki was a doubtless well-meaning Japanese gentleman who noticed soon after the Second World War that all the children seemed a bit miserable. And so he set about trying to cheer them all by teaching them the violin. (He was himself, it must be said, a violinist. I'm not accusing him of self-interest, merely helping you to understand why this theory represented something less of a logical leap than it might have done to others). He thought that young children ought to be able to learn to play music in much the same way as they learn languages, namely in small steps, often by ear and in large groups. He started, in effect, a revolution in learning. He devised a detailed and prescriptive method of teaching in which young children were immersed in music, and more and more instruments have over the years been added to the International Suzuki Association's list – cello, viola, harp, recorder, flute to name but five.

His work is, of course, quite admirable. To my mind, attempting to revitalise a culture devastated by huge losses of human life and the demoralising surrender in August 1945 following the invasion of Manchuria is an extremely noble aim. But where does it all lead? I'll tell you. By the early 1980s every prep school in Britain was filled with class upon class of uninterested pupils sitting on chairs and trying to scrape out 'My Bonnie Lies Over the Ocean' in unison on tiny violins. This was not, I feel, a desirable outcome. The resulting noise, if heard by the wrong sets of ears, could easily have led to a resumption of hostilities. If Mrs Thatcher had banned the Suzuki method rather than milk, she might have won herself more fans.

I attempted to partake in a game of playground football on more than one occasion and was never left anything other than tired, tearful and confused. For a start, up to fifty people could be playing, so the whole thing was a complete whirlwind of activity and the playing area was, frankly, over full. This is, I assume, why in real football the number of people playing is limited to (thirty.)* Also, it was completely impossible to tell which side anybody was on, as everybody was dressed identically. Utter chaos. Not a fan.

Is this right? Please can somebody check?

I felt, when I first arrived at the school, a pressure to join in, a desire to be part of something and to simply do as others did. My younger brother Ralph was always absurdly, terrifyingly good at sport, but I didn't seem to have any sporting genes in me whatsoever. Some people, I notice, are not fazed by the thought of a ball of any size coming towards them at considerable speed. They instinctively catch it. Or stop it with their foot. Or kick it somewhere else with their foot. Or sometimes with their head. It's unbelievable really. If I see a ball coming towards me, even now, my first instinct is one of self-preservation. I will dive out of the way. Or duck. Or run off. Sometimes I get in a no man's land of indecision as to which of these options to take, and then end up getting hit. It's dreadful really.

Queen's Park, near to where I live, is generally a fairly placid sort of place. Yes, there is some sort of pitch and putt facility. Yes, there is a very well used play area and yes, there is a petting zoo. There's also a bandstand (underused in my opinion). But the open areas are generally quiet and relaxed. It's somewhere where I can go to feel safe and indeed content. Anthony and I have had so many memorable picnics there that it would simply be impossible to remember them all. Other times, on those rare occasions when I find myself with a deadline-free stretch, and there is no keeping house to do – perhaps I've put something in the oven at a low temperature, lamb perhaps, very occasionally pork, but it certainly isn't my favourite, and there's nothing to do for hours but wait – I will take myself off to the park with a book, often having stopped en route for a takeaway coffee it must be said (and you're certainly spoiled for choice round our way, so that can add anything up to forty-five minutes to your journey time), and sit on a bench and read. It is pure bliss. But if a game of football starts up near me I will always get up and go *instantly*. I simply do not want that thing, or indeed the sort of people who play with it, coming anywhere near me. I have been hit by footballs in parks on *many occasions*, and any apologies that I have received in such instances (and one doesn't, sad to relate, receive apologies in all such instances) have always been delivered laughingly. Not nice.

Sometimes a football rolls across one's path, and societal conventions dictate that one must return it in the direction of the owner. But I don't. Can't, even. If I ever hear the words, 'Could you possibly kick our ball back, sir?', I pretend to be deaf. I do hope that this isn't offensive. Each time I do it I pop into the newsagent and drop a couple of pounds into the box for Action on Hearing Loss, so I hope that offsets any ill-feeling.

Occasionally in the playground during one of these riotous and unregulated free-for-alls, and definitely more by fortune than design, the ball would come towards me and stop at my feet.

'Pass it to me, Damo!' someone would shout, and I would endeavour to prod the thing in their direction. They nearly always turned out to have been on the other team. I despise trickery, and always have done. I once got wind of a rumour that Anthony was planning on holding a surprise birthday party in my honour. I had the thing closed down immediately. Even the thought of coming home to find thirty of my close friends or family members screaming 'SURPRISE!' at me in my own kitchen is enough to make me get twitchy, so heaven knows what the result of actually experiencing such a trauma would be. An overnight stay in a hospital, I shouldn't wonder.

On about the third occasion I played football at school, I was struck in the face so hard that the game briefly stopped. I had fallen to the ground instantly, and a small crowd gathered around. I had shut my eyes long before the moment of impact, and they were still tightly shut now.

'Is he all right?' somebody asked.

The moment I opened my eyes, someone said 'he's fine', and the game just started up again. I couldn't believe it. I hadn't demonstrated that any other part of my anatomy was in working order and yet just from a couple of blinks they thought that it was perfectly acceptable to carry on. It could have been a *Diving Bell and the Butterfly* situation for all they knew. I limped from the playing area in some distress, but I already knew where to go.

Only the day before I had had my first lesson with Mrs Kensham. She had struck me instantly as one of the nicest and most wonderful people that I had ever set eyes on. She had dark hair, and dark eyes, and the gentlest manner imaginable. She told us that she wanted us to enjoy whatever we did in her classroom. We didn't always have to be drawing or painting. Sometimes, it was just enough to think about these things, or indeed about something else. But whenever we did put pen or brush to paper, we should make sure that we were using these implements to express how we were feeling.

'Even if it's just a drawing of a chair?' said some wag, sniggering.

'Even if it is just a drawing of a chair,' said Mrs Kensham, immediately picking up a wicker chair and placing it in the centre of the classroom. 'There are lots of different ways to draw a chair like this, for instance. What does this chair make you think of?'

'My grandfather,' said the sniggering boy, who instantly broke into floods of tears.

Such an exciting way to learn. And so as soon as I had limped from the playing area, it was to Mrs Kensham's classroom that I fled.

'Is it all right if I come in?' I asked her.

'Of course,' she said. 'You can always come in here. Anyone can.'[2]

And so I always did. Mrs Kensham's art classroom contained everything the aspirant artist or even keen hobbyist could ever wish for: paper, pens, pencils, crayons, oils, watercolours, ink, easels, plaster of Paris, batik equipment. I loved it.

But Mrs Kensham didn't just enable us to enjoy our own art. She taught us to appreciate (all) art. I don't know how on earth she did it, but she persuaded the headmaster to let her take the (entire school) on an art trip once a term.*

We'd be packed into a series of coaches, and head into the centre of London. It was utterly fabulous. I was incredibly fortunate to see so many of the great art exhibitions of the late 1980s and early 1990s as a result of Mrs Kensham's enthusiasm and indeed encouragement: I saw Leonardo Da Vinci at the Hayward and *Visions of Japan* at the Victoria and Albert. We went to *The Age of Chivalry* at the Royal Academy, and the *Pop Art* exhibition. We saw Rembrandt (the way he painted light!), Franz Hals, Inigo Jones, Bridget Riley, Georgia O'Keeffe, Monet. Possibly even Manet. In fact many of those I may even have seen long after I'd left Mrs Kensham's tutelage, for it was she who had got me into the habit of going to such exhibitions and it was a very hard one to get out of – not that one would ever wish to.

2 Technically, this wasn't actually sensible advice. I heard one story about some people bursting into her classroom to find her sketching a nude adult male.

110

Awful lot of italics here, Damien. Would it be possible to scale them back at all?

As I said, it's for the audiobook.

That reminds me, Martin Jarvis has pulled out.

Oh dear. It'll have to be Plan B. I shall start steaming my vocal cords!

No need. Paul McGann is going to do it.

Marvellous news. No complaints from my end at all. All I ask is that, as with Martin J., I can sit on all recordings.

No can do, sadly. Owing to time constraints we have been forced to book the smallest sound studio in London. Possibly Europe.

OK. I look forward to the results. If for any reason he can't do it, then I would be more than happy to step into the breach.

No need. We've also got Sean Pertwee on a pencil just in case. Please stop worrying about this, and just focus your time and energy on the text.

I'm not worrying.

Of course.

Mrs Kensham was much in my mind recently, as it happens, when Anthony and I took a long overdue trip to Chicago. Chicago is a wonderful city, and if you haven't been then you really must. Don't be put off by the threat of mobsters. The theatre is splendid, the opera divine, the food really rather heavy and meaty (more to Anthony's taste, it must be said, than mine. There's something called a Chicago Pizza Pot Pie that he ordered one day when we stopped for an early lunch and he only just managed to finished it. It weighed a pound, and left him very little room for pudding) – but the art ... oh, the art. We spent three days wandering the floors of the Chicago Institute of Art, and I have to say it wasn't anything like long enough. Even without any art in it, the building would be fabulous enough, standing as it does rather grandly on the shore of Lake Michigan, and somehow managing to combine robustness with a huge amount of natural light. The restaurant on the third floor is excellent, by the way, with a terrace that gives one a fabulous and lofty view of Anish Kapoor's *Cloud Gate* and there are simply *heaps* of cafés and toilets.[3]

3 It might seem odd to mention the restaurant or lavatory facilities in an art gallery before making reference to any art that is actually within the building, but I happen to believe that these sort of things matter. Lavatories, cafés, toilets, restaurants – call them what you will – are part of an art gallery's infrastructure, and it is jolly hard to enjoy or even appreciate art without having them in place.

It is simply not in my nature – and indeed never has been – to be a moaner, but the fact remains that a staggering number of both galleries and museums in the developed

But the reason that Mrs Kensham was often at the forefront

world, certainly here in Britain, are very badly let down by their cafés to a degree that is, in all honesty, extremely upsetting. There are a huge number of considerations that need to be taken into account when arranging a gallery café, and all too often these considerations are ridden roughshod over in the pursuit of profit.

The quality and range of food is, of course, very important. If something bills itself as a café, then nobody in their right mind would be expecting the food to be heavy or even the range of food available to be extensive. What you need in such instances, as indeed is so often the case in all walks of life, is just a few things done well. Some pastries are essential. Cakes are also absolutely essential, although in an ideal world (and Lord knows we do not live in one of those) you will be able to have the cake sliced to order. The sight of a cake already sliced and laid out on plates is not an appealing one. How long has the ruddy thing been sitting there, one wonders? A slice of cake left on a plate and then kept refrigerated for hours would be no more appealing to me than a joint of meat left under the heat and light all day at a carvery. That is to say, not very. What they should seek to do in a museum or gallery café is have a selection of three cakes; a chocolate one perhaps, something along the lines of a more conventional filled sponge with perhaps a touch of lemon and some decent icing, and then a third more off-beat choice (gluten-free, perchance, if you're feeling in the mood to be inclusive). Then as a customer you can take a look at the cakes, say to the man or lady behind the counter 'Could I have a slice of the chocolate, please?'

'Certainly, sir,' they will doubtless respond.

And then you have the satisfaction of watching them slice a piece for you there and then. The sight or feel of a sharp knife slicing through a cake should always be satisfying, much as with plunging a cafetière. It's also an opportunity to assess the cake. If any cake other than a fruit one takes a great deal of human effort to cut through then, hello, I think we have a problem. If a knife goes through a cake too easily, and a cake that shouldn't have a fondant of my mind as I wandered about looking at such incred-

centre turns out to possess one, then this is the time to find out. (Actually, someone should have stuck a fork in the thing when it first came out of the oven, but there we are.) If all is well, they can pop it on a plate for you and then Bob very much continues to be your uncle. The plate that the slice of cake is popped on to, by the way, should be at room temperature. A warmed plate on which to serve a hot entrée is a good thing. In fact I'd even go so far as to say that it is the *right* thing. A slice of cake served on a chilled plate is not a good thing, and upsets me almost as much as the destruction of historic buildings by Islamic State.

Any pastries on offer should be fresh. There are an awful lot of excellent bakeries about the place, and there is simply no excuse not to have one of them as your stockist. We have all eaten mass-produced croissants over the years, haven't we? And if we're completely honest with ourselves and indulge a little bit of calm and thoughtful reflection, we have never once enjoyed them, have we? Do you serve jam? Then serve it in a ceramic pot or a mini-jar. Don't serve it in a little plastic container with a fiddly lid, for goodness sakes. It simply isn't nice. I don't take sugar in my hot drinks but I know that a number of people still continue to do so. So there should be a pot of sugar on each table, and not a cup full of paper sachets. I despise sachets, and I very much hope that you do.

I will not eat a cake or brownie that is sold in a packet. Sorry, but no.

A lot of cafés serve sandwiches and soups. I am perfectly capable of seeing the temptation, but unless you're in a position to be able to prepare sandwiches to order, then this essentially amounts to spitefulness. Removing cling film is an unpleasant overture to any immediate consumption. You might as well be eating out of a shower cap. As for soup, you will be hard pressed to find anyone in the world who is a greater admirer of it than me (unless that's a claim about himself that Donald Trump also makes).* But the sight of one of those enormous, black ten-litre soup kettles always puts me right of the stuff. Any large containers of liquid make me

* What on earth does this mean?

It relates to comments made during the American Presidential election of 2016.

About soup?

About women.

I see. Does it need to be made any more explicit?

Pardon?

As in clearer?

Oh. No.

ible things was that because of her I had already seen so

---

feel incredibly uneasy. I can practically hear my bladder creaking. I don't know why. I'm not at all fun to be around when I'm at an aquarium, I can tell you. Anthony installed a water butt last year, but every time I walked past the thing I found myself involuntarily gulping at the thought, and so it had to be got rid of. A great ruddy enormous pot of soup gives off the whiff of mass-production, and again, how long has it been sitting there for?

Also, and it might just be me and my sensitive tongue, but any soup that I've had to have out of one of these things as a necessity has always been far too hot, and led to no little embarrassment, either because I have to blow or flap wildly at the stuff in an attempt to get it to cool down, or because I have thoughtlessly taken a spoonful to the back of my throat and found myself suddenly capable only of gasping furiously and waving my arms about. I've no idea why this happens, actually. But it is how I invariably behave whenever I am struggling to find the words I need for any particular situation but am unable to locate or voice them. Perhaps it's a symptom of some disorder or other. But the minute I start to fluster, up go the arms and then there's little that I or my companions can do, but wait for the storm to pass. If it happens in a restaurant then a waiter will often come over, assuming that there is an emergency. But if the emergency, for instance, is that my mouth is full of incredibly, dangerously hot soup, I am not in a position to say this. I just point at my mouth and try to explain the predicament by bulging my eyes which is, I realise, an ineffective technique and open to misinterpretation. Twice in my life I've been visited at a dining table by doctors believing that I was in the grip of some sort of serious attack. In each instance it has been, in all honesty, a little embarrassing, and I've had to send a bottle over. I don't have a solution to how to serve soup for large numbers without using a soup kettle, as very few café kitchens have a hot ring handy. Therefore, I suppose, my only advice is: don't.

The most important aspect of running a café is – and it really ought to go without saying but I'm afraid that these very many of them. It was extraordinary to stand in a

---

days it still sadly doesn't – the *coffee*. If you don't serve proper coffee then you're not a proper café. (Gosh, I rather like that actually. 'If you don't serve proper coffee then you're not a proper café.' That rather has the rhythm of a slogan from one of those lovely commercials of the 1980s, doesn't it? 'Better Buy Hitachi.' 'Happiness is a cigar called Hamlet.' 'A home's not home without Homewheat!' 'Scream for Cream.' 'Is your house a Maxwell House?' It isn't actually, no.)

These days, there's really no excuse for not making proper coffee, and there is a vast array of seriously good coffee-making machines on the market. At home we prefer, as I think I may have occasionally remarked elsewhere, to use a cafetière, but sadly cafetières are not used in all contemporary cafés. I'm prepared to forgive them, but only if they have something decent to take its place. A filter coffee machine, unless you're serving the coffee at once, is simply not acceptable. Again, the coffee just sits on the hotplate for far too long. If you're serving coffee, then serve it fresh. (Another slogan? Could D. Trench be in the wrong business?)

Instead of a filter coffee maker one ought really to think about a decent bean-to-cup machine; one of those Heath Robinson devices with an inverted tin on the top (why don't they sell them with the writing upside down, by the way? Optics in pubs got there in the end).* And for anything that requires an espresso, given that we've established that you're unlikely to have a hot ring or gas burner and have thus, sadly, no possible choice to use a stove-top percolator (we call ours the Vesuvius), you'll need to invest in a Gaggia, an Astoria, or a Nuova Simonelli. Other brands are, of course, available, but when it comes to espresso I think it makes sense to leave it to the Italians, don't you? Yes, the machines are expensive. But they're also good. That's what you're paying for. You can often pick up a second-hand one if another café has had to close owing to, for instance, a rates hike, a bereavement or someone having some sort of major mental wobble and realising that they simply cannot cope with the stress of running a café any more. (You do occasionally hear about people who find running cafés stressful, which I must

*Damien, I really have no idea what you're talking about here.

Stay with me. You will. And you'll thank me. Especially if you're likely to open a café in the near future.

Unlikely.

room full of Monets (many of which are *overwhelming*),

say I find a little hard to understand. Personally I think it sounds like a dream, but perhaps some of the customers are incredibly demanding? If so, that is both a shame and, if you don't mind my saying, inexcusable.)

You don't need to serve a wide range of coffees; you're a coffee shop, not a coffee shop.* A rich roast, a medium roast and a mild roast. Perhaps a decaff roast, although you have to wonder quite what they're doing to coffee beans to decaffeinate them. I sincerely doubt it's at all healthy. Anthony, who reads a lot about this sort of thing, says that decaffeinated coffee is not good for your bladder, and I've absolutely no reason to disagree with this thesis. Do not underestimate the importance of good coffee, and the vital role that it plays in the lives of others. If you encounter people who think that it isn't important, disabuse them of that notion as swiftly but gently as possible.

We once needed some emergency building repairs done – a stair joist I think it was, or perhaps it was to do with shower tiling – and – this is frankly a nightmare scenario – our regular builder Mr Mullaney was unavailable on account of his somewhat unexpected but at the same time perfectly understandable decision to take a short family holiday to Ghana. We asked our neighbours for a recommendation and were duly visited by a fellow called Stirling, who was very much to our liking and who quoted for the job promptly and reasonably. It felt a little odd not using our regular builder, a little like sleeping in a hotel bed or using someone else's bath, but I think we coped pretty well, actually. All things considered. He was a perfectly decent man, Mr Stirling. But he was not Mr Mullaney. I once asked Mr Mullaney what sort of coffee he would like and he replied, without hesistation, 'Sumatran'. By contrast I asked Mr Stirling what sort of coffee he would like and he looked baffled and mumbled, 'Coffee's just coffee, isn't it?' Oh dear. Coffee is many things, but one of the things that it is certainly not is *just coffee*. I didn't know where to start with the poor fellow, but I took a deep breath, sat him down and forty-five minutes later I would like to think that he saw the world rather differently.

What does this mean, 'coffee shop, not a coffee shop'?

Exactly what it says.

Which is?

Well, a coffee shop is a café, but a coffee shop is a shop that sells coffee. A stockist.

Not sure this is totally clear in the current form. Would you consider a change?

Yes. Call me on Wednesday.

and realise that because of Mrs Kensham's enthusiasm

And what's more he then nipped upstairs and did whatever he had to do extremely quickly, taking less than half the time he predicted. Couldn't have seemed to want to do the job any faster, which I thought was both impressive and thoughtful.

You should also pinpoint a brand of coffee that you like, and stick with it. Too much choice is actually rather distressing for customers. But do your research and trust your instincts. Buy Fairtrade, I think it goes without saying. And avoid things that are over-complex and have silly and inappropriate spices added to them because that is just stupid.

Use your own preferred method of steaming milk for lattes or cappuccinos, and don't be tempted to use a stencil when sprinkling chocolate. If indeed you think sprinkling chocolate is a good idea. I happen to think, although I am by no means a prescriptive sort of a person, that it is, as Princess Anne would doubtless say, naff.

Then there is the ambience to consider. You can play music in a café if you wish to but I certainly won't be going there. What I'm more concerned about are acoustics and airflow. If you're going to be using big thrusting coffee machines and endlessly pumping steam into the atmosphere, then you'd better be pretty damned sure that there's decent airflow in the place. If the whole place is full of coffee steam then, lovely as coffee is, it actually becomes somewhat oppressive. I don't know about you – I certainly don't imagine for a moment that I speak for everybody but at the same time I would never think of myself as particularly *odd* – but too much coffee steam in a café makes my sinuses absolutely *throb*. That said, I'm not a fan of air conditioning either as a result of once losing an uncle to Legionnaires' disease, so – and here's a thought – how about opening a ruddy window?

As for the acoustics, if your café is high-ceilinged then you simply have to find a way of dampening them. I cannot bear an echo in a room with clattering crockery and indeed cutlery, and in which gossip and cackling hangs long in the air rather than just instantly dying as it should. I don't know if you've ever stopped for a coffee at the National Gallery and dedication I was seeing so many of them for the

---

but, by crikey, the place is absolutely deafening. It's like trying to relax in a steam yard. Bash, crash, toot.

I went not all that long ago at all to the National Gallery to see *Goya: The Portraits.* The *Telegraph* called it 'electrifying'. The *Guardian* described it as 'momentous'. But for me, superbly bleak as many of the pictures were, the whole experience was completely ruined by an utterly unforgiveable flapjack in a packet that I bought at the cafeteria. I don't know what the hell I was thinking, in all honesty. Such a purchase was breaking all my rules. Anthony, bless him, kept on suggesting as we queued that I opt for the carrot cake. But in a rare moment of stubbornness (I blame fatigue. I'd written 400 words on endives for the Soho House magazine that morning and had then not found a seat on the tube), I plumped for the aforementioned flapjack and the whole exhibition and show was – not to put too fine a point on it – ruined. I can't even see a Goya reproduction these days – not even one from the *Disasters of War* series – without feeling the ghost of sweaty oats at the back of my throat.

The café there is also positioned far too close to the gift shop and this lack of proper zonal demarcation makes for a very unrelaxing and restless experience. Keep the two things separate, I beg you. I like to browse, and I like to sit and reflect. But I don't think anyone should be forced to do both these things adjacently. They require two such completely different mental states that I'm genuinely amazed that anyone else can cope.

Not that the gift shop there is in itself a bad one. It's actually very good. It's not as good as the one at the V&A, but then frankly, where is? An honourable mention must also go to the gift shop at the Baltic in Newcastle, which is fabulous. I went there a few years ago to see the Turner Prize shortlist and it was only the gift shop that prevented the visit from being a complete disaster. I bought so many items – gifts mainly – that they had to call me a taxi.

One other thing – it's a jolly good idea to have non-slip trays. There we are then. Is any of that too much to ask? I really don't think so.

second time. Walking into a room full of Monets is like stepping into the path of a ray of glorious light.

'You seem to know a lot about all this,' Anthony kept saying as I dragged him from one canvas to another, pointing out various subtleties and effects.

'It's Mrs Kensham!' I kept saying. 'She opened my eyes!'

'Marvellous,' he would say. 'All we need now is a lady who can shut your mouth and I could enjoy these pictures in peace.' Ever the wag.

But truly, all my appreciation for and understanding of and engagement with art stems from the five years that I spent as a pupil of Mrs Kensham. And the frankly astonishing collection at the Chicago Institute of Art gave me much to reflect upon.

At Willesden Grammar, where I later went, the walls of the sixth form study room – intended as an area for academic fervour but used, generally, as a place for frankly filthy chat – were decorated with a number of framed prints of the paintings of Pierre-Auguste Renoir – *Two Sisters (on the Terrace)*, *Dance in the Country*, *By the Seashore*, *Bal du Moulin de la Galette*, *The Skiff* and several others the names of which have unaccountably slipped from my recollection. Goodness only knows how long they had been hanging on those wretched walls, because the frames

---

The gift shop at the Chicago Institute of Art is utterly splendid, of course. Anthony and I went completely *bonkers* in there. There was a machine at which you could type in a code and have reproductions of much of their collection sent straight to your door. All too tempting, I'm afraid.

had long been divested of any glazing. Smashed, I presume, as a result of unsupervised shenanigans. Probably while *some* people were trying to get on with some work. I used to think, as a teenager, that those Renoirs were utterly and irredeemably dreary.[4] Walking through the Impressionist area of the Chicago Institute, however – and there are just *rooms and rooms* of the stuff – I suddenly had the sickening feeling that I had done Monsieur Renoir an enormous disservice (perhaps in its own way as great a disservice as those boys who had insisted on daubing his works with boorish and indecent imagery). Because in the flesh, as it were, the work of Renoir is anything but dreary. It is frankly effervescent. All those years at Willesden Grammar I had been looking at renderings of his work that must have been sun-bleached and horribly aged. They had become gloomy, and the sight of them depressed me. To stand but inches away from a real Renoir is actually an incredibly emotional experience. They are so bright (but not too bright), so rich

4 They had also, I might add, been horribly defaced with graffiti. I shall never understand quite why teenage boys are so utterly amused by the sight of crudely drawn phalluses. Penises provide a number of necessary functions including, but by no means limited to, pleasure. But they are most certainly not there to amuse. I have always been utterly bewildered by those people who find naked body parts, or even references to nudity, in any way a cause for mirth. Frankly, if you are the sort of person who finds yourself tittering at a poor quality Biro sketch of a seemingly disembodied priapic member in a state of discharge, then I simply cannot even begin to imagine what the hell must be wrong with you.

(but not too rich) and so, so vibrant. They postively sing at you. (It was Mrs Kensham who had taught me that paintings could sing. I'd quite honestly had no idea.)

Chicago was a place to be reacquainted with some works I had seen before, of course, but also a place where I could see in the flesh for the very first time works that I had longed to witness close up for simply ages. My admiration for the work of Alfred Sisley, for example, is long held, and I have always been inspired by his absolute and stubbornly singular dedication to painting *en plein air*. Now that I think about it, in many ways every picnic that I have ever assembled has been in some way a tribute to the man's work and attitude, the backdrop to a picnic being, to my mind, almost as important as the food. If not more so.*

I had first been introduced to the work of Georgia O'Keeffe by Mrs Kensham at, I think, the Hayward Gallery in the early 1990s where O'Keeffe and Bridget Riley were being exhibited together. Riley's work gave me headaches, in all honesty, but then I was a very sensitive child. I've actually grown not just to respect her as I've got older, but also to love her. We have used some extremely bold colours in our downstairs lavatory over the years, and some people have emerged from the room looking a little shocked. It's an understandable reaction to such a lively colour scheme in what is traditionally in most houses a restfully appointed space, but the keen-eyed amongst our visitors always instantly recognise that it is actually a nod to Riley's work *Nataraja*. Whatever I've gone in there for I nearly always come out absolutely enlivened.

* Damien, might it be sensible at this point to draw some parallels between art (which you are discussing in rather a lot of detail here) and cookery?

I don't think so, no.

As you wish.

My fascination for Georgia O'Keeffe has only grown in the years since. In fact I harbour a very serious desire to one day emulate her travels in New Mexico in a Model A Ford. Not that I can actually drive, you understand. But perhaps we could rent a reproduction automatic model and then Anthony could convey me about the place. I'd love to see Ghost Ranch, and Abiquiú, and of course the San Francisco de Asis Mission Church at Ranchos de Taos, places only familiar to me through her paintings but that I would relish the chance to see up close. Perhaps we could summer at Lake George one year, although we'd have to find our own version of the Stieglitz family or it wouldn't be the same at all!*

In many ways it is Georgia O'Keeffe *the person* who intrigues me as much as the work. I absolutely love her landscapes and portraits. But if I am completely honest with you, and I really do hope that I can be, some of her paintings – specifically the giant close-ups of flowers – have always made me feel a little unsettled and uneasy. There is something about larger pictures or even sculptures of smaller things that disturbs me very slightly. Something rendered in actual size always seems to be majestic in some way. Something made smaller is comforting. (Can this be control freakery? I do hope not. I simply couldn't cope if I were ever accused of such a thing). But I have always found staring at, or indeed into, Georgia O'Keeffe's mighty petals to be extremely intimidating indeed, as if one is being confronted by the ovules within. I think we all know how Freud would have inter-

* I do not get this reference.

It's an attempt at levity. Hence the exclamation mark.

In what way, levity? Who are the Stieglitz family?

They were great friends of O'Keeffe. And then Alfred and Georgia became lovers. All a bit awkward, I'm afraid. But the art that resulted was divine.

Does that really count as levity?

I understand your reservations, but I think that those of my readers who are at all familiar with the work of O'Keeffe – and I suspect that we have quite a large crossover demographically speaking – will be thrilled by it.

As you wish.

preted that. But that said, I have always refused to be judged by the standards of bourgeoise Vienna in the 1920s, and will continue to fight against those members of my social circle who insist that I should.

Few things have made me think so much about art as that trip. Walking around that wonderful Institute – and I could hardly believe that it had never even occurred to me before – I was suddenly struck by the realisation, and I made sure to confide this to Anthony, that Charles Biederman spoke to me as a child, in much the same way as Toshiko Takaezu did as a young adult: loudly and clearly, but never aggressively, always nurturing. Thank God.

'I see,' said Anthony.

I could tell that he understood instantly. He didn't need to say anything more. Which is, I expect, why he remained completely silent for some hours until we found ourselves looking at some Jackson Pollocks. Anthony absolutely loves the work of Pollock, but I have to say it leaves me totally cold. In a cold sweat even.

Is it because it looks like carelessness? It could be. It looks, without I hope coming across as overly obvious, a bit messy. If you found a Jackson Pollock on your work surface I'm pretty sure that you'd try and clean it off instantly with a J-cloth and a domestic cleaning product of your choice. (I've started using Ecover recently for environmental reasons, although you do have to scrub just that little bit harder. And I suspect that they're aware of this.) Even thinking about Pollock's work and the

Damien, I do not mean to be rude – so please do not take this to be anything other than constructive – but I genuinely fail to see how the last few pages could be of any interest to anybody.

You forget the humble connoisseur, for whom this book is written. And will I hope be marketed. Speaking of which, any news from the marketing department? I do hope that they're getting on with things.

Absolutely, Damien. Everybody is very excited. We're just taking rather a lot of time choosing an individual who we feel would be best equipped to deal with the requirements of working with an author as unique as you. We really are looking for someone who is also unique.

Well, good luck with the search. Glad to hear you're being so thorough.

knowledge of how he created them never fails to make me feel extremely dizzy. Often to the point of nausea and beyond.

I had hoped that this aversion to his work was something that I had overcome but sadly this isn't the case. Anthony and I recently went to see the Abstract Expressionism exhibition at the Royal Academy. I was in high spirits and feeling perfectly relaxed, but the moment that I set eyes on his *Blue Poles* I instantly became so discombobulated and anxious that I genuinely believed that the world was about to end. I whispered as much to Anthony, who simply uttered the words, 'Oh for goodness' sake. If you don't like it, *go.*'

This was absolutely not the response that I was hoping for.

'I'm serious,' I said. 'This picture made me feel funny in 1997, and now it's happening again.'

'Then look at something *else,*' Anthony said.

'I can't,' I replied. 'It's just too ruddy mesmerising.'

He was right, of course. I should have dragged my eyes away from the painting, but somehow I just couldn't. I was lost in it. The colours drew me in and then tossed me about in their chaos, as if daring me to have a panic attack. I could feel myself becoming faint, Anthony started tutting and then the next thing I knew I was lain prostrate upon one of those benches that sits in the middle of all right-thinking galleries, presumably for moments exactly like these, having commandeered all available seating space and uttered the sort of low cries that are more generally associated with sea sickness. But that is the effect that Pollock has on me – he plays complete havoc with my balance-sensing system which has always been a little bit suspect at the best of times. I was dizzy, I was nauseous, my skin became pale.

'We've got to get you out of here,' said Anthony. But I refused to move, and he knew damn well that I wasn't capable of going anywhere for at least forty minutes. Despite this manifestation of symptoms, Anthony was still not wholly sympathetic to my plight, but after a short but robust exchange of words, he agreed to go off and hunt for some mineral water.

'San Pellegrino if they have it,' I shouted after him. 'But absolutely *not* Hildon. I'd rather die. Or have tap water.'

'You'll have what you're given, you mewling infant,' Anthony spat back over his shoulder and then stomped off.

Regrettably, there were large numbers of school children visiting the gallery that day, and as I slipped in and out of consciousness, cast adrift on choppy seas made rougher by Pollock's drip painting techniques, I attracted an awful lot of attention that I could frankly have done without, and that also struck me as somewhat unwarranted. One cocky teenage girl asked me if I was merely elderly or suffering from the effects of a drug overdose.

'I'm just a little dizzy,' I replied, before blacking out again.[5]

5 I came to in the dining area of the education department which had had to be evacuated for the purposes. Everyone

Therefore I could tell that Anthony's insistence on stopping in front of the Pollock in Chicago was an act of needless aggression, and so I quietly took myself off to the basement to explore the Thorne Miniature Rooms. This is a quite sumptuous collection of small-scale reconstructions of a wide variety of European interiors that were built in the 1930s. They are astonishing took at. They are so incredibly detailed and small, and they made me nostalgic for the little dolls' house that my sister was given for her seventh birthday, absolutely hated and then gave to me. I completely loved it, and spent many happy hours playing with it, adjusting the décor and repositioning the furniture. After not too long Anthony came down to meet me, all was forgiven, and we enjoyed the Thorne Miniatures together. Anthony was rather taken with the English Great Room of the Late Tudor Period and I, meanwhile, was utterly smitten by the French Bathroom and Boudoir of the Revolutionary Period 1793–1804. It looked awfully comfortable.

Is this section just a little bit too 'What I did on my holidays'?

It is what I did on my holidays. Problem?

I could have stayed down there for absolutely hours but eventually I became utterly incensed by the sheer

---

was extremely nice about it, it must be said, and one lady told me that I had caused no trouble whatsoever. Words I had no reason to take at anything other than face value, even if the rather harassed primary school teacher muttered something a little unkind about my arrogant usurping of resources intended for others. I put her behaviour down, not to an aggressive personality, but merely as a result of the stress cause by having recently served under Michael Gove. Anthony finally tracked me down. He was carrying, bless him, a bottle of San Pellegrino.

numbers of people taking photographs. Why on earth can't people just live in the moment a little more? People ought to make sure they read some Susan Sontag before going out and buying a camera, but for reasons that I cannot even begin to imagine, they simply don't. A little hushed silence is, I like to think we can all agree, generally rather a good thing in an art gallery. And this state cannot hope to be achieved if the respectful atmosphere is continually being perforated by the sound of little machines going click, click, click, click, click. No sooner had one been looking at a miniature for five minutes than you suddenly felt yourself being elbowed out of the way by someone 'just wanting to take a photo'. Utterly sick-making. I had, eventually, the most enormous tantrum. Not that anybody noticed because as usual and in line with pretty much all of my tantrums, my protest was silent and undemonstrative. That said, it was a super place to visit, and I thought of Mrs Kensham and her wisdom pretty much non-stop.

Later that day Anthony was violently sick on the observatory deck of the Willis Tower. One hundred and three floors up, and no kitchen towel in sight. I ask you. That's what happens if you follow up a pound of pizza pie with pudding, I told him.

Whilst in Chicago, we were also fortunate enough to visit the home of one of my idols, the great Frank Lloyd Wright. It was just dreamy. If I could have a house in Oak Park, I'd be there like a shot. What I love about Frank, apart from his clean lines and his strong understanding of the concept of 'the journey',[6] is his complete and utter commitment to space. Designers and estate agents often talk about a sense of space, and they are usually talking complete rubbish. What, in my experience, tends to give a 'sense of space' is almost always 'actual space', and buildings and homes designed by Lloyd Wright always have this in absolute spades. The centre of every reception room, with the obvious and understandable exception of the dining room, is completely clear. In his children's playroom he even set a grand piano into the wall (it juts out over an adjacent stairwell), so as to create and free up as much space as possible. I love him for that. He also hated his next-door neighbours' house so much that he completely redesigned his windows so that he would never have to see it, but still kept as much natural light. I love him even more for that. At home in Queen's Park my own clean-cut and empty lawn is inspired by Frank Lloyd Wright. It's a perfect green square, so you might think it to be inspired by Miles Mathis.* But it isn't.

Who he?

Google him.

But it is not just my appreciation of art that I have to thank Mrs Kensham for. She also did me another great service. On one of our termly trips to a London gallery, we were in a coach making, as all coaches must do, its interminable way down the A5. I was reading a book (I

6 Not to be confused in any way with Tony Blair's concept of *The Journey*, the audio book of which we once listened to in bank holiday traffic driving back from Bude in Cornwall and which sent us both quite mad.

can generally manage about seven pages before I feel sick when reading on coaches. All I have to do is close my eyes tightly for fifteen minutes, and then I can have another go). The boys up the back of the bus were being a little bit rowdy, and singing a few mucky songs, but it was nothing too crass, and so Mrs Kensham, who was sitting at the front of the bus, just let them get on with it. But then something happened. The boys started using the word 'gay', and laughing. 'Oh, this is so *gay*.' 'That is so *gay*.' 'He is so *gay*,' etc.

Mrs Kensham got up from her seat, and walked down to the end of the bus (probably illegal now, but anyway), and coughed quietly. The boys stopped what they were doing and looked up at her. She had, I genuinely believe, the respect of all.

'I couldn't help noticing', she said, 'that you all keep using the word "gay". Would one of you like to tell me what it means, please? No one?'

Nobody said anything.

'Well,' said Mrs Kensham. 'If you don't know what a word means, then I don't think you should be using it. But, if you like, perhaps I can tell you what it means. If somebody is gay, then it simply means that they like or love or are attracted to people who are the same sex as them. If men like men, then they are gay. If women like women, then they too are gay. That's all it means. It's not something to snigger about. It's just normal. It's natural. And people who make a fuss about this sort of thing are very silly indeed.' And with that, she turned on her heels and left the boys at the back of the bus looking a little shame-faced.

'Ah,' I thought as she walked back to her seat. 'There's a word for it.'

Chapter 8

BACK TO MISS PROCTOR

Well, I hope you enjoyed that little diversion. It certainly did me the world of good. I now feel refreshed and ready to recommence the Proctor Saga. When we last left the story, she and I had just exited the changing room of the swimming pool together to return to school. So enraged was Miss Proctor already that I had not dared tell her exactly what was on my mind. But the fact of the matter was that I was actually in desperate need of the lavatory. The stress and rage that had been building inside me during the last humiliating quarter of an hour had taken something of a hold on my insides. Stress and nerves have affected me in this way all my life, and I'm not remotely minded to imagine that this will ever change.[1]

---

1   I am not alone in this. My partner Anthony reacts to moments of stress in much the same way and, if anything, he has it far worse. Driving on motorways upsets him greatly, and we have probably had to make forced stops at most service stations in the country. Tebay is our favourite. Leigh Delamere we enjoy rather less. The problem is that using 'public conveniences' is also something that makes him panic, so we can occcasionally get trapped in something of a vicious cycle. We once spent nearly an entire afternoon at Heston Services, and as our visit entered its third hour I became so demented and frustrated by the experience that I ended up luring him

The journey back to school generally took, as I mentioned only a few short pages ago, a smidgeon under twelve minutes.*

* Not sure you need to repeat this detail. Extraneous.

How can something be detail AND extraneous? Clarity is, as ever, my watchword.

Mais bien sûr.

Grand merci.

I was partnered at the front of the line with a boy called Edgar. I can't remember his surname, but I can certainly recall that he recognised the practicalities of using a briefcase to convey one's exercise books and stationery and so forth around school buildings almost as early as I did. His was black faux-leather, and mine was brown faux-leather, but other than colour scheme there was little to choose between them. I also remember that his parents ran some sort of a cash and carry on the borders of Barnet that sounded like a veritable Aladdin's Cave. We were holding hands, as were each pair of boys, as the school's policy for outside journeys determined.

'Are you all right, Damien?' Edgar asked as we set off.

He was always one of the more perceptive boys in my class. Like me he was short for his age, and also like me, had a certain sensitivity that was hard to mask.

'I'm fine, Edgar,' I said, 'but thank you for asking.'

'That was a nasty thing of them to do back there,' he said. 'I'm sorry that I wasn't able to stop them.'

'Do you know who it was? The person who threw them up there?'

'It was the usual gang,' he said.

'I suspected as much.'

---

out of the bathroom with a twelve-pack of Krispy Kremes. Dreadful things, but we didn't have to stop again until Gloucester and so the expense was justified.

The usual gang were four boys called Iain Jenkins, Patrick McHugh, Thomas Renwick and Kenton Tucker. I still get LinkedIn requests from them to this day, and I have no intention of replying to them. This makes them, of course, no different from any of the other LinkedIn requests I get (who, quite seriously, *are* these people? Who on earth wishes to 'join the network' of a management consultant, or a 'brand officer'? Not I). But even so, I hope they get the message. They were bastards then, and they're probably no better now. In fact they're probably the sort of feckless pin-striped men who drink outside city-centre pubs on Fridays, cackling and jeering and ruining it for everyone. It's possible that they're nothing like this, of course. I might have them pegged all wrong. Perhaps they have matured into the most delightful fellows. We're all capable of change, after all, and no one recognises this better than I. I've even experimented with a Nespresso machine recently, and I wouldn't have thought *that* possible five years ago. I still much prefer the good old cafetière, but I try not to be a stick in the mud about it.

'Were your pyjamas all right?' asked Edgar.

I was silent for a moment, but eventually managed to collect enough strength to reply, in a hoarse whisper: 'They have been torn.'

I blinked in shame, and a single tear escaped from the corner of my left eye, and slowly made its hot track down my cheekbone. Edgar was on my right-hand side, fortunately, and couldn't see this. I took a deep breath through my nostrils and attempted to remain calm.

'Torn? Where?'

'Right up the back,' I replied tersely. 'And I'd rather not talk about it if it's all the same with you.'

'Sorry,' said Edgar.

Poor Edgar. He was only trying to show concern. I, however, wanted to banish all memories of recent events at the swimming pool from my mind for the moment, and concentrate on the suddenly rather more pressing fact that I was absolutely bursting to sit down on a lavatory, whilst burdened with the knowledge that our journey was still going to last another ten minutes. I had little confidence that I was going to last another ten minutes without serious mishap, and so I was mentally running through some of the worst-case scenarios that I could envisage and trying to dream up ways in which they might be resolved. Could I dash into a shop? Did we pass a public lavatory perhaps? Or was there somewhere wild we might pass where I could do my business *en plein air*? A bit of wasteland maybe, or some scrubland? What would be the ethics of relieving oneself in a skip? (I had tissues with me after all. I always carried tissues. Still do.) Would Miss Proctor allow me to delay things any further by breaking away for some respite? It seemed extremely unlikely. Perhaps I would just have to make a break for it like an escaped POW and hope that I didn't get shot attempting to climb the wire? Or maybe, just maybe, I could cling on for dear life and see if I could possibly manage it.

My partner Anthony and I recently began a course of pilates exercise classes with a quite delightful young lady who is extremely patient, very hands on, a quarter Portuguese and an absolute fount of information on all manner of things (introduced us to Freecycle, as it happens, and I've not had to pay for a seedling pot since). One of the many benefits that pilates has brought to both Anthony and I (in addition to finally gaining the confidence to walk down a high street in sportswear) is a significant improvement in our core strength. We lie on the mats waving our legs and arms about as instructed, and have both become aware of muscles that we barely knew we had. How on earth have I got to my age in life without realising that I possessed a pelvic floor? It's been an absolute revelation, and not a day goes by that I don't make a little bit of time to work it. Anthony has suffered from quite debilitating back pain for as long as I have known him. Sometimes it has been so bad that the poor thing has to spend entire evenings lying on his back on the sofa incapable of doing anything apart from watching the television and drinking rum through a straw. We even had to completely rearrange the layout of our sitting-room furniture so that he could reach the occasional table on which I like to place the cheese board. Occasionally, and much to my regret, I have found myself incapable of being entirely sympathetic to his condition, and have verbally attacked him (unfairly) for being lazy and (rather more fairly) for eating miniature Babybels in the way that some people eat pistachios. This has all changed since we commenced our pilates classes. He rarely mentions back pain, stands up beautifully straight and has really cut down on the Babybels. But what I find to be extraordinary is that the muscle group one exercises the most when one does pilates is the very same muscle group that one uses the most in order to control one's bowels and bladder. This has made such a positive difference to our lives both at home and on the road. We no longer have to pause television programmes so often, and nor do we need to stop at every service station we pass as a matter of course. It's fabulous. So long, Leigh Delamere! Hasta la vista, Newort Pagnell! Sayonara, South Mimms!

How I wish, then, that I had known about pilates when I was so much younger, or things might have turned out very differently on that fateful walk back from the swimming pool. Nowadays, I like to think that I would be in with a reasonably good shout of lasting twelve minutes even if in pretty dire need. That day, however, I simply couldn't cope. I had been trying my absolute damnedest to hold it in from the moment we left the swimming pool, but five minutes into the journey I could simply take no more. The inevitable occurred. And at pace.

'Gosh, you're holding my hand very tightly,' said Edgar.

I felt a great swathe of emotions sweep over me, but to my surprise the greatest of these was just relief. The worst thing that could possibly have happened had happened, and so now all I had to do was deal with the consequences. It suddenly seemed so simple. I would say nothing about it, walk back to school as best I could, and once we were safely back I would excuse myself, find a spacious cubicle and clean myself up. My underpants would probably have to be disposed of once I'd removed the nametape, but that was just a hit I was going to have to take. 'Going commando', as I believe it's called, has never been my style, but it seemed a far more comfortable and less unsanitary prospect than the alternative.

'Are you sure you're all right?' Edgar said. 'You're walking funny.'

'Funnily, you mean. I am walking *funnily*. But I'm not, anyway. This is how I walk. It's how everybody walks. Just a matter of putting one foot in front of the other.'

I was playing it, I felt, pretty bloody cool.

'But you're not really putting one foot in front of the other, are you? You're sort of sticking your legs out sideways.'

'I'm practising a new walk, Edgar. Leave me alone.'

'Fine, fine. Only asking.'

'I can get away with this,' I thought, 'just as long as Edgar stops asking silly questions.'

We walked on, the pair of us silent, but the boys behind us chatting away merrily. Suddenly Miss Proctor appealed for silence and asked us all to halt.

'I'm sorry to have to ask you to stop,' she said. 'We're already behind schedule thanks to young Mr Trench's inconsiderate attitude to timekeeping. But I'm worried that somebody might have trodden in something unpleasant. We seem to be carrying with us a lingering smell, and so I can only assume that somebody has – rather unfortunately – trodden in a dog mess.'

Some boys sniggered at the thought of this, and so Miss Proctor silenced them with her customary ruthlessness.

'QUIET!' she bellowed so loudly that a passing shopper figuratively jumped out of his skin.

'Dog mess is *not* funny! And neither is lateness. I need everybody to check the soles of their shoes and make sure that they are not the person walking about with the dog mess on. It is unhygienic, and it is smelly.'

'This,' I thought, 'is very serendipitous.' I had been becoming increasingly concerned that the sizeable lump of misfortune that I was now carrying on my person might give itself away by smell. The fact that somebody had now trodden in some 'dog mess' as the lady insisted on calling it had, quite by chance, created a helpful distraction. The olfactory equivalent of a smokescreen.

There was much muttering from my contemporaries, as people leant against a wall in order to raise their soles to each other and check for the offending substance. I checked Edgar's shoes and found no sign of any misstep. He then checked mine. He gave me a look but said nothing. All along the line the cry went up: 'Nothing here, Miss.' 'Mine are clean,' etc. One fool said, 'Have you checked yours, Miss?' and then instantly regretted it.

'I don't need to check my shoes, because I look where I'm going,' she said, stepping backwards into the path of an elderly couple, who she then stared at until they apologised.

'No problem!' she called after them, sarcastically and as if no apology had been forthcoming.

'She seems strict,' the old man said to me and Edgar with a wink, as he passed us.

'Do not talk to any strangers!' Miss Proctor bellowed down the line at us. 'Now then, does anybody have anything at all on their shoes that they ought not to?'

'No, Miss.'

'Not me, Miss.'

Miss Proctor walked up and down the line, surveying us with a scornful look, as if we ourselves were <u>dog mess upon the sole of her shoe of life.</u>[*]

'Really?' she asked. 'No one? No one has *anything* on their shoe? Because I can still smell whatever it is and it is not very nice *at all*.'

'I can smell something too,' said Kenton Tucker. 'Something disgusting.'

'Yes, all right, Kenton. Thank you for demonstrating that I am not imagining things, but we don't need any more commentary. Everybody carry on, and we can sort this out when we get back to school. And walk quickly please. We are getting later and later. Damien and Edgar, you set the pace please.'

Edgar absolutely lurched off at a pace I found incredibly difficult to keep up with, almost as if he were trying to get away from me.

'Slow down a bit, Edgar, please,' I said, struggling to maintain my usual top speed whilst trying out my new walk. Then the penny suddenly dropped. There had been no fortunate smokescreen. If Miss Proctor could smell something unpleasant and nobody had anything unpleasant

[*] Not sure that this analogy/ metaphor quite stands up.

You didn't know her.

Bit clunky.

Please expand?

I think the sentence could just end with 'scornful look'. Stands up fine without any addition.

My feeling is that if I take it out it could change the feeling of the entire book. And not for the better.

If you say so . . .

Please avoid ellipses in future. They are a little aggressive.

Noted.

on the bottom of their shoes, then what Miss Proctor could smell (and she could still smell it, she helpfully reminded us every two hundred yards) could only be that rank burden which I was still hoping to keep concealed.

Normally when we got back to our school, we were instructed to go straight inside, hang up our swimming bags and convey ourselves back to our classroom as briskly as possible. But not on this occasion. As we approached the steps leading up the front door of the school, Miss Proctor overtook Edgar and myself and demanded that everybody stop.

'Whatever it is that is causing this most unpleasant smell is still with us, and so I am going to have inspect the shoes of each and every one of you before you can be allowed back into the school.'

This was absolutely not what I wanted to hear. I wanted to get to a lavatory as fast as possible, and try and get this horrendous ordeal over with, with a minimum of fuss and, presumably, a maximum of toilet tissue. The thought of Miss Proctor finding out what I had done filled me with a terrible dread. She was not a discreet woman, and she'd probably blame *me* for having normal bodily functions, in much the same way as she'd blamed *me* for stealing my own pyjama bottoms.

Miss Proctor climbed to the top of the stairs, and we all waited at the bottom. This, in my view, turned the whole thing into far more of a performance than was strictly necessary. A show trial almost. There was a great deal of anticipation from the boys assembled at the bottom of the stairs as to who it was that had failed to own up to excrement on their shoes, and a hushed silence fell.

'Edgar,' said Miss Proctor. 'You first.'

Edgar climbed the stairs towards Miss Proctor, looking a little nervous, but not even half as nervous as I was feeling. My life could be about to change forever. Miss Proctor told Edgar to turn around and face away from her, and then to slowly raise each foot in turn.

'Edgar,' she said when she had finished her inspection. 'You may go in.'

The boys behind me all clapped. I braced myself.

'Damien, you next please.'

I mounted the stairs like a condemned man mounting the scaffold. The crowd beneath me bayed. Although only, it must be said in fairness, in my imagination.

I reached the top of the stairs and tried to look as breezy as I could in the circumstances, which was not very at all. These were the first stairs I had attempted to climb in this exact state, and it was not a happy experience.

'Turn around please, Damien.'

I turned around so that my back was to Miss Proctor, and offered her up each of my feet in turn without being prompted. My dearest hope was that she would see that there was nothing on them, and send me inside the building. But I heard no words emanating from her. Instead I heard a cough, and then a gentle sniff. And then a less gentle sniff. And then finally a gagging noise.

'May I go in please, Miss Proctor?' I asked. Bravely.

But Miss Proctor did not answer my question. At least,

not directly. Instead she turned to the pupils below and said, 'Right. Damien does not have any dog mess on his shoes, but I think that we can safely say that we have found the source of the smell. You may all go inside now. Hurry please. And Damien,' she said, turning to me. 'You just stay exactly where you are.'

As all the other boys processed past me, I had to stand at the top of the steps with Miss Proctor, like a sort of shamed Highland Chief. A couple of them even saluted, which was uncalled for. When the last boy had gone through the door (Kenton, possessor of quite the cruellest of laughs), Miss Proctor said to me, though extremely gritted teeth and in a voice so strangulated that I wondered that she wasn't cutting off the oxygen supply to her own brain, 'Damien, why on earth didn't you go to the loo at the swimming pool?'

'I didn't think you'd let me,' I wept.

'Of course I'd have let you.'

'But you were already cross with me for making everybody late.'

'Yes I was. You'd made us all *very* late. But that doesn't mean I would have prevented you from going to the lavatory. I would far rather that than … than this,' indicating my crying form with a wave of the hand.

'I'm sorry, Miss,' I said.

'Are you going to be able to get cleaned up by yourself?'

'Yes Miss.'

'Then go inside, and sort yourself out at once. Come to the classroom as soon as you can.'

I mumbled some thanks, heaven knows what for, and then dashed into the building, down the stairs and into the loo. I shall spare you the details of what followed, but it was not the most fragrant of circumstances in which I have ever found myself. Still, I got myself cleaned up, picked the nametape off my underpants and disposed of them before going back to class. Miss Proctor said nothing as I eased myself behind my desk, which was good of her, and nor did any of the boys, which was frankly suspicious. I wish that it was not the incident that defined my time at that school the most, but sadly it was. I was reminded of that incident every single day thereafter that I spent at that institution. I have no wish to go into the treatment handed out to me by the other boys as, all too sadly, I'm sure you know what boys are like. But I don't really blame the boys anyway. I blame Miss Proctor.

I often used to wonder if the incident – which really was traumatic, and I have skimmed over a number of details – didn't have some kind of profound psychological impact on me in later life. I have been assured, by a medical health professional, that it hasn't. For a brief period in the early 2000s I underwent a short course of psychotherapy. I wasn't depressed – far from it, I have always made an effort to be one of life's celebrants rather than cynics, a champion of the human spirit, in fact, and never knowingly down on anything. But I was, if not clinically depressed, then perhaps clinically a little upset some of the time. My relationship with Anthony was at an early, difficult stage – we had been through our phase of exultance and obsession and passed into a period of doubt and questioning. In truth, I think that at the time we had each become terrified of losing the other, and so were trying rather too hard. A friend of mine (sadly no longer with us) had found psychotherapy to be helpful, and wondered if it might be something I'd like to consider, and so I went along for some sessions with – as ever – a completely open mind.

We had a couple of good sessions, and whilst discussing my childhood I began to tell him the story of the swimming pool incident. He seemed fascinated at first, and listened in complete silence. Then, however, he became slightly restless and suddenly got up – claiming that he had just remembered that he needed to let the cat out. He had – quite by chance I'm sure – an appalling coughing fit out on the landing, and then returned wiping the edges of his mouth with a hanky, and saying that as far as he could tell, I was absolutely right as rain and needed absolutely no further sessions at all. I just needed to try to worry slightly less (this insight, as far as I was concerned, completely justified the whole therapy experience and its accompanying fees; up until that point I had no idea that I *was* a worrier), and that possibly there might be something to be said for me to avoid any tendencies I might have to overshare. I have done as he said from that moment to this. I hope.

I do not know what became of Miss Proctor. For all I know she is still called Miss Proctor, and failed to ever find the happiness that a long-term meaningful relationship can bring. Perhaps she sits surrounded by hungry, mangy cats and empty bottles of the cheap spirits that she buys from her local convenience store. But I do hope not. I am not, and nor have I ever been, one to bear a grudge.

Spaghetti Bolognese

Time to think about something nicer. God, I love Italy. I would happily move there tomorrow. If the admin wasn't likely to be such a nightmare. And it wasn't such a big commute. And if aspects of its political system were reformed. And if the pound was a little stronger against the euro. And if, as my partner Anthony has just pointed out, they definitely have decent broadband. But otherwise – there like a shot. Just try and stop me. You won't be able to. You might think you can catch me, but it will be impossible. Because I'll have taken the precaution of covering myself in some of their excellent extra-virgin olive oil, and I'll be too damn slippery. Gotcha.

Back when I was a child, we had an au pair from Italy. (Technically, therefore, I should refer to her as being an *alla pari,* but then you might not know what I mean. Who knows why it is the French term for this role that has become almost universal, but it has.) Up until that point in my life – I think I was eight, but as I say, I'm not good with dates – I had been labouring under the quite unfair impression that all that the Italians had given the world was dried pasta and frozen pizza. I had been wondering, quite frankly, what all the fuss was about. And then along came this girl from a village outside of Milan with a week's worth of clothing and a ready smile, and she changed the way I thought about Italian cuisine very rapidly indeed. (Again, I'd rather use the word *cucina* than cuisine as it looks silly to me to have French words to describe Italian things, but there we are. What a minefield language is.)

She wasn't with us for very long, sadly, but I personally learnt a lot in those four days. (She never even got through that week's worth of laundry, as it turned out, and that ready smile soon vanished from her face to be replaced by the look of someone absolutely haunted. In retrospect, by the time my father took her back to the airport she was absolutely broken.)

It was a shame that she had to leave when she did, but I think she and my mother realised very quickly that their ways of going about things did not overlap a great deal. Additionally, my brother Ralph had slapped her bottom, and my sister punched her several times. She still sends my parents a Christmas card every year, so life has presumably moved on for her. Or perhaps it indicates that she still spends much of her time dwelling on the past, and Christmas is the one time of the year when she feels able to voice it. Gosh, I hope she's OK. She certainly deserves to be, because she was a wonderful cook.

The afternoon she first arrived, and before she had experienced the way that my brother and sister behaved at bath time and the tears began to flow, she volunteered to make supper. And what a supper it was. I have had many dishes of spaghetti Bolognese since, and many of them have been vastly superior, but I shall never forget my first experience of Italian food that was cooked by an actual Italian.

I've been making Bolognese for years, often experimenting and fiddling about with quantities and cooking times – even herbs – but I've now reached a stage in life where I'm completely content with my Bolognese recipe, and am unlikely to change it again. Not too drastically, at any rate. There's room for improvement in all aspects of life. Last weekend, by way of an example, we finally took the plunge and chose new escutcheons for every door in the whole house. It took our beloved builder Mr Mullaney all of Monday and Tuesday to affix them. I supervised, naturally, offering help and guidance wherever it was needed and very occasionally changed my mind about things (your escutcheons don't need to match your door knobs exactly, for instance, but they should always complement them. Things were looking a bit tricky on that front in the guest bathroom for a spell, but the obstacle was eventually overcome). I have to say, every penny and minute of the entire experience was absolutely worth it. I was making use of our small downstairs lavatory this morning, and took the chance, while sat, to admire Mr Mullaney's handi-work. Quite honestly, it has brought that room alive. Just goes to show.

Now then. A short word, if I may, about pasta. I know a lot of people make their own, and I have, for many years, been proud to count myself among their number. But I am also acutely aware that not everybody has the time, the inclination, or indeed the drying space. This is a perfectly acceptable stance, and in no way a reason to hate yourself. I would urge people that do have the chance to make their own pasta, though, to think very hard about giving it a shot. It's a wonderful, if sometimes strenuous, process. But then so are lots of things that I enjoy. Spaghetti, however, which we are about to be thinking about, is absolutely not the place to start. Even if you do have a pasta maker, making spaghetti requires an additional attachment. You're far better off making sheets off the stuff, and cutting them up to make ravioli, or even fettuccine. I suppose that what I am trying to say – in, uncharacteristically it has to be said, a somewhat long-winded way – is that although I urge you to start making your own pasta, it is perfectly acceptable, in my book, to use shop-bought spaghetti. There, I've said it.[2]

2 Seriously, though, DO ask someone to give you a pasta maker as a birthday or Christmas gift. Or invest a chunk of inheritance money in one. Hours of fun. We use a brand called Imperia, and we've never had a moment's problem with it.

For this you will need ...

   Butter, salted, 2 oz of

   Olive oil, extra-virgin, 5 glugs (approx. 2 tbsp) of

   Onions, big, 2

   Carrots, likewise, 2

   Celery, sticks of, 3 if they are of a size, 4 if they are not

   Bay leaves, dried, 4

   Garlic, peeled and chopped, 7 cloves. I know that sounds a lot, but stay with me.

   Pancetta, 8 oz of. You could use lardons, but don't tell anyone I told you. And do obtain them, as with all your meats, from your local butcher. Your local *good* butcher, at any rate. Not the type that sells pre-packaged meat.

   Some beef mince, about 2 lb of. Some people only go for lean, even extra-lean, mince. I am not of this persuasion. I like a bit of fat on my mince, as it gives flavour. Not too much, mind. But a bit.

Save for the time we returned late one summer from an extended holiday in Normandy (not recommended) to discover that we had mice. The little blighters had taken up home in our pasta maker, and being latrinal, had turned the thing to rust. Not a happy discovery. We borrowed a cat from my good friend Marion and that dealt with the mice, but the pasta maker was damaged irretrievably.

I can see the attraction of the pasta maker to mice, if I'm honest. If you're that sort of size then the inside of a pasta maker probably feels a bit like being inside a Frank Lloyd Wright building. Or – at a stretch – the Bilbao Guggenheim. Not, I realise, that the mice would appreciate this entirely. Or even at all. But I do wonder.

Mushrooms, your favourite type. About 10 of the things. They're going to be chopped up into pretty small pieces though, so do bear that in mind. I often use porcini.

Good red wine, ½ pint of. That's about two large glasses. N.B. Remember the 'there is no such thing as cooking wine' rule. There is good wine, and there is other wine. Cooking requires, nay deserves, the best.

Some sea salt

Your pepper mill

Some fresh thyme

Perhaps some oregano?

Plum tomatoes, peeled, 2 tins of. I really do advise that you don't use the chopped variety. Tomatoes gain sweetness as a result of being heated. So don't chop them or break them up until they've been cooked for a while.

Beef stock, ½ pint of

Tomato puree, 1 tsp of

Double cream. *Seriously?* Seriously. As much of the stuff as you dare. We all have to be naughty sometimes. And where better to be naughty than the kitchen? If I can't persuade you, then I can't persuade you. I shan't be cross. But if you can be tempted, then get a little pot and keep it ready. I make my own double cream, actually. (Not really.)

Serves ... Oh God, about eight. Twelve? I really

don't know. Sorry to be unhelpful. Feel free to halve it. But then, why should you?

Right then. Shall we begin?

Take down a nice large, heavy pot that has a decent lid and a pleasingly heavy bottom. Pop it on a low to medium heat, and then drop in the butter so that it melts. Once the butter has turned to liquid, but before it has started to bubble, add the oil and mix the two together with a wooden spoon. Then add your onions and let them soften for a moment or two – perhaps long enough for you to enjoy a short reverie set in the Sabine Hills – and then also add the carrot and the celery. This would also be the optimum moment to add your bay leaves. Keep working it all together and watch with pride as it slowly turns golden. (Well, the onions will turn golden. Good luck turning bacon golden without the addition of chemicals.)

When, and only when, you are completely and utterly thrilled with the colour of your chopped veg, you may now add the minced beef and the – what the more I think about it sounds like an absolutely terrifying quantity of – garlic. You are not so much seeking to brown the mince, as to stop it being pink. Add the pancetta at this point, making sure that you keep everything moving around the pan so that the pancetta gets its turn having some direct contact with the hot metal. Always let your meats share the heat.

Some people like to add the mushrooms *after* the wine. I am not of their number. Rather I prefer to put them in now and have a little bit of a fry (only a little, mind; don't let them cook through) before I add the wine. This too is a sensible moment to add salt, pepper and the remaining herbs. Turn the heat up just a notch to allow the liquid to reduce by just a smidgeon.

While that reduction is happening all by its little self, gather together your tinned tomatoes and your beef stock, and add the tomato puree to the latter, so that it combines thoroughly. Then add all of them to the pan at once and give the whole mixture a decent stir.

The most important ingredient is not, however, one of those that I have listed above. It is, in fact, *time*. (Not to be confused with *thyme*.) Put the lid on the pot, and reduce the heat under the pan to the lowest possible temperature that you possibly can without your gas ring giving you funny looks. You can let it sit there for a minimum of two hours, and are welcome to do so for a little longer. All I would say is that it can be a good idea to add a little more liquid if you cook it for longer. Some people put some water in. I put some wine in, which I think makes rather more sense. Especially if it's Italian wine.

It's easy to become impatient while you're waiting for all the beautiful flavours in a dish like this to come together, but I promise you that it is *absolutely* worth the wait. And two hours is easily long enough time for you to fit something really useful in. You could crack on with a bit of admin, or even sit down and watch a film. We watched Derek Jarman's *Caravaggio* last night. Utterly baffling, but you'd be amazed who pops up. Dexter Fletcher's in it, for instance.

When it's been on the heat for two or more hours, you may turn off the heat, take off the lid and give it a lovely big stir, not least because that may well help you to locate the bay leaves which really do need to be removed at this stage. It is now, with the addition of as much cream as your constitution will allow to it, and the addition of spaghetti under it, ready to eat. But may I make a little suggestion? Thank you. Don't eat it now. In fact don't even take the bay leaves out now. Put it to one side and let it sit for a whole extra day. It becomes *even more* flavour-some. Then remove the bay leaves, heat it through and add the cream. And whatever you do, make sure you've some Parmiggiano-Reggiano to hand to grate straight on to it or you are missing out. *Buon appetito, ragazzi e ragazze!*

Chapter 9

ADOLESCENCE

Apart, of course, from Mrs Kensham there was nothing that I missed about the place when I left that school. And apart from what I learned from Mrs Kensham, nor am I at all sure that I gained anything from the experience other than a hatred of team sports and of group-taught violin playing. Thanks entirely to Mrs Kensham's sensitivity and tact, though, I now knew and understood rather more about myself than I might have done otherwise, so I must at least be grateful for that.

I don't think that I have ever managed to express coherently enough to my parents what I thought of that school. Whenever the subject of it comes up, my mother always says, 'You had a good time there, didn't you?' And: 'You were always very friendly with that Edgar boy, weren't you? Chalk and cheese, you were. He was a very sensitive soul.' And even: 'That's where the marvellous Miss Proctor taught you. What a sensible woman she was.' Whenever I mention Mrs Kensham, my mother always looks a little tetchy and describes her as 'that communist woman'.

But what of life beyond school? My home? Those summer holidays before school stretched out forever?

How did we spend our time as a family? Ralph, as I said, was usually away playing games but Angela and I were always around, often restless and needing to be entertained and fed. I have no real idea what it must be like for young people these days, but from everything that one reads in the newspapers one gets the impression that it must be thoroughly depressing. If one takes a moment to look back at the seventies and eighties, one would be quite mad to think of them as times of happiness and contentment. But at the same time, when it came to young people I still believe there was an optimism for the future. A sense that people who had children believed that their children's lives would be better than theirs. Certainly, my parents made numerous attempts to give me that impression.

'Your life will be better than ours, Damien,' my mother would tell me.

'Easier, too,' my father would say.

'Unless you turn out to have allergies,' my mother would add, by which time I would be feeling rather less optimistic than I had when the conversation had begun.

I am extremely unlikely to become a parent any time soon. Certainly not via the traditional method. Anthony does, very occasionally, talk about adopting but I soon silence him on the matter. Besides, we haven't the space for a nursery. We'd lose a spare room, and then where would the guests go? The whole thing would be a logistical nightmare, quite apart from all that business of powdered milk.

'We should discuss it properly, Damien,' Anthony tells me. 'It's not just about spare rooms.'

'No, no, you're quite right,' I say and generally do my best to change the subject.

The fact of the matter is, I have never once heard Anthony raise the subject of our adopting a child until after he has consumed a minimum of three large glasses of a particular white wine. Which usually takes him all of about fifteen minutes. Sometimes after a fourth glass he says that we should perhaps see if we could get twins.

'What are you talking about? Why are you being like this?' I'll say.

'I'm just feeling broody,' he'll say.

What Anthony doesn't realise is that what he thinks of as broodiness is actually just hunger. This sort of misunderstanding on his behalf is, I am afraid, not at all uncommon. There are all sorts of things he comes out with that really just boil down to the fact that a certain peckishness has once again risen up within his vast frame. The man is a slave to his appetite. Actually, *I* am a slave to his appetite. Because he really does get hungry a lot. Honestly, it's like keeping a blue whale.

'Shall we stop for petrol?' he'll sometimes say when the tank is half full. What he means is, 'I am craving a Twix.'

'I think I might pop out for a walk,' he'll sometimes say. What he means is, 'I am going to go out to our local independent coffee shop and bring home two almond croissants in a brown paper bag. For myself.'

'Do you want me to tidy up the fridge?' he'll sometimes say. What he means is, 'If there are any leftovers in there I am going to eat the ruddy lot.'

'I'm a little bit worried I'm coming down with a cold' means 'I am going to go out for a hot curry'.

'Did you have any plans for those brownies?' means 'I have eaten every single one of the things'.

In fact, almost anything he says means that he wants to eat something. If, on the other hand, he says that he's feeling a little sleepy it means that he has somehow managed, against all odds, to eat too much and is suffering the consequences.

'This is not a sensible way to live your life,' I often tell him. 'Anyone that regularly needs to "sleep off breakfast" is not making the best use of the day.'

So when Anthony turns to me, looks me straight in the eye and says 'I think we should adopt twins', I know that what he really means is that he's probably about to slip out of the house and come back with a very large kebab. That he is not allowed to eat in the sitting room.

I would feel very troubled indeed about raising a child in this modern world. Will there be enough jobs to go around for all the children born today? What on earth will have happened to the local high street? How far away are we from nuclear war? Perhaps I'm being pessimistic. Perhaps Brexit will foster a new spirit of self-sufficiency and more people will start growing their own veg than ever before?

When I was young, though, we always had things to

do. Some of that, of course, was simply down to our imaginations. I loved to draw, I loved to read. I loved trying to help out in the kitchen. My sister liked shadow boxing and experimenting with her chemistry set. But there were also a huge number of after-school clubs. My sister and I could choose one each a term, on the proviso that we both attended. I opted that we join a singing group. It was marvellous fun. There were about thirty of us, and as a boy soprano (a voice I could claim to be until I was fifteen) I used to sing really quite lustily. I enjoyed the camaraderie of it, and the thrill of unaccompanied, often close harmony, singing. I might have hoped for more of a classical repertoire perhaps, as we mainly seemed to sing what might be termed 'rock gospel' and indeed the songs of Boney M.

My sister, it must be said, did not get as much out of it as I did. She has quite a narrow, and surprisingly deep, vocal range, and so was never allowed anywhere near the melody but instead often more likely to be asked to sing the background parts, the 'la la las', and to provide necessary percussive effects. She used to become very bored at times, and fidgety. I asked the group leader if I could never be positioned in front of her as she used to like whispering rude words into my ear when I was trying to listen to all the other voices. Once, when I was singing a solo, she punched me so hard in the kidneys that I was forced to let out an astonished cry. I did not sound so much like somebody sitting down by the rivers of Babylon and weeping as somebody sitting down by the rivers of

Babylon and howling about the need for a trained first aider. There was a boy she liked in that group, though. She used to whisper naughty things to him, and once I saw her lick his ear. He looked, I must say, absolutely haunted.

My sister opted for us to join an after-school judo club. For my part I expressed reservations from the very start.

'It'll be good for you,' my father said. 'Toughen you up. Make up for all those years you spent vomiting when you were little.'

'It'll be a chance for you to understand about the East,' my mother said. 'China, or wherever it's from.'

'It's Japanese,' my sister said. 'I'll learn how to immobilise someone.'

'I think I might get killed,' I said.

The judo classes were held in a draughty church hall (is there any other kind?), and were taken by a man called Dennis who could not have been less Japanese if he'd tried. There were thin blue mats laid out across the floor, and on our first lesson we were handed judo uniforms, or *judogi*, and instructed to put them on. Mine was not flattering, and nor am I ever particularly happy to be bare-footed in the presence of others. It makes me feel intolerably vulnerable. Shy, even. (This can, awkwardly, be misread by some as coquettishness.) We were then ordered to form a circle, and Dennis explained what we were all there for. It sounded as if we were preparing for some sort of imminent attack. From that moment on it was a matter of us all taking it in turns to grab each other and try not to end up on the floor. Although of course I always did, accidentally at first but increasingly deliberately as I realised that the quicker I submitted then the quicker the whole ordeal would be over.

Angela absolutely loved it, but frequently had to be taken to task by Dennis for being less than magnanimous in victory. Where possible I tried to avoid any situation that involved the two of us being paired together. At home I spent a disproportionate amount of my free time trying to prevent this girl from physically attacking me and from picking me up and dropping me on my head, so I was distraught to find myself in an environment in which this sort of behaviour was endorsed and applauded. Every week I would come home with an appalling headache, and exquisitely tender ribs. I will forever rue the day that my sister was taught a chokehold.

At weekends as a family we would often go off on little outings to country houses.

My parents have been devotees of the National Trust for as long as I can remember. That lovely little windscreen sticker denoting our membership was a source of as much pride to them as the 'GB' sticker on our boot. In fact, it was probably even more of a badge of pride actually, as its mere presence entitled us to free parking at hundreds of sites nationwide. Not to mention entry to a fabulous array of marvellous houses of historic interest and, it goes without saying but I will anyway, places of 'natural beauty'.

As I child, I absolutely adored visiting stately homes

and their gardens, and I like to think that I made a point of always showing due deference to the many volunteers (some of them of quite an age, it must be said) who devote their time to the upkeep of these wonderful places. If there was a guidebook, I would splurge my pocket money on it. If there was an audio tour, well, I was good for nothing else. I was only eight years old when I first saw the Palladian Bridge at Prior Park in Bath, and if I've been struck by anything as possessed of such sheer beauty and perfection since, then I've forgotten it. Kedlestone Hall in Derbyshire was also a favourite, and Little Moreton Hall in Cheshire makes me giddy to this day.

My sister was always more of an English Heritage person, as their sites always tended to be weatherbeaten ruins, which rather suited her temperament. She liked to jump about and scramble over things, and generally let off steam. Whereas I liked to have a picnic and then have a gander at some really super wallpaper. Horses for courses, I suppose.*

Did you know that at Stonehenge, the stones themselves are in the care of English Heritage, but the ground is looked after by the National Trust? Such a state of affairs kept both my sister and I happy, but more to the point also, I think, serves as a splendid example of what can be achieved in the spirit of cooperation. Happily, I was actually remarking on this unlikely but very satisfactory position of compromise that has been reached in – of all places – Wiltshire only the other day to my partner Anthony. Anthony are of one mind across a whole range

* I would love to hear more about the qualitative differences between the National Trust and English Heritage. Could help us get a bit of traction when it comes to publicity. The more outspoken the better, frankly.

You are mercenary. No.

of issues, both at home and abroad, but inevitably we occasionally find ourselves at odds in the most surprising of circumstances. Cheese is one area (I like mine runny, he likes his hard), vests is another (he likes to wear sleeveless, I prefer a quarter-length-sleeve T-shirt). We've also had the odd quibble about the situation in the Middle East. (This is perhaps inevitable given Anthony's background in the world of finance. He has a tendency – and I'm not saying it irritates me, but God I really wish he wouldn't do it – to make economic cases for his arguments, whereas I just want everyone to get along. As per.)

In this particular instance we were having a bit of set-to in an antiques shop that, on the advice of a dear, dear friend (a lady who has overcome adversity like no other to achieve her dream job as a home economist) we'd driven all the ruddy way to Crystal Palace to visit. I'd seen some mirrors that rather caught my eye, and also a wonderful wardrobe that I thought we could put into service in our spare bedroom (partly for guests to use, and partly for us ourselves to use as additional clothes hanging space and also for laundry cupboard overspill. We have too many sheets at the moment, because *someone* cannot stop buying bedding. It's me. And I don't like the fitted ones. I know they're convenient when you're actually making up the bed, but when it comes to folding the things they are – if you'll forgive me – a bugger).

Anyway, I measured the wardrobe and realised it wouldn't fit. Anthony, meanwhile, had stumbled across a Chesterfield three-seater and declared that he had *always* wanted a Chesterfield. This was news to me, I must say. We've bought six sofas (four new, one vintage and one ex-display in need of re-upholstering) since we've been together and not once has he even *mentioned* his so-called 'love' of Chesterfields. I told him this, using rather economical language. 'No, no,' he insisted, 'I have *always* loved them, I just didn't know what they were called.' This sounded like a funny sort of love to me. I didn't rise to this bait, although on another occasion I very easily could have (like that time when we were having a weekend in Cheltenham and he suggested that for lunch we could 'just grab a panini'. Apoplectic). If you've been on this planet for over forty years, as Anthony has, and don't know that a Chesterfield sofa is called a Chesterfield, then in all likelihood there is something quite seriously wrong with you.

I let all that pass, and simply pointed out that I, speaking as someone who had always known perfectly well what they were called, simply did not like them. This cut, I'm surprised to say, no ice whatsoever. 'I'm going to buy it,' he said, 'and you can like it or lump it,' or words to that effect. In Anthony's defence, I have chosen each of the other six sofas that we've bought together, so I saw, as usual, absolutely no point in kicking up a fuss. 'Fine,' I said, 'but I shall choose the cushion covers.'

'Fine,' he said.

'It'll be like Stonehenge,' I said.

'What?' said Anthony, and so I explained the simile in appropriate detail. I was just about to squeeze out a quick anecdote that I had once heard about Octavia Hill, when the man who ran the antiques shop came over and said that if it was all right with us, then he really rather needed to lock up. 'Can we quickly buy the ... what is it called again, Damien?' said Anthony.

'Chesterfield,' I quietly reminded him.

'Have you a way of getting it home?' said the man. We realised that we didn't. I bought some rather nice basil seeds (Genovese) from a shop next to where we'd parked the Uno, however, so it was by no means a wasted journey.

Stonehenge, though, I would very much recommend. As I would all National Trust sites. And indeed those of English Heritage. And indeed those of its Welsh counterpart, Cadw. And indeed of its Scottish counterpart, Historic Scotland. There's also a Manx National Heritage on the Isle of Man, but I've not actually been there. I'm sure it's fine.

Quiche Lorraine

I have always been – for as long as I can remember – absolutely daft about quiche. Hot, cold – lukewarm even – if it's a handmade quiche then I'm a fan. I suppose that it's their transportability that makes them so perfect for picnics, but frankly who gives a fig about boring old practicalities when you've something as delicious as a quiche at stake. I think that it's the combination of textures that does it for me, just as much as whatever the flavour might be (and trust me – there are many). I love that feeling of the soft, eggy, possibly even cheesy, filling giving way to the light, starchy crunch of the pastry; the way that their yellowy pale surfaces are dashed with occasional evidence of oven browning. Good quiche can be a hard thing to pull off. Lord knows that I have presided over some absolute catastrophes in my time – a smoked salmon and asparagus effort I made during the summer of 2005 still gives me cause to wince at its wretched memory even now – but the practice (could one say *art* even? Perhaps) of making quiche is one that is most definitely worth pursuing.

It could have easily gone so wrong for me at the very start, as my earliest introduction to quiche was a supermarket one that my mother must have brought home from one of our Saturday morning expeditions to the giant Sainsbury's in Camden Town in the early eighties. I mean I like onions, but these things were ridiculous. So often these shop-bought quiches seemed to me to be utterly without nuance, the textures so samey, the pastry so damp, the exteriors burnt to a cinder, the interiors as cold as ice, any meat within of such dubious provenance. And what, in all honesty, could be more depressing then a flan tin made out of foil? You are right. Almost nothing. But I happened to go to a funeral of a relative when I was about eight, and at the reception afterwards miniature handmade quiches were served. I could hardly believe that these things were from the same family as the packaged nonsense that we regularly consumed at home. They were heavenly and also piping hot. (As, given that the funeral had been at a crematorium, would the deceased have been by this point.) I cannot remember who the relative was, or even what they died of, but the buffet was a cracker. It was a Damascene moment for me, setting me on a lifelong path of belief in quiche.

I never pack a picnic without one. And I hope you won't too. Let's keep it simple, shall we, and start with a Quiche Lorraine.

For this you will need ... well actually, the first thing that you'll need is some shortcrust pastry. And I'd like you to make it yourself, please. If that's all right with you. Thank you so much.

So, for the pastry you will need ...

Plain flour, organic *bien sûr*, 4½ oz of

Some sea salt, ground as fine as you dare and then some

Butter, ideally at room temperature, 1 oz of

Lard, very much likewise, 1 oz of

And 1 bowl of water, iced

(Also, some baking beads)

Pour the flour and salt through your sieve into a large bowl, and give it a right thorough sifting, shaking it about merrily but not so merrily that your face and apron are covered in the stuff. You are doing this not just to make the flour as fine and smooth as possible, but also to aerate it, so keep that in mind when you are considering which of your many wrist actions to employ.

Then slice the butter and the lard into relatively small pieces and drop them into the mixing bowl with the flour and salt. Take a knife and chop the butter and lard into even smaller pieces and in so doing start to incorporate it into the flour and the flour into it. When you have done this to your satisfaction, and everything seems to be pretty well as thoroughly mixed as you can manage, then put the knife to one side, and blend and rub everything together further using the tips of your fingers. Don't go at it hard, mind. This sort of pastry, as indeed we all do at times, requires a gentle touch. Allow as much air into the mixture as you can by lobbing it all about a little, but don't go mad. When you've a nice crumbly mixture, take up your knife once more and using your spare hand gently drop a teaspoonful of water into the mixture and mix it in with the knife.

Then rid yourself of the knife once more, and go at it with your fingers. This process of adding a small amount of water and mixing it together needs to be repeated painstakingly until you have what is unmistakeably some pastry before you that you can scoop out of the bowl without leaving any sticking to the sides. The moment that you achieve this particular consistency is a most satisfying one indeed, and you could be forgiven for allowing yourself a short burst of celebratory hollering. Then having regained control of yourself, take the ball of pastry and wrap it in some cling film before placing it into your fridge to relax.

It shouldn't need more than half an hour of resting time, but this provides you with more than ample time to carrying out a few light stretches, have a little bit of a tidy, and then assemble your other ingredients …

Streaky bacon, smoked, 4½ oz of

Large eggs, free range, 2, and the yolk of a further one (but what to do with the leftover white, you may well ask. Pop it into a ramekin, cling film it and leave it in the fridge. Either you'll soon find a use for it – perhaps an egg-white omelette if you're on some sort of dastardly health kick – or, in a few weeks' time, you'll happen upon it, have a brief think about how long it's been there and then pour it down the sink). You will also need a little extra beaten egg for the pastry.

Double cream, ½ pint of

Salt and pepper to season

Gruyère cheese, 2¾ oz of

Grill the bacon so that it is just on the verge of hardening but still very much pink, and then remove from the heat, allow to cool and cut it into pleasingly small pieces.

Once your pastry is rested, remove it from the refrigerator and roll it into a neat ball with your hands. (That sounds like obvious advice, but I do know people that can roll pastry with other parts of their anatomy. My friend Trevor does it with his knees as an – admittedly rather niche – party trick.) Sprinkle some plain flour on a flat surface, and then take your best and newest rolling pin, and begin to slowly roll the pastry out. If you do this carefully you will be able to keep the pastry in a round shape and thus save yourself an awful lot of faff later. The key here is to make it as unsticky as possible, so do not be afraid to keep adding more flour. In order to make sure that the pastry is evenly rolled, make a point of rotating it every now and then as you go.

You will either have a tin or a ceramic quiche dish to hand, probably a shade under twelve inches in diameter. Personally, I like a ceramic one, but I am very much aware that I am not necessarily like everybody else. Whatever you use, lay the round pastry over the top and then press it gently into the dish using your fingers, which you should work all around the sides, making sure that the pastry is pushed snugly against the dish all around the edge. There will be some inevitable overhang, but this is not a reason to panic. Now this pastry needs to be prevented from expanding when you are giving it its initial cook, so this is when your baking beads will come in handy. Having first pricked the pastry base with a fork fairly rigorously, pour your ceramic baking beads in so that they are weighing the pastry down. Some people like to place baking parchment inside the dish first, but I am not remotely concerned about this. Perhaps I should be, but I'm not. Sorry.

Your oven, I should have mentioned previously, should now be at gas mark 5. Slide the dish into it, and let it cook for at least a quarter of an hour, after which the pastry should be nice and firm – you can test the outer edges to see if this is the case. When you're convinced that it's solidified, empty out the baking beads (which will be jolly hot, so do watch out), then brush the floor and walls of the pastry with a little beaten egg before returning the dish to the oven for anything up to ten minutes until the pastry has coloured a little to a nice biscuity hue. (That's a nice combination of sound, isn't it? If I had a friend called Hugh, I would definitely start referring to him as 'Biscuity Hugh'. If he seemed in the right frame of mind for a bit of repartee. Anyway, I don't have a friend called Hugh. Bit of a galling thing to suddenly realise at my time of life, actually. It's something I should probably seek to rectify.)

When you remove the pastry from the oven, reduce the heat to gas mark 4 or your nearest equivalent. And turn your attentions to the filling. You've already attended to your bacon needs, but take your two whole eggs, crack them into your mixing bowl and add the additional yolk. Whisk them thoroughly, and then pour in the cream and whisk it all together with your doubtless characteristically wristy finesse. Season this mixture to your taste with the salt and pepper. I like to go at it fairly hard with the pepper. Don't be tempted to overdo the salt, even though the piquancy it will add is most urgent.

Well, well, well, it's assembly time. Take the pastry case that you have so lovingly prepared and cooked, and fill its bottom by coarsely grating most but not all of the Gruyère into it. Gruyère really does have the most delightful smell. It's a little harsh to naïve taste buds, but you soon warm to it if you value a density of flavour. I also like to put the odd chunk in amongst the gratings to give someone a nice surprise. Make sure that the cheese is spread evenly, and then add the bacon, which you must also arrange as evenly and fairly as possible. An inconsistent quiche is no quiche at all in my book. Then pour the egg and cream mixture over that and you'll hopefully fill the case almost up to the very brim. If you are especially lucky you might achieve an inverted meniscus. Now grate what remains of the Gruyère all over the top, and it's ready to be cooked.

Slide it into the oven on top of a tray as gently as you can given how sloppy it will be, close the oven door and then – if you're anything like me and your oven light is in good working order – you can watch it cook. It will need upwards of half an hour (possibly as many as thirty-seven minutes) but you can always test it to see if it has hardened sufficiently. You don't want it to be actually hard, of course. It must remain a little wobbly in the middle. When it has achieved its ultimate consistency, remove it from the oven to allow it to cool for a quarter of an hour.

Serve it in its cooking dish, and it should be the centrepiece of a delightful picnic spread. Slice it with as sharp a knife as you have, and do take the great care when removing each slice and placing it on a plate. Quiche is easily angered.

And remember, you can never take too many blankets to a picnic. Or quiches.

Chapter 10

ANIMALS AND TREES

I said earlier that I would describe my sister in more detail, but I'm not entirely sure how wise that would actually be. I think I can perhaps more easily shine a little light into her soul by describing her relationship with animals. If I can accurately relate that, then it would I feel give some insight into what her relationships with humans are like.

My parents have always been pet lovers, but it was never something that my sister and I were at all capable of getting our heads around. In most families it is the children who beg the parents to let them have a puppy, but in our case it was the other way round. Every year in the run-up to Christmas, the same conversational topic would suddenly arise out of nowhere, like a corpse that has been dumped in a lake suddenly breaking free from whatever weight has been holding it down and popping unexpectedly to the surface, startling a fisherman or perhaps a picnicking family. We might be having a family meal together, or sitting in traffic on the way back from doing the weekly shop at ruddy Sainsbury's. My ideological opposition to the supermarkets didn't come, I'm embarrassed to say, until I was much older, thirteen or fourteen perhaps, and the whole family was brought low by rather unpleasant digestive issues triggered by a somewhat uncharacteristic impulse decision that my mother had made to purchase some frozen, oven-ready cannelloni that were 'on special'. I suspected that, rather than being a lone incident, our appalling experience (more than one pair of good trousers was ruined) was symptomatic of wider malpractice and poor attention to ethical detail that all major supermarkets were guilty of. And I was right. It would be lovely to say that things have improved since I was a child but, despite many years of people like myself and George Monbiot trying to bring this to the attention of the great British public, I'm not at all sure they have. The meat scandal, anyone? Self-checkouts?

Anyway, we were on our way either to or from Sainsbury's when one of my parents (whichever had drawn the short straw, I suspect, usually my father) would say apropos of nothing whatsoever: 'We were wondering if it would be a good idea to get a cat?'

'Cats make me cough,' I would say, not altogether disingenuously. Because they did. And indeed still do. A really dry hacking thing. The sort of cough that it's dangerous to do near soup.

'Oh,' my father would say.

'If you get a cat, I will kill it,' my sister would say. And I believe she meant it.

'Well, what about a dog then?' my mother would ask.

'I am, in all truth, a little frightened of dogs,' I would say. And this was indubitably the case. I'm better now, it must be said. But as a very young child I was once barked at by a bull mastif in a campsite, and had lived with the fear ever since.

'Oh,' my mother would say. 'Still?'

'Still,' I would insist, no longer able to hold back the tears.

'If you get a dog,' my sister would say, 'it will be harder to kill than a cat, but I promise you I will find a way.'

I'm not sure where Angela's loathing of pets came from. My indisposition to them was grounded in genuine fears caused by real events that had scarred me or made me wheeze. My sister had no more reason to fear cats and dogs than she did anything else. And she feared, as far as I could tell, absolutely nothing else. Perhaps she was just being spirited, or maybe she was joking. But then when she was younger she had once killed all of the fish in our pond by emptying a whole can of WD-40 into it. By accident, she claimed. My parents never did get a cat or a dog until we left home, so she was never put in the position of having to carry out her threats. She never, as far as I'm aware, hurt any of the cats or dogs of our friends or relatives, and if she did, then the matter must have been hushed up. I do have, however, a very vivid recollection of her once in Spain, throwing rocks at a donkey, although this could well be a dream.

'Right,' my mother would say, and the journey would continue in silence.

But you're never too far from the pets of others in London, because of the abundance of parks and green spaces. London, for all its manifold faults, happens to have the most wonderful parks. There is a veritable *abundance* of them. Brockwell, Brockley, Hyde, the Regent's, Greenwich, St. James's, Victoria, Battersea, Crystal Palace, West Ham, Clissold, Burgess, Dulwich, Southwark, Queen's, Alexandra, Golders Hill, Holland, Thames Barrier, Kennington, Richmond, Haggerston, Finsbury, Norwood, Green, Hammersmith, Mile End: these are all, I'm quite sure I'm right in thinking, the names of parks. And jolly nice a number of them are too. There are commons as well, such as Clapham and Wimbledon. And there are fields, such as Lincoln's Inn, Highbury, Coram and the vaguely named 'London'.

But there is one which, to my mind, tops them all. Barcelona has Gaudi's Park Güell, Lisse has Keukenhof; the good burghers of São Paulo probably skip daily and gaily about Oscar Niemeyer's fabulous Ibirapuera Park, whilst the habitants of Munich can do pretty much anything they fancy in the Englischer Garten and the very best of luck to them, I say. None of these though, for my money, can hold so much as a candle to the vibrant green sprawl that stretches between Hampstead and Highgate in the north of London: the majestic Hampstead Heath. Truly, it is arcadia.

We used to go there for walks pretty much every Sunday afternoon when I was a child, and I have simply never tired of the place. Its 790 acres are replete not just with beauty, but also with history and joyousness. It is managed by the City of London Corporation, and whatever else you may think of them they actually do it bloody well. All human life is there, as well as a variety of fascinating wildlife. I know the heath like I know the back of my hands. I could probably find my way through it by smell in pitch darkness should I have cause to go there after dark. Which I don't. The only time I have ever got lost on the heath was when walking there with my family after the storms of '87, when so many trees had been knocked down by the those mighty winds that Michael Fish so famously told us not to fret about that I completely lost my bearings. I had, in my characteristically foolhardy fashion, wandered away from the rest of the pack, got distracted by some flowers or bushes or somesuch, and then looked up and realised that I did not have the foggiest where I was.

'HELP!' I wailed. 'I am lost!'

I repeated this phrase for some minutes, until I could finally hear my calls being answered.

'Keep shouting, Damien!' my father was calling. 'Keep shouting and we'll find you.'

'And don't panic!' I could hear my mother shrieking.

The next thing I knew I felt something hard strike me in my right temple and I went down like a sack of King Edward's. Then I heard the sound of Angela laughing, and breaking out of the undergrowth.

'Thanks for shouting, Damien!' she said. 'It made it easier for me to aim at you.'

My mother then arrived at the scene, took one look at me lying prostrate on the ground and began wailing like someone out of the New Testament. My father subsequently appeared, appealed for my mother and Angela to stop their respective noises and, when relative calm had descended, inspected my injuries.

'He must have tripped,' said my mother.

'No,' said Angela. 'I threw a stone at him.'

Then my father scooped me up, and carried me about for a bit like Mr Darcy holding Elizabeth Bennet on a moor.

I had assumed until then that I had always used the paths to navigate my way about the place, but that day I realised how much I had come to depend on the trees as landmarks, in much the same way as an old sailor could navigate by the stars. The storms were, and I don't completely blame Michael Fish for this by any stretch, absolutely heartbreaking. So much damage done to so many trees in so short a time. Some were knocked over and now leant at ungainly angles, others were broken clean in half, and now protruded like bones sticking out of the mud of a battlefield. Horrible, really. Others were torn up from the root, and now lay flat on the ground like the dead after a natural disaster. I had no idea where I was, but I sat down and wept for some time, like one of those aforementioned people from Psalm 137 remembering Zion by the river of Babylon, whose story was so vividly brought to life by Brent Dowe and Trevor McNaughton, and then irreparably seared on our hearts by the members of Boney M. The song should have been ruined for me by my own agonised experiences singing it in the choir with my sister, but mercifully it hasn't been. True art transcends pain. When we got home, arnica was applied to my wounds, and I was allowed to stay up late and watch a costume drama.

The views of and indeed from the heath, especially that from Parliament Hill, are simply stunning. There are, contained within its neat boundaries, an astonishing twenty-five ponds, four of which you can swim in. I prefer the Parliament Hill Lido, but have been in the men's pond, the mixed pond and once, as a result of a picnic that simply got out of hand, the ladies' pond. Which is lovely. I have, as an adult, always loved open-air swimming, both at home and abroad. It has an almost timeless quality, and is refreshing in the way that a dunk in an over-chlorinated municipal swimming facility never really can be. I think the most marvellous place that I've ever swam in the open air is at Brienzersee in German-speaking Switzerland where I had an experience that, though I could not possibly describe in detail here, was positively both life-changing and affirming. Such clean air.

Anthony, I am sad to relate, is rather less keen on open-air swimming, or indeed swimming of any kind. He has never really found a pair of swimming shorts in which he feels completely comfortable, mainly because of his considerable heft, which is a shame as most swimming pools insist upon their being worn. People of Anthony's dimensions are catered for relatively well when it comes to smart, formal or leisure wear, but the swimming trunk manufacturing community have, it must be said, been rather slow on the uptake in this regard. I did once have a pair made up for him as a surprise gift, but it wasn't a great success. The amount of material required in order to give him a level of coverage that he would feel safe in – anyone of Anthony's substantial height really needs their swimming trunks to be worn long,* as if they are of a normal length then, in proportion to the wearer's height, they look skimpy which is certainly not a look that Anthony has ever been able to pull off, and I'm not sure that even if he could I'd want him to – was simply astonishing, and although we both felt that they looked marvellous on purely aesthetic grounds, once Anthony was in the water, they turned out to be incredibly impractical. Anthony found that carting around that much wet cloth behind him caused considerable drag. He could just about swim in a straight line, albeit slowly, but turning was completely beyond him. In the end he was forced to just tread water, and eventually lifeguards had to become involved, and the experience was ultimately a humiliating one for pretty much everybody in or around the pool that day. But hey ho. I still think it was worth trying, and I still love surprises. Well, giving surprises. Being surprised, as I think I mentioned earlier, absolutely infuriates me and I simply will not stand for it. Anthony has often accompanied me to the Hampstead Ponds; never, alas, with his swimming gear, but usually with a thriller to read and, thankfully, pretty much always with a picnic.[1]

* Even if Anthony's swimming shorts can't be, is there anyway this this clause should be a little shorter?.

I'll think about it. But no promises.

1 I, generally speaking, have to make up the picnic, as if I left it up to Anthony we would be sat there drinking cider from

There is so much to see and do on the heath. Kenwood House, a former stately home on the northern boundary of the heath, is packed full of the most exquisite art. (Actually, 'packed' isn't quite the word. It's all very tastefully arranged and mounted.) It's generally Old Masters, but there is also a good smattering of sculptures by the likes of Henry Moore and Dame Barbara Hepworth, who I adore. Unusually for a stately home, I think it looks more impressive from the rear than it does from the front, but sometimes life's like that. Personally I am rather more excited by the derelict Caen Wood Towers site, over to the north east. There's something rather fabulous, I've always thought, about a ruin. 'Decay is a kind of progress,' Alan Bennett once wrote, and you're not about to read me arguing with him.

The heath is made up of many areas, not just the aforementioned Parliament Hill Fields, but also the Kenwood estate, the Heath Woods and a wonderful area known as the Vale of Health which was, until the early 1800s, known as 'Hatchett's Bottom'. Splendid. The history of the place is sometimes mindboggling. Karl Marx and his family used to walk there. There are even some who say that Boudicca may have been buried there, and you'd have to agree that whatever faults she had (and she did seem a bit on the surly side), she's certainly not chosen a bad spot.

---

cans and eating the contents of a family-sized pack of Doritos dipped in convenience-store taramasalata. It's always a bit of a lottery as to whether the cider or the taramasalata will turn out to be the fizzier.

But for me, it's really all about those Sunday walks as a child. In many ways the saddest part of every week for me, as a child, was the journey home from the heath on a Sunday evening, and knowing that it would be nearly a whole week before I could be back there again. Whatever life might throw at you at school and at home, a Sunday afternoon on the heath was a chance to decompress. We went there when it was sunny, and we went there when it was rainy. Presumably we went there when it was grey and overcast, as that is what the weather always tends to be during recollections of my childhood.

We'd have an early lunch on a Sunday, usually a roast of some sort. I would beg my mother to let me help, but she was easily flustered in the kitchen and so we generally left her to it. Sometimes I would see my father emerge from the kitchen, carefully shutting the door behind him and looking a bit shaken.

'Is everything all right in there?' I'd ask.

'Your mother's … cooking,' my father would say, and we'd look at one another sadly.

When my mother felt that the food had been cooked enough (that was always how she judged food, incidentally. She was never concerned with cooking it well, she just wanted it to be cooked 'enough'. She didn't concern herself with the taste, ever, rather with just ensuring that none of us were going to come down with beriberi. I'm not sure why she thought that beriberi was something caused by eating undercooked food rather than Vitamin B1 deficiency, but no one ever challenged her on this), I would be instructed to go and fetch my sister down from her room and tell her that 'lunch is on the table'. My sister would normally respond to this news by punching me to the ground, and then running past my stricken form, and sprinting down to the kitchen to sit in the seat that she knew I preferred. I would come down to cry, and then we'd eat. We would talk about the week that we'd all just had, my sister would call us all idiots, and then we'd have some fruit. Traditionally, the meal ended with my mother remembering that there was still gravy warming, and my father would be forced to remove the absolutely scalding and usually over-full gravy boat from the oven, using both oven gloves and additional tea towels to try and insulate himself from the unbearable heat.

'SOMEBODY OPEN THE BACK DOOR!' he'd shout. I would always go and open it, whilst my sister sat there calling us all names and my mother, quite needlessly, got on with wafting the air with a tea towel. My father would burst out into the garden, muttering something about a failure to learn any lessons from history, fling the thing on to the lawn and come back in nursing a fresh injury and barking at us not to attempt to pick the gravy boat up for a few hours.

'I'm so sorry,' my mother would always say. 'Do you think it needed gravy?'

I usually fell silent at this point, as gravy made from granules and served at a nuclear temperature was quite far down my own personal list of improvements that I would make to my mother's Sunday lunches. (Number one was a serious review of cooking times, and numbers two through seven were a variety of seasonings. Also, and I have written reams about this elsewhere, you must choose your roasting potatoes *carefully*. Personally, you can't go wrong with a Maris Piper. Different potatoes are for different things, and you treat all potatoes as equals at your peril.)

'It was delicious,' my father always said. 'Why don't we save the washing up for later and go to the heath?'

And then we'd pile into our big red car – a Volvo possibly? Is that a make of car? – and nip round to Mum's friend Andrea and borrow her dog. Because of my sister's attitude, the thought of a pet living with us permanently was quite out of the question, but Andrea offered a compromise. Every Sunday she would let us borrow her dog, and in return we … actually I'm not sure that in return we did anything. Perhaps no further deal had to be struck because our borrowing the dog was mutually beneficial. We, that is to say my mother and my father, loved dogs, but were unable to provide one with a safe place to live permanently. The dog, Graham, certainly need to be regularly exercised and Andrea didn't seem all that keen on being present when exercise was being taken by anyone. Graham was a Norfolk terrier, and rather an animated one at that.

The first time we ever took Graham with us to the heath he attempted to leap over the divide between the boot and the back seats and had the great misfortune of landing into my sister's lap. She said nothing, but wound down the window, and attempted to force Graham out of it. Graham bit her, and then she bit Graham. My father, from the driving seat, appealed for calm, but was drowned out by my mother telling him that he was going the wrong way. I attempted to wrestle Graham from my sister, and for my troubles, I was bitten. By both of them.

It was an inauspicious start. The first few times we took Graham out, my mother used to absolutely panic about him being let off the lead, but my father, who was the one holding on to the lead, and thus being dragged all over the heath by an increasingly frustrated Graham, eventually persuaded her the dog could be trusted not to run off. As soon as Graham was let off his lead, however, he did run off, which was when we first realised that Andrea hadn't taught Graham his own name. The four of us wandered about the heath in a line like a forensics team combing the scene of a crime and chanting 'Graham! Graham!' over and over again (which is something that presumably forensics teams don't do unless it's absolutely necessary). My sister was saying that it was a waste of our time searching for such a dumb animal, and suggested that the kindest thing we could do in the circumstances would be to go home and leave the creature to die. The rest of us overruled her, and we eventually found Graham swimming in a pond at the foot of the Vale of Health.

It was my father who was ultimately forced to wade in to retrieve him as it was beginning to get dark and the heath, my mother insisted, 'turned into a rather different sort of place at night'. Paranoia, I'm sure, but she wasn't going to back down and thus my father, at her insistence, walked into the pond – the water was up to his chest – and successfully grabbed hold of Graham. Graham, of course, could shake himself dry, but that wasn't an option available to my poor father, who my mother made drive home trouserless and pantless to avoid damage to the car's upholstery. This was a great shame for him, as when we got back to Andrea's house, she had put on a tremendous spread by way of a thank you for us taking Graham out. Being naked from the waist down, my father had to remain in the car while we went in for tea, and when we eventually emerged from the house again some ninety minutes later he was in a very agitated mood. Apparently some police officers had shone a torch in his face and asked him what exactly he was doing, and had been somewhat unsympathetic to his plight. I hadn't been at all unsympathetic, and had brought him out a slice of Battenberg. It has always had, oddly, a very calming effect on my sister but I must say my father looked rather miserable as he ate the thing awkwardly with one hand whilst driving home, as my mother berated him for getting crumbs on the car and indeed himself.

Nevertheless business gradually improved as these outings continued. Graham eventually began to learn his own name, and would come galloping excitedly back to us with a stick in his mouth for us to throw. My sister, perhaps inevitably, always threw the stick *at* Graham rather than to him, but luckily Graham remained oblivious to her malicious intentions and instead thought it was some sort of a game. We let Graham swim in the ponds knowing that he'd eventually come back, and we always took with us a box of Terry's Neapolitans, which I still love even though they're rather hard to find these days and not generally in date when you do. We only saw Graham once a week, but he steadily became part of the family, and all of us began to relish the Sunday afternoon walks with the funny fellow. I succumbed surprisingly soon to Graham's charm, and Angela learnt to tolerate him, but then she generally wore her Walkman on family outings and took very little part in conversations. My parents insisted that she removed her Walkman while we were having tea with Andrea, and my sister relented, although in the car afterwards she often told us all how Andrea was clearly 'evil'. Perhaps she was, but she could certainly bake.

There were, sadly, some traumatic incidents as a result of our Sunday afternoons with Graham. From my father's point of view it was the time that we collected Graham from Andrea and she said, vaguely, that 'he's been in a bit of a funny mood today'. It turned out, once we had arrived back at the car park after our walk, that what Graham had actually done that morning was to eat an entire ball of string which had now worked most of its way through his digestion system, but was clearly going to need a little help making those last few vital twenty yards or so. The string had to be slowly extracted from Graham like somebody unravelling the wool from a jumper and it took my poor father forty-five minutes for which he wore an extremely pained expression. Graham also looked rather pained, and my father found it very hard to explain to the animal exactly what it was that he was doing back there. As a result of this communication problem, Graham kept jerking around, which disturbed this somewhat delicate operation. All we could do was sit in the car and watch. When we finally got back to Andrea's, my father looking as if he had been wrung out and Graham looking, well, strung out, there was a slightly tense stand-off.

'Graham had eaten an entire ball of string, Andrea,' my father said.

'I know,' said Andrea. 'Didn't I say?'

'You said that he'd "been in a bit of a funny mood".'

'Yes,' said Andrea. 'That's what he does when he's in a bit of a funny mood. Now, I've made Battenberg.'

My father went off to clean his hands, but didn't come back from the loo for a very long while indeed, much of which time he could be heard shouting and kicking the skirting. It seemed if not an appropriate response to events, then at least an understandable one.

The other trauma involved, unfortunately, me. My sister, as I'm sure you would be able to glean from everything that you have already read about her in these pages, was not the happiest of teenagers. Nor was she particularly safe to be around. She had, I think even she would admit now, a propensity for quite astonishing mood swings. One minute she would have you up against the wall by the lapels, and be screaming obscenities at you from such close range that you could actually feel your inner ear humming. Other times she would suddenly be cold and distant, taking to her room for hours – sometimes days – at a time. When she would come downstairs for meals, she would sit at the family dining table, but refuse to speak. Instead she communicated by sighing, tutting and rolling her eyes. She often used to make a sort of gagging sound when eating something that my mother had cooked, but this could have been unrelated to her mood, and simply, I'm afraid, an honest response. Then suddenly she'd be off again. Either of my parents would make some, to me at least, perfectly innocent-sounding remark, and my sister would fly into an instant, hot fury. Doors would be slammed, books and ornaments would be flung from their shelves and extremely unpleasant language would ricochet about the house.

She was also prone to sudden and completely unprovoked violent outbursts. Once, when I was getting scones out of the oven, she hit me over the head with a rolling pin. I was out cold for several minutes, apparently. The strange thing is she *likes* scones. Another time I was sitting out in the garden reading the collected letters of Lady Diana Cooper, and she set fire to me. When I protested, she turned the hose on me, ruining the book and leading to the first of many library fines.

I always found this behaviour quite unnecessary, and – because of the unpredictable nature of these outbursts – it was impossible to know how best to prepare for them in advance. Once, after a succession of attacks in the night

– cold water, stones, yoghurt and so forth – I asked my parents if I might have a lockable bedroom door. I would have one key and my parents would have the other, so that they, and they alone, would be able to open the door from the outside in case of emergency, such as if I overslept or fell over and inadvertently swallowed the key. A handyman was duly sent for and he called when my sister and I were out at school and attached the lock. That night I lay in my bed feeling safe for the first time in about a fortnight, when I suddenly heard the most frightful noise. My sister had somehow managed to cart my mother's hostess trolley up the stairs, loaded it up with the heaviest items she could find, and turned it into a battering ram. She took the whole door clean off its hinges, said simply, 'How's your new lock working out, Damien?' and then went back to bed, leaving my bedroom looking utterly war-torn.

This sort of behaviour was, oddly, confined to when my sister was at home with us. At school she was completely delightful, apparently, and never a moment's trouble. Hard-working, conscientious, etc; helped old ladies across the road, volunteered for various responsibilities. My parents once asked her head teacher if they thought that my sister should undergo child psychology and were told that she was 'an absolute model pupil'. It was only when she was at home that she really struggled. Perhaps my mother or father or I were annoying her somehow. Heaven knows why this could have been the case. With me, incidentally, it was very much the other way round. At school I was self-conscious, and easily flustered (two things I'm very glad to say that I've grown out of). School was where people spoke loudly about things you had no interest in, where people jeered at you, pushed you over when you stooped to tie a shoe lace or bent down to pick up another pupil's litter, and where personal items were stolen not out of need but out of malice. At home I was always far, far happier. My sister and I were and indeed remain, in many ways, yin and yang. (Not that I subscribe to many ancient Chinese systems of belief but you will, I am sure, get the gist.)

Now, my sister has always had the most amazing head for heights and a sense of adventure that can sometimes appear to the onlooker as plain old foolhardiness. When we were young she absolutely loved to climb trees. Still does, for all I know. She seemed able to practically dance up the side of even the highest and most challenging tree like a monkey, leaving those of us still at ground level clutching at our figurative pearls and wondering just how the devil she managed it. Impressive a sight as this was, though, she would then often demonstrate something of a reluctance to come down again and would spend hours alone at the top of a tree cheerfully or indeed moodily sitting in the branches that swayed in the breeze while the rest of us looked up and wondered just what to do. Hampstead Heath, when she was in the mood for this sort of thing, represented quite the temptation and this sort of behaviour could often eat into the day somewhat.

On one occasion we were just coming to the end of our walk, and my mother said that it was probably time that we were getting dear old Graham back to dear old Andrea. Hearing the news that Andrea's Battenberg was in the offing, my father and I found it hard to think of much else, and quickened our pace. My sister, however, had other ideas. She scanned the horizon for the tallest and most challenging-looking tree that she could find, and having chosen one that met her criteria, suddenly sprinted off towards it. We knew what was coming, of course, but though we all jogged after her (Graham rather quicker, it must be said, than the rest of us) we were powerless to stop her. By the time we reached the foot of the tree my sister was some fifteen feet or so above us, and in no mood to stop her ascent. Higher and higher she climbed, like a surly koala, until we could barely see her.

'Well, that's not the best timing, is it?' said my mother.

My father said nothing, and instead went looking for a tree of his own that had a sufficiently soft-looking bark that would enable him to kick it repeatedly whilst making the usual utterances about a wasted life, and so forth.

Minutes went by, and there was no sign of movement at the top of the tree, other than wind-induced oscillations. My father eventually came back from kicking his tree.

'Any news?' he said. 'I just want to go and eat Andrea's Battenberg.'

'You eat too much sugar,' my mother said and we all fell silent, except for Graham who was barking excitedly, as he did pretty much of all of the time.

'You're going to have to go up there and get her,' my mother said eventually.

'Who, me?' my father and I chorused.

'I'm not climbing *that*,' my father said. 'I'll break my bloody neck.'

'What about you then?' my mother asked me.

'I just … I just don't think I could. And what if I do manage it? She might push me off the top.'

'Is there someone we can call?' my father asked. 'Mountain rescue or someone?'

'Just how far do you think we are from the nearest mountain?' my mother said.

'I don't know. The Brecon Beacons?' he said.

'The Peak District National Park?' I proffered.

'Both hopeless,' my mother said.

'They're not hopeless,' my father said. 'What's wrong with the Brecon Beacons?'

'Not the mountains, you idiot,' my mother said. '*You*. You're both useless.'

My father looked crestfallen at this diagnosis, and went and sat down on a log.

'What about the fire brigade?' I said.

'Not open on a Sunday,' my mother said.

'Of course the bloody fire brigade are open on a Sunday,' my father shouted. 'It's an emergency service. Not a bloody florist.'

'Don't be rude, Samuel,' my mother asked.

'Don't be stupid then,' my father replied.

Another silence fell. I called up to my sister, but there was no reply.

'If we're not there by five Andrea will eat all the

bloody Battenberg,' my father said, sadly. 'She's like a wolf.'

'My friend Andrea is not remotely like a wolf,' my mother said. 'She's just had a hard life.'

'She's like a big fat wolf,' my father said, and Graham barked at him.

I took another look up at the tree. Maybe it wouldn't be as hard to climb as it had first looked? Yes, it was tall, but it had a lot of branches on it. They weren't the thickest-looking branches, but there were plenty of them. I'd have several options once up there, and could cling on to one branch while checking the steadiness of another.

'I'm going up,' I said suddenly.

'Don't,' said my parents in unison.

'We don't want two of our children stuck in a tree,' my mother added. 'That wouldn't look at all good.'

'I'll be fine,' I said. 'I'll go at my own pace, and I won't take any risks. Once I get near her, I'll coax her down.'

'What with?' asked my father.

'The last of the Neapolitans,' I said. 'She loves them. Eats them with the wrappers on sometimes.'

And off I strode to the foot of the tree.

'I'll need a leg up,' I said.

My father came forward and held out his clasped hands. I stepped on to them, and heaved myself up on to the first branch, and then pulled myself up on to another one. Then another. The branches were thicker than they looked from the ground, and nice and dry so they were easy to get a good grip on. Up and up I climbed, calling out to my sister as I went. 'I've got Neapolitans,' I called up, but she didn't reply. I climbed slowly, but steadily.

'Careful!' my mother called up. I looked down at her. She must have been ten foot below me now, and had a worried look on her face. My father was sitting on the log again with his head in his hands.

'Mind you don't fall!' my mother said. She needn't worry. Compared to my pyjama-bottom-retrieving incident at the swimming pool, this was child's play. I might not have had the aptitude for this sort of thing that my sister had, but I wasn't a total idiot. It was just a matter of being alert at all times, always holding on to two different branches at once and making sure I didn't …

Suddenly, the branch that I was standing on snapped. I fell fifteen feet without having time to even cry out. It was my head that hit the ground first, I was later told, followed nanoseconds later by the rest of me. I blacked out on impact.

When I opened my eyes, I saw my parents kneeling down over me looking incredibly concerned. All I could hear, though, was the hysterical laughter of my sister, as she shinned effortlessly down the tree and then dropped down next to me. 'Where are the Neapolitans then?' she asked.

My father carried me back to the car, while my mother fretted and shouted at my sister. Graham carried on barking excitedly. I was strapped into my seat, and my mother and father asked me questions in a frenzy.

'What's your name?'

'Damien.'

'Where are we?'

'Hampstead Heath.'

'What's the name of this dog that won't stop barking?'

'Graham.'

'How many fingers am I holding up?'

'Which one of you?'

'Samuel, put your fingers down.'

'Sorry.'

'Three.'

'What's the capital of France?'

'Paris.'

'Mozambique?'

'Don't ask him that.'

'Maputo.'

'You see?'

'He might not have known that before he hit his head.'

'What's your favourite food that I cook?' my mother asked.

'I really can't answer that,' I said.

'I don't think he's well,' my mother said.

'I think he sounds fine,' my father said. 'Let's go and have some Battenberg. If Andrea's left us any.'

And so off we went to Andrea's. My head ached. All of me ached, in fact. My vision was largely blurry, but whenever it came into focus all I could see was my sister smirking at me, so I preferred it blurry.

My father has always said that he regrets not taking me to hospital for a check-up, and frankly I can see his point. I did, after all, keep asking him to. But I don't know if the fall has had any lasting effect on me. I don't absolutely love heights, but then who does? I was never very likely, all things considered, to have been destined for a life as a steeplejack. I have, as an adult, climbed to the top of most of the highest cathedrals in France, for example, and coped – if you don't mind my saying – admirably. Anthony and I both got a bit wobbly visiting the late-Gothic cathedral in Strasbourg, but then a lot of people do apparently. Also, we'd had *un plateau de fruits de mer* the night before, which given Strasbourg's location was possibly not the wisest of choices to have made from a purely geographical point of view. (You wouldn't eat a bivalve in Switzerland, now would you? And that's less than 100 miles away.)

I think the incident has not so much changed my relationship to heights as my relationship to trees. I have become both more intrigued by them and more respectful of them as a result of my fall. And also, I like to think, they are of me. We're regaining each other's trust, I suppose. I find them simply fascinating. Ever since my fall, I've liked to spend a lot of time extremely close to trees. Right up against them, in fact. Not hugging them exactly, just with one ear pressed hard against them. (It would be quite hard to press both ears up against a tree though, wouldn't it? Unless, I suppose it was one of those trees that suddenly branches off a couple of feet up into two different trunks; it happens with yew trees quite often. For reasons I cannot even begin to imagine. But if you had a tree like that you could put your head between the two divergent trunks and then gently lower it until it your head could go no further, by which stage, I like to imagine, both of your ears would be very snugly pressed against a tree. I don't know why it's never occurred to me before. How maddening. Now I come to think of it, there's a tree like that – an oak I think, although it could be a fruit one – over in Queen's Park. It can't be more than ten minutes' walk away. I could stop typing, head over there, test my theory and be back in less than half an hour to write up the experience in anecdotal form. Unless I got stuck, of course, in which case the story would have to take the form of a cautionary tale, and heaven only knows how long I'd be there. The thought of having to phone the emergency services from the park fills me with nothing less than dread. Worse still would be someone else having to call them on my behalf, if I managed to get my head stuck in such a way that I couldn't actually reach my back pocket with my arms. Or in such a way that I could reach the phone, but then couldn't get the phone to my ear. What am I thinking? My ear would be pressed flush against the tree; I might not be able to hear anyway. I never want to have paramedics called to the park on my behalf again. That was actually one of my resolutions, one new year, the winter after the summer when I'd had a panic attack in the petting zoo and clasped the spindle on a bench so tightly there were many who feared it would snap. I think it must have been 2009, as Brown was prime minister at the time and my hay fever was at its absolute worst. I'd had my medication dose upped and didn't respond at all well. I don't think I will test my tree theory now that I think about it. There's simply too much at stake, and I've lunch to think about.)

Battenberg

There are some who think that Battenberg cake is a bit tacky, but I resolutely refuse to count myself among their number. Admittedly, it's not a cake that goes with many people's colour schemes, but if you happen to keep things neutral in that regard then you should just about get away with it. If I'm serving Battenberg in the kitchen I never worry too much, but if I'm serving it in the sitting room then I will usually make a point of removing all of our brightly coloured cushions from the room or it can all be a bit much.

I became so obsessed with Andrea's Battenberg that I became ambitious to make my own.

'Can we make our own Battenberg?' I asked my mother late one Sunday afternoon as we drove away from Andrea's.

'No,' she said. 'It has to be done with a machine.'

And like a ruddy fool, I believed her. Years later, when I was looking through an early Mary Berry, I discovered the truth. I was absolutely astounded by my own naïvety and set about making up for lost time.

Incidentally, Anthony and I once visited the town

of Battenberg, on a sort of pilgrimage. It's a pretty little spot in the Waldeck-Frankenberg state of Hesse, although no one is much interested in talking about cake there. I tried to discuss it with a waitress but she was rather more interested in talking about us paying our bill. There's another Battenberg in the Rhineland-Palatinate where – although not related in any way to the cake – they might be more a little forthcoming, but I've not yet had a chance to find out.

Now then, I'm not saying that making your own Battenberg cake is straightforward. But if you pull it off, then it is a truly wonderful feeling. An even more wonderful feeling is placing a Battenberg cake down in front of some ravenous yet refined afternoon guests and hearing one of them say the words, 'Gosh, did you make this yourself?' and being able to answer, 'I did, as it happens. Shall I slice?'

For the cake, you will need ...

Butter that is already in a softened state, 6 oz of. I sincerely hope that most of you always keep in your kitchen a sensible quantity (at least one pack of butter, but I tend towards two) outside of your fridge. (In winter, at least until the complete melting of the ice caps, just keeping the butter out of the fridge isn't necessarily enough to keep your butter soft and so you'll need to find somewhere in the house a little warmer to keep your soft supply. Please, please, *please* make sure you put it in a butter dish though. We had an absolute disaster earlier this year in the airing cupboard when I got distracted by Jehovah's Witnesses whilst trying to hurry the butter-softening process on a cold day. I never slam the door on anyone who comes to the house even if I don't agree with a single thing they have to say, but on this occasion I got rather too stuck into a chat about the historical Jesus and before I knew where we were I was putting the kettle on. It was only as I was waving them off that I suddenly remembered the butter. I dashed back up there as fast as I could, but it was hopeless. We had two sets of double sheets and duvet covers in there as well as numerous pillow cases, and months later I am still coming across upsetting yellow stains.

Caster sugar, golden, 6 oz of

Flour, self-raising, 5 oz of. I must say, I don't always keep a supply of self-raising flour in the house. It is, after all, merely normal flour with some baking powder added to it. I tend to add a very slightly heaped teaspoon of baking powder to every 5⅓ oz of flour and I generally get away with it.

An extra ½ tsp of baking powder

Almonds, ground, 1⅔ oz of. You can do this in your blender or, if you're feeling like expending a bit of energy, you can do it yourself with your pestle and mortar.

Some lovely eggs, 3. Free-range, but not too big.

You also need some extract of almond (maybe as much as 1 tsp, but certainly no more).

And some pink food colouring. It really is worth thinking very hard indeed about the exact shade of pink that you think will suit your cake and indeed your interior décor. Although scientists insist that the colour of food doesn't *really* alter the taste, I personally think it makes an enormous difference. All colours are suggestive, and if you have a particular colour in your mind when you eat something, then it really can have an impact on your taste buds. If you don't believe me, then trying eating a boiled egg whilst even thinking about dark green or rusty brown and I can guarantee that you will struggle to finish it. I appreciate that this is a somewhat nuanced point, however, and all too rarely does science have room for nuance. But as far as I'm concerned, your shade of pink really matters. All sorts of shades are available, including rose, rose water, pink lemonade, cotton candy, strawberry shake, fuchsia, dusky pink, baby pink – and those are just the ones that I can name off the top of my head. Some people sell it simply as 'pink'. Unhelpful. Avoid.

That's all for the cake, but what about when you come to assembly?

For the topping, you will need …
    Apricot jam, 3½ oz of (not many people make their own apricot jam, no idea why)

A little icing sugar

Marzipan, 17½ oz of

Now then. Can you buy marzipan in the shops? Yes. But should you? Well that is a different question altogether. No. ('You really made this all yourself? Even the marzipan?' 'Of course.')

So here we go. This is a recipe for as much as you'll need for this particular Battenberg. There are never leftovers with marzipan. Not for long, anyway.

For the marzipan, you will need ...

Ground almonds, 9 oz of

Caster sugar, golden, 4½ oz of

Icing sugar, also golden, also 4½ oz of. And you must really give it a thorough sieving.

An incredibly large egg. Or, at a push, 2 little eggs. Or, I suppose, 1 medium egg and 1 absolutely tiny one.

Some lemon juice, a little over 2 tsp I expect

Some sherry, perhaps a thimbleful. (Is there a little thimble in the corner of *your* kitchen? I know there is in mine. As Alan Bennett once almost, but didn't quite, say.)

A little bit of vanilla extract, to taste

To make the marzipan, all you need to do is take a large mixing bowl, pour in the ground almonds, golden caster sugar and the sieved golden icing sugar, and mix them together thoroughly. Then elsewhere combine the wet ingredients with a fork or whisk. Pour them into the dry ingredients, and give them a bit of a stir and then put your spoon aside and go at it with your hands. Knead it. Knead it some more. Then knead it again. It should eventually become beautifully smooth. Take a few moments to admire it, then cover it, and put it to one side.

Is it really necessary to buy something that is that easy and indeed pleasurable to make? Answer me honestly. You are quite right. Of course it isn't.

There is, you might not know, such a thing as a Battenberg tin. They tend to come with neat, removable dividers and they cost less than twenty pounds. Nice as they are (and some of them really are *lovely*), they are a luxury item and you can quite definitely get by without them. I have a number of good friends who have downsized in the last couple of years, and all of them have felt able to dispense with their Battenberg tins and not looked back. They all, incidentally, offered them to me but I had to graciously decline their generous offers as I already have seven of the things, and thus already have one, possibly two, too many.

I'm going to make the assumption, not unkindly I assure you, that you *don't* have a Battenberg tin. Not because I am judging you, but purely because those who *don't* own their own Battenberg tins require slightly more guidance. Those of you who *do* own your own Battenberg tins have, quite frankly, a simpler task ahead of them, and – that being the case – might see their way to patiently bearing with us.

Begin by popping your oven on to gas mark 4 or equivalent. Then, have a rummage through your collection of square baking tins and select the eight-incher. You then need to take a length of tin foil, or even aluminium foil if you are that way inclined, and fold it over so that it becomes decently rigid. Concertina this to make a neat dividing line down the centre of your baking tin, folding back a tab at each end to go flush against the base. What you are aiming for here is a sort of a rigid barrier down the centre of the tin, which divides the tin in two. I can't pretend that this isn't a bit of a faff, but if you're not happy with your efforts, just keep trying until you are. It's not as if anyone's watching, is it? (Or perhaps they are? I am, as you must expect, completely unfamiliar with your home arrangements.)

Once you are happy with the divider, line each side of the tin with some baking parchment, pushed in as neatly as you can possibly manage. Always trim away loose baking parchment before inserting your bake into an oven by the way, otherwise a stray bit might make contact with the filament and then you've a small fire on your hands and ash in your cake mix. Not nice.

Then put the butter, the sugar, the flour, the extra baking powder, the ground almonds, the eggs and the almond extract into a mixing bowl, and go at it with a hand whisk until smooth. You could, of course, use an electric whisk. I went through quite a lengthy electric whisk phase, but I have now passed well and truly through it and am safely on the other side. I think it was the noise that did for me in the end. And the mess around the bowl. One false move and you've got work-surface mayhem, and I spend enough of my time cleaning up as it is. I now look back on my electric whisk phase I the same way as I do on some early love affairs, and find myself wondering just what on earth I can have been thinking. Still, you live and learn, don't you? And if you do use an electric whisk I wish you – much as I wish my former lovers – well.

Once you have whisked the cake mixture together, pour exactly one half of it into one of the compartments in your baking tray, and then mix in the food colouring you chose (I'm stuck on dusky pink at present, but I've no doubt I'll change to something else when the time is right) with a certain degree of haste, and then pour it into the other compartment of your baking tin. You then need to invest a bit of time in making sure that you spread the mixture on each side so that it is sitting evenly in the tin, has as flat and smooth a surface as is feasible, and that the mixture absolutely meets all the sides. It is worth using a different spatula for each side so as to avoid colour contamination. There is, I'm afraid, simply no room for messiness in Battenberg. If you like your cooking messy, then you'll just have to stick to pulled pork.

Once the tin is looking *perfect* – a neat flour-coloured rectangle and a neat pink one happily sitting side by side – you may put it bang into the centre of your oven, close the door and pray to whoever you pray to that you've got it right. It might take as long as half an hour to be just right. If you're using a fan-assisted oven God himself might just be able to help you with your timings, but I certainly wouldn't have the confidence to. Once it's past the twenty-three minute mark, check it regularly by putting a fork gently into the mixture. You want it to come out hot, but leave no residue.

When the cakes are done, remove the baking tin from the oven, put it to one side for anything up to twenty minutes and then very carefully transfer the cakes on to your cooling rack and leave them until they are at room temperature. How long this will take depends both upon the season, and your own central heating. (The kitchen has its own thermostat in our house precisely for this reason.)

Depending on how neatly you were able to spread the mixture when you first poured it into the tin, you will either already have straight edges or you will have to straighten them yourselves with a knife. Then cut each of the rectangles directly down the centre *lengthwise*. Do whatever is in your power to make these cuts as neat as possible. If you really trust your eye, then you could perhaps chance it, but don't be afraid to use a ruler, some string, even a spirit level or a set square just to make absolutely certain that you're performing your slices in exactly the right place. Then get down on your knees and look at your four rectangles side on. Actually it only occurs to me now in the writing that the same effect can be achieved by just turning the cakes over. But there we are. You want them to be, when viewed from the end, perfect squares, and thus should not be afraid of doing as much as you can with your knife to make this the case.

This wonderful little cake is going to be held together by your doubtless superb apricot jam. But jam that is just right for spreading on sourdough toast or dropping a nice big globule of in your morning porridge is not, sadly, in the optimal state for holding sponge together. In order to achieve this state, it needs to be gently, slowly, heated, and then put through a sieve. It will then have the perfect consistency for the job in hand.

You need to take approximately one third of the marzipan that you have made and roll it out. (N.B. When rolling pastry you would do so with a little bit of flour on your board in order to prevent it sticking. When working with marzipan, icing sugar performs the same function.) Form the rolled marzipan into a rectangle that is eight inches by four, and then give it a good coating of the apricot jam with a brush. Then take one of your plain sponges and lay it down along the top half of the marzipan rectangle. Brush more apricot jam along its edge and then fit one of the pink sponge pieces alongside it. You should now be looking at something structurally reminiscent of the flags of Ukraine or Poland, although with different colours. (Perhaps there is somewhere with a flag that is pink and yellow, but I've not yet come across it. It could be Battenberg's flag. If they were a bit less stand-offish and rather more interested in their own heritage.)

Brush more apricot jam atop the plain sponge, and put the remaining pink sponge on top of it. Then put jam on its inner side and fit the plain one alongside it. (Am I making this sound more complicated than I should be? I freely admit that while writing this I am having to keep closing my eyes, scrunching up my forehead and really thinking very hard indeed about it. Not always a wise move, as if I shut my eyes during the daytime I have a dreadful tendency to drift off into extremely odd yet vivid daydreams. I had one last week about Grant Shapps and some egg boxes that left me feeling so out of sorts I had to cancel a dental appointment.)

Take the remaining marzipan and roll that flat too, and form it into a rectangle that is eight inches by seven. Smear jam over all available bits of sponge and then drape the rectangle of marzipan over the top of the sponge cake, folding it as neatly as ever you possibly can around the three long sides of the cake. The flatter you have rolled it, the easier this will be. In fact, if you're so inclined – and I've a number of friends who *are* – then you could lightly score this piece into thirds to make this part of the process ever so slightly simpler. You've already got your marzipan base, and so gently meld this new layer of marzipan to it, either using a little water, or giving it a light crimping. Don't forget, you could always trim a bit of marzipan away with a knife if it's become messy. You should take a thin slice off each end of the cake as well, in order to make it as smart as possible. And then there we are. Wasn't without stress, was it? But it's done. Breathe a sigh of relief, pop the kettle on and get ready to welcome some guests. Actually, maybe it is easier just to buy it? No matter, it's done now.

Best shared with friends and a pot of decent tea. Lapsang Souchong between the hours of two and four, and then Earl Grey any time after.

Chapter 11

THE WHEEL TURNS

Before leaving the independent preparatory day school that I do not wish to name, I had secured a place at Willesden Grammar School. This achievement absolutely delighted my parents as it meant that I would not have to be privately educated for my teens. I myself was also extremely pleased. I think private education is morally wrong, ethically repugnant and not even financially astute. Based on my experiences of it I cannot help but feel that it represents absolutely appalling value for money. Money can buy you a lot of things, such as – happily – a KitchenAid or antique cloche, but – sadly – one of those things is also an ill-deserved sense of entitlement. Best keep away, I say.

But the summer holiday between my finishing at one of these schools and starting at another positively yawned out in front of me. Ralph was, of course, going to be away. Perhaps playing rugby in South America or even cricket in Zimbabwe, this being a time when much better relations existed between our two nations. But my sister was going to be at home, and so it was generally felt it might be beneficial if I could be away too.

A French exchange trip was my mother's idea initially,

but it was a suggestion that I absolutely leapt at. I had learnt some French whilst at the unmentionable establishment but not, I think it's fair to say, to an acceptably high level. The French teacher was a man called Terence Smith who, though possessed of a sturdy grip on the technical aspects of the language, had very little grasp of its romance. He somehow made speaking French sound about as attractive and interesting as speaking computer code. He was, I'm sorry to report, not hygienic. He is now, I'm also sorry to report, dead.

My French exchange was with a boy called Gabriel who lived in a village on the outskirts of Toulouse with his mother Pascale and his stepfather Jacques. Gabriel and Pascale collected me from the airport in a battered old yellow Citroën (this is a guess, but that's the only French car I can think of) and drove me for three quarters of an hour back in the direction of their home. I could tell after just a few minutes of faltering conversation in the car that I was going to learn an awful lot, as they seemed to speak no English whatsoever. Gabriel – blond and lanky, eyes like a young Jean Reno – and I sat side by side in the back together as Pascale – a sort of elongated Fanny Ardant only with sadder eyes – hunched over the steering wheel and smoked continually.

The sad eyes were, in point of fact, completely unrepresentative of her actual emotional state. Instead she seemed incredibly jolly. She would ask me a question in very slow French, I would attempt to answer, and then she and Gabriel would discuss what I had said in breakneck French before bursting into peals of laughter. I attempted to join in with their laughter on the basis that the language of laughter is universal. But whenever I began to laugh, they would suddenly stop, like people concealing a guilty secret. We stopped outside a little supermarket, and Pascale bounded in, her long tanned arms swinging. While she was in I asked Gabriel some questions.

'Elle a combien d'ans, ta mère?'

'Je ne sais pas,' said Gabriel and broke into yet more laughter.

'Elle a beaucoup d'ans?' I asked, presuming this to be the joke.

'Non. Non. Je ne sais pas. Ma mère, elle est comme une petite enfant.'

Then he laughed more. I joined in, and this time he let me. After a few more minutes Pascale re-emerged, carrying some French sticks and several packets of cigarettes and wearing a floppy and inexpensive-looking straw hat.

'Qu'est ce que vous en pensez?' she asked, posing for us on the pavement.

Gabriel shrugged and I ventured, 'C'est un bon chapeau.' Pascale and Gabriel exchanged a few speedy words at this and then collapsed into yet more laughter.

'Déjeuner,' she finally said, and slung a French stick through the open window into the back seat. Gabriel broke it into two halves, gave one to me and began to greedily gorge on the other. I took a few tentative bites of mine. It was delicious. The little supermarket did not look at all promising, and yet the bread they sold was superb – of a far better quality than the hats they stocked. I dearly wished to articulate that French supermarket bread was clearly vastly superior than that sold in British supermarkets, but sadly did not have the necessary French, and so instead made a series of noises to suggest that I was extremely happy.

'Tu aimes bien le pain, Damien?' said Pascale, and she and Gabriel collapsed into further giggles.

Gabriel then offered her the heel of his half, but she waved the offer away.

'Je ne mange pas,' she said to me, by way of explanation.

'Pas du tout?' I asked.

'Pas du tout!' she guffawed, lit up another cigarette and then started up the engine. Somebody then knocked on the window, and she turned it off again. It was a tall man with a cheeky smile. He was wearing, despite it being a very hot day, a leather jacket. Pascale leapt out of the car again and embraced this man, who then began entreating her in a soft voice. She made a few minor protests, but then turned around and marched back into the supermarket and came out with two cans of fizzy drink which she passed into the back of the car to us, said, 'Vingt minutes,' giggled and disappeared with the gentleman.

'Qui est ça?' I asked Gabriel.

'Ma mère, elle connaît beaucoup d'hommes,' he said quietly and then opened his fizzy drink.

I opened mine too with a great degree of difficulty (we

never had such things at home) with the end result that it began to spray everywhere.

'La fenêtre!' said Gabriel, and so I held it out of the window in order to minimise the damage to the car's interior. In so doing I managed to spray the fizzy drink over a little old lady who was passing the car. When the can had finished spraying she stuck her head through the window and screamed angrily at me in words I could, thankfully, not understand.

'Je suis désolé,' I offered meekly, when her invective had finally come to an end.

'Il est anglais,' offered Gabriel.

'Il est anglais?' said the lady, in a tone that suggested that this news confirmed her very worst suspicions. She barked some more words at me, finally wound her neck in and then stormed off. I suddenly felt an incredibly long way from home and burst into tears. Gabriel looked at me with eyes full of pity, and said, 'Ce n'est pas grave.' But it had been grave. It had been very grave indeed.

No sooner were my tears dry than Pascale came skipping back to the car, leant in through the window to give Gabriel a kiss, and then slipped back into the driving seat. She started up the engine, lit another cigarette and then pulled out into the traffic. A few minutes later, we parked up on the dusty drive of a large, whitewashed bungalow. Pascale took my suitcase from the car and carried it towards the house for me, up the drive and past old tyres, bits of wood and tarpaulins.

'Bienvenue!' she said, and opened the door to their

home which was, I noticed, unlocked. What a different world.

The interior of the bungalow was all higgledy-piggledy, and so very different from the ordered world that we inhabited back in London. There wasn't clutter anywhere as such, but things looked like they'd been allowed to land where they dropped without any immediate pressure to put things away. It seemed relaxed. Gabriel showed me to his bedroom at one end of the home. A camp bed had been set up for me in there. I laid down my suitcase on the bed, and looked at these new surroundings. He had posters of footballers up on the wall and a tank with two rather sad-looking fish in. Perhaps, though, like Pascale, they were actually much happier than they appeared and knew 'beaucoup d'hommes'.

No sooner had I sat down on the bed to repose after my travels, than Gabriel began removing his clothes and changing into swimming trunks.

'La piscine?' he said, and ran out of the bedroom.

Gosh. It hadn't occurred to me that there would be a swimming pool. What better place could there be than here in France for me to lay the ghost of my upsetting swimming pool experience to rest? Surely Pascale and Gabriel wouldn't steal my trunks. And if they did, surely they wouldn't have a high diving board. I hurriedly pulled my own swimming trunks on, and found my way out to the garden. And there it was. Oh, to be French at that moment. It was a large pool, possibly twenty metres long, with semi-circular steps leading into the shallow end nearest the bungalow. At the far end was a small diving board, from which I saw Gabriel hurl himself athletically into the pool. This all seemed gloriously, impossibly, decadent to me. And I loved it. I gingerly made my way in at the shallow end, bracing myself for the water to be cold, but it was wonderfully warm. Gabriel noticed my surprise and laughed at me.

'C'est chaud!' he said, and pointed to what looked to me like a run-down garden shed but which must in fact have been some sort of pump house. Next to the pump house was a shower under which Pascale was washing herself. I had been looking at her for some moments before I suddenly realised that she was only wearing the bottom half of her swimming costume.

I had never seen a woman's breasts before. Nor have I seen all that many since, it must be said.[1] People simply didn't behave like this at swimming pools in Britain. But then I suppose there's a world of difference between the freezing and gloomy environs of Willesden Baths and a secluded bungalow in France. Pascale saw me looking and smiled at me, but made no attempt to cover up. I looked away in shame, despite my interest in her append-

1   A producer with whom I have often worked, Marion Duffett, used to make a habit of showing me hers when we were enjoying evenings out. I've no idea why. Possibly in an attempt to wind me up, or maybe as a traffic-calming measure. Anthony always thought that this sort of behaviour was hilarious, but then he used to work in the banking sector in which all sorts of unseemly behaviour passes as entertainment. Marion has a child now, and has mellowed considerably, I am pleased to report.

ages being purely scientific. For all I know – and I am by no means an expert in these matters – they were absolutely terrific examples of the genre. But I already knew very deep down that they were absolutely not my thing.

What did instantly impress me about Pascale was her extraordinary sense of freedom. I'd barely known her for an hour or two and yet I could already tell that she and my own mother could not have been more different. My mother was vehemently anti-smoking, and yet Pascale apparently puffed away almost ceaselessly. My mother did not condone the consumption of fizzy, sugary drinks, and yet Pascale had positively pushed them on us. My mother generally wore several layers and was about as likely to take a shower in our garden as she was to swear allegiance to an Islamic Caliphate. My love of French cinema stems, I often think, from meeting and knowing Pascale. I can hardly watch any French films without being reminded of her *joie de vivre*, body confidence and infectious, scurrilous laugh. For the rest of the afternoon we all romped* merrily in the pool.

Gabriel's skills from what was really a very low diving board were virtuoso, and he and Pascale had a very tactile relationship, often wrestling in the shallow end, and ducking each other under the water. When my own mother swam she held her head above the water almost religiously (she claimed that all water was bad for her face), and would generally turn pretty savage if someone splashed her even inadvertently. Pascale, on the other hand, would pounce from nowhere, and drag one under,

* Damien, I'm not sure the word 'romp' is quite what you're after here? It has unhelpful connotations.

Really? To romp: (especially of a child or animal) to play energetically or roughly.' Problem?

Might be worth you occasionally having a little look at an online urban dictionary.

Just done so. And I completely concur with you. Suggest 'frolicked' or 'capered'.

Let me come back to you.

tickling furiously and grabbing hold of one's feet. Gabriel would do the same to her and me but I had little strength to fight back, occasionally having to swim to the edge of the pool and cough up large quantities of water. It was one of the happiest afternoons that I can remember.

At about half past five we had all just finally climbed out of the pool, wrapped ourselves in towels and arranged ourselves on rickety plastic sun loungers at the shallow end of the pool when Jacques himself returned. He kissed Gabriel and Pascale and then removed his oily, mechanics' clothing before showering and then hurling himself naked into the pool, creating the most almighty splash, big enough to extinguish the glow of Pascale's cigarette. Pascale and Gabriel leapt in after him and proceeded to drag him under the surface, but I stayed where I was, too fatigued by the day's exertions, and felt that wrestling with a naked man that I had only just met was hardly my place. I felt far more comfortable just watching them intently.* I had occasionally heard the phrase 'touchy-feely' used back home in England, and never quite understood what it could have meant. Lying back on the sun lounger as these three French people thrashed about at the deep end, I suddenly understood – even if their behaviour was at the more extreme, nuder, end of the 'touchy-feely' spectrum.

Slightly strange phrasing if I may say, Damien. May I offer 'just looking on' as an alternative?

Good suggestion. Will certainly have a ponder. In due course.

At last some sort of halt to proceedings was called, and Gabriel and I were encouraged to go inside to have a bath or shower before supper. It was only as I was about to lower myself into a nice hot bath that I realised the extent to which my skin was stinging. I removed the towel in front of the bathroom mirror, and saw to my shock that my chest, shoulders and face were a terrifyingly vibrant pink colour, even red in places. In my excitement to dash out to the pool on arrival, I had completely neglected to cover myself liberally with sun cream as per my mother's lengthy and repeated instructions. As I lowered myself into the bath I rued that neglect even more. The stinging was so unbearable, that I began to imagine that I might need to be hospitalised. My screams had alerted Gabriel, who came barging into the bathroom – no locks, of course – to see the cause of my agony. When he saw me in the bath, all pink and shrieking, he pointed at me and laughed hysterically.

'C'est mal,' I said weakly. 'C'est grave.'

'C'est drôle!' he replied. 'C'est très drôle,' and ran off to find his mother and Jacques, who soon appeared in the doorway and also took turns to point and laugh.

'Il est comme un petit homard!' said Pascale squealing and, I noticed, still clad only in her bikini bottoms.

I had, as I have already remarked, seen Pascale do a lot of things that afternoon that my own mother would not have done, and this was another of them. In this instance, though, I felt that my own mother's attitude to medical emergencies was a rather more understandable one. I had never once seen her laugh at the sight of any of her children in pain, and I was glad of it. True, she had a tendency to panic about accidents, but at least she was empathetic. My father would go beyond mere empathy on occasion, and is still prone to faint at the sight of blood. I was used to sympathy and concern. The sight of three French people pointing and laughing at me was suddenly all too much, and I burst into loud sobs.

Jacques looked incredibly embarrassed about this, and backed away muttering something about 'les anglais' that I suspect was none too complimentary. Gabriel looked shocked and also backed away. It was left to Pascale to lever my wet body out of the bath, pat me dry with a towel and then cover me from head to tea in a lotion that she had taken from the cabinet beneath the sink. I stood there, numbly, as the unguent slowly did its work and I could feel my skin become cool again.

'Merci,' I mumbled.

She gave me a sad little smile and indicated that she would see me at dinner.

I was very quiet at dinner, partly because I was embarrassed by my behaviour in the bathroom, partly because the sun cream felt sticky under my clothes and partly because the pace at which Pascale, Jacques and Gabriel spoke French. I must have understood less than one word in seven, and was incapable of understanding any of the many, many jokes that left them all paralytic with laughter. We ate salad and grilled sardines outside, the sun somehow unable to finally set. Finally it became too cold to stay out any longer, and Gabriel and I helped Pascale carry the things back to the kitchen. She and Jacques then commenced the washing up, and Gabriel and I retired to his bedroom. I was exhausted and fell asleep almost instantly, only waking briefly in the middle of the night at the sound of Pascale and Jacques arguing outside the window. A bottle or glass was smashed, and shouts were exchanged.

'Gabriel?' I whispered.

'Ne t'inquiète pas,' he said. 'C'est comme d'habitude.'

It was like that for the rest of the week. We didn't go anywhere other than the supermarket or the little bakery a mile and a half away for breakfast croissants. All day long, Pascale and Gabriel lounged by the pool, swimming and roughhousing. I would lie by the pool under a fairly filthy-looking sunshade, reading my books and absolutely caked in sun cream. Occasionally I slipped into the pool and did a few lengths or joined in with the tomfoolery, but otherwise I stayed put. We had siestas at lunchtime – God, how I wished we had those in Britain – and then returned to the pool for more high jinks. Jacques would return at the same time every night and there'd be one final splashabout and then that would be it.

I envied their lifestyle dreadfully, but at the same time began to tire of it a little after a few days. Couldn't we perhaps go to a museum, or visit a working farm? Didn't Pascale want more from life than beer, cigarettes and the occasional male visitor? It's hard to think how that would satisfy anyone, but she never seemed anything other than deliriously happy. Apart from in the night, of course, when the shouting would start up. One night there was another voice in the mêlée that didn't belong to Jaques or Pascale; a man who spoke in a deep voice and occasionally spat. More glasses and bottles were broken that night, but by morning time all had been forgotten and forgiven, and Jacques gave Pascale his usual lengthy and passionate kiss at the breakfast table before giving Gabriel a peck on the forehead and my cheek a playful pinch, and heading off to the garage with a spring in his step.

Despite their apparent unusualness, I was extremely upset to bid farewell to Jacques and Pascale at the end of the week. Their marriage was clearly an extraordinary one and yet it somehow made them happy. Gabriel occasionally looked dismayed by their antics, but a lot of the time they just seemed to have the most enormous, often naked, fun. They had – apart from all the laughing and pointing – been incredibly kind to me, and I'd learnt all sorts of surprising phrases from them. They both took Gabriel and me to the airport for the return leg of our exchange. Before we headed into departures, Jacques gave both of us a little hug and a squeeze of the cheeks. Pascale clutched Gabriel to her for a long time and then – to my surprise – did the same to me.

'Damien,' she said, 'tu es un petit garçon très spécial.'

'Merci,' I replied. 'Tu es une femme très magnifique.'

We had done almost nothing, gone almost nowhere and barely scraped the surface of French cuisine and yet I'd had the most marvellous *temps*. But I was also looking forward to returning to England, and the bosom of my family, and to introducing Gabriel to my family too …

It was raining when we arrived at Heathrow. My parents and my sister were waiting for us at the arrival gates, my mother holding a macintosh for me.

'I hope you've brought one of these with you,' she said to Gabriel. 'Or you'll be drenched through.'

He hadn't, and he was. Gabriel sat in the middle of the back seat between Angela and me. She seemed impressed by Gabriel, although he rather less so by her in part because of the way that she sat with her legs so far apart and in part because she kept telling him that he was about to have the worst week of his life.

'Nonsense,' my mother bellowed from the front. 'Do you like museums, Gabriel?'

'Yes,' he said tentatively, 'but the football is … better.'

'Oh, do you like football?' said my father.

'Be quiet,' said my mother, 'and concentrate on the road. How the hell do we get out of this godforsaken place?'

'Do you have a piscine?' asked Gabriel quietly.

'There's a municipal baths,' said my mother. 'And it's filthy.'

'Only because Damien wees in it,' my sister said.

'Don't be unpleasant,' my mother said.

'That was ages ago,' my father added. Not altogether helpfully. 'Damien's much better at adapting to sudden changes of temperature now, aren't you?'

'Yes,' I mumbled.

'I hope you're all right with a bit of weather, Gabriel?' he asked. 'It's forecast to be like this for the rest of the week.'

Gabriel gazed out of the window and looked bereft. He seemed consumed by an ill sense of foreboding.

He was not, it transpired, without good reason to feel

this way. Even I was not aware of how many museums there were in London until that week. As the rain hammered down outside, we visited one every day of his stay from opening time until closing, an itinerary organised and decided by my mother with, it seemed, no input from my father whatsoever.

There was simply no let-up. At the end of the first day, spent entirely in the British Museum, Gabriel asked if he might go straight to bed without supper.

'It's shepherd's pie,' said my mother. 'You'd be mad to.'

'I cannot eat with my feet hurt,' said Gabriel falteringly.

'Nonsense,' my mother said. 'Lamb mince is famously restorative.'

I happen to agree with her, but it seemed a little unfair to force-feed the poor boy. Gabriel ate in silence, while Angela kicked us both under the table and my father – somewhat unwisely – raised the possibility that we perhaps might go to a museum only every other day.

'Nonsense,' said my mother. 'The boy's here to learn. And we'll all benefit.'

'Do you like museums?' Gabriel asked me that night as we prepared to brush our teeth in the bathroom.

'Sometimes,' I said.

'I do not,' he said. He was asleep within minutes.

On the second day we went to the Science Museum. As we were eating our sandwiches on a bench near the cafeteria I asked Gabriel how he was enjoying it so far.

'Your sister. She keep want kiss me.'

'Right,' said my father. 'Is it time for the history of aviation?'

'Agriculture,' said my mother.

My father said nothing, but dropped the remainder of his sandwich into a bin.

The next day we went to the V&A. Which I loved, but everyone else hated.

The day after that was the Maritime Museum at Greenwich, where Angela made such a great attempt to kiss poor Gabriel by the sea clocks that my father had to forcibly separate them.

On the fifth day we went to the Natural History Museum. I don't think Gabriel spoke all day. At one point in the afternoon we came across a glass cabinet housing Guy the Gorilla, a British cultural icon. Now taxidermied and glass-eyed, he had spent his entire life in captivity.

'I know how you feel,' said my father and, closing his eyes, pressed his forehead against the cool glass.

'You'll make a mark,' said my mother. 'So stop it.'

At breakfast on Gabriel's final day my mother told him that, as he was flying back tomorrow, it was his choice how he would like to spend the day.

'I will sleep,' he said and immediately withdrew from the table.

'Shall I go and see if he's all right?' my sister asked.

'NO,' we all said.

My parents and I took him to the airport the next day, my sister refusing to travel with us on the completely spurious grounds that she had a headache but which in the circumstances my parents were all too happy to accept.

'I have had a very interesting time,' Gabriel said, as he shook my father's hand.

'I will never forget you,' he said to my mother.

'Bonne chance, Damien,' he said to me and headed off towards departures.

'What a strange boy,' my mother said, and we all walked back to the car together.

A Genuinely Appetising Shepherd's Pie

This is, and I kid you not, a serious bit of cooking. You've got to really love meat. And you've got to love unguency. And you shouldn't be afraid of a little bit of hard work and of allowing things to take their time. One aspect of this recipe that makes some people absolutely leap out of their skins is the fact that it doesn't involve the purchasing of lamb mince. This is, I think, a good thing. A lot of the big chefs these days advocate this sort of approach to a shepherd's pie, but some of us have been doing it this way for years. I started out of necessity as my mincing tool wore out, and I have to say I've never looked back.

But it is not just about the lamb. It's about everything else. Because this is a recipe that does not skimp on *anything*. And why should it? You'll need to have a big nap after making this, and then probably another one after eating it. I have dreadful recollections of eating shepherd's pie as a child. Always with carrots that were simply too crunchy. And lamb that was probably rather grey to begin with and unconscionably so to end with. Moisture, moisture, moisture. Need I say it again? I think I do. Moisture. (I'm referring to the meaty sauce within, by the way. Not the potato crust. That needs to have some crunch, and nothing in the way of slop. Crunchy above, succulent below. That's how I like it. Always have done.) It is, I am afraid, rather a lengthy process, but I'm so confident that you'll find it a worthwhile one that if you find that it's not, I'd be only too happy for you to knock on my front door and call me a time-waster, a bounder or a charlatan. Although, ideally, not all three.

For this you will need ...

Olive oil, extra virginal

Shanks of lamb, 4

Homemade beef stock, 1½ litres of

Bay leaves, pair of

Potatoes, 3⅓ lb of, a waxy variety, but not overly so, skin off and chopped into pieces about the size of an ice cube

Butter, unsalted (I *know*), ½ lb of

Milk, full fat, ½ pint of

French mustard, 1 tbsp of

Large onions, 3, chopped awfully thinly

Nice carrots, pair of, diced

Celery sticks, 3 of, likewise

Garlic cloves, half a dozen, almost obliterated with your smallest, sharpest knife

A star anise

Mushrooms, porcini, dried, ½ oz of and soaked in boiling water. (When they have properly saturated, remove the mushrooms from the water, and chop them up, but *do not* get rid of the water. Please.)

Tomato purée, 1 tbsp of

Big glass of *vin rouge*

Mint, handful of

Rosemary, 4 sprigs of

A touch of cornflour

Salt (Maldon) and pepper

Sorry that was so much prep. Right then. Pop your oven on at gas mark 4 so that it's ready when you need it, and then put a little heat under a casserole dish and pour in some olive oil. Brown your four shanks in the olive oil, grind some pepper over them, flake some salt over them and then pour in the stock and add your bay leaves. If your oven has reached the desired temperature, place the lid on the casserole and then put the whole thing into the oven. In about three and a half hours' time the meat will be practically falling off the bone without you so much as even having to ask it nicely to. But, don't rest on your laurels, because in the meantime there's more work to be done.

Boil up a kettle, then put the potatoes in a big pot and pour over the boiling water and some cold so that they are covered in warm water. Don't put much heat under them – just enough to bring it to the verge of a simmer and leave them like that for a good half hour. Then drain them, and add some fresh, salted water to the pan and bring that to the boil. This method, though it may seem perverse, does wonders for their eventual consistency. (Just don't ask me what the science is. Haven't a clue.) Now gently but not timidly lower the potatoes into that and keep them there until they crumble at the touch of a fork. Drain them very thoroughly *indeed*. Take a nice big bowl, place your unsalted butter in it and cut into chunks. Then put the drained potatoes on top of the butter and mash the two together gently but with purpose. Put the milk in a pan and warm it a little, and then slowly add it to the mash. Only add what you need – which might not be as much as you have. What we're after here is the creamiest mash you have ever seen. But not the wettest. Crumble some more of your salt flakes on to the mash, and also stir in your French mustard.

Leave that to one side for the moment, take a deep breath, and then dive straight back in. (To the fray, not the mash.) Get another cooking pot, pour in some more of your olive oil and start cooking the onion, carrot, celery, garlic and the star anise. It needs to be stirred continually, or you'll end up burning it and hating yourself. After approximately nine minutes, add the porcini mushrooms (remembering to reserve the water used for soaking them) and also the tomato purée and keep stirring it all together for another five minutes before adding the wine and reducing the whole lot. It will become surprisingly thick, but don't let this panic you. This is, however, time for us to bid farewell to our star anise. It has done great service, but it has come to the end of the line in terms of what it can offer and we must now go our separate ways. Drop it into your food waste bin with appropriate gravitas and then get back to the job in hand. The kitchen is no place for sentimentality.

I've no idea how long this will have taken you. An hour? An hour and a half? Anyway, the lamb shanks need to have three and a half hours plus cooling time, so you may well have some spare time to yourself now. That said, you've already used rather a lot of cooking pots and utensils, so I don't think that doing a little washing up would be the worst idea in the world. But then nor would reading be. Or, if the mood takes you, a brisk walk and some star jumps.

When the time comes, remove the lamb shanks from the oven, and let them cool in the stock. Then take out the shanks, reserving the stock, and let the meat just fall off the bone into a bowl. This bit is delightful. Chop it up into nice-sized pieces or, if you prefer, just sort of break it up in your hands and then put it to one side with the mash and the vegetables.

Pour the water left over from soaking your mushrooms (ensuring there is no grit in it) into the stock that the shanks just cooked in. Put a high heat under it and reduce it hard, so that only a quarter or so of it remains. Then turn the heat right down and add the herbs – in a bag if you fancy. Don't break them up as you'll be taking them out and flinging them in the food waste bin after a quarter of an hour.

Now put your oven on again at gas mark 5 so that it's ready for you in a few minutes. Take some of the stock and add a little cornflour to it and then put it back in with the rest of the stock and keep stirring it as it thickens. Then add the meat and vegetables to this, as well as some more crumbled salt and a few generous twists of your pepper grinder. Mix it all together. If you want to keep a little stock back to avoid the whole thing being too wet, this would be understandable. Then pour this delightful mixture into a lovely and appropriately sized piece of oven-to-table ware with flat sides. Spread the mash over the top of it, and distribute it fairly. Quite how you finish it is up to you. Some like to make patterns with a fork; others like to leave it smooth liked skimmed plaster. I don't have a preference, myself. I just do what my waters tell me. It needs just twenty-five minutes in the oven, by which time it will be absolutely piping.

Serve it absolutely as is. The only other thing I put on the table is red wine, water, wine glasses, tumblers and an absolutely enormous bowl of peas with butter on them. *Délicieux*.

Chapter 12

GRAMMAR AND NONSENSE AND LEARNING

At the end of that summer holiday I started attending Willesden Grammar School. It was not a prospect that I particularly relished. For years I had been used to the sight of the Willesden Grammar boys slouching around the streets of our area in their school uniform, and never once did they look anything other than intimidating and a little brutish.

I felt absolutely sick with nerves on my first morning as I walked up the street to my new school, and it was a feeling that I was unable to shift for my entire time there. The place just seemed so terrifyingly *big*, and so did the other boys. 'Am I ever going to make any friends here?' I wondered as we all filed in to our first assembly. It was a question that I was unable to answer definitively until my last day at the place. But the answer was no.

There were people with whom I regularly associated, of course. Once a week I liked to make a batch of biscuits and bring them into school in some Tupperware, and a small circle of people always seemed genuinely grateful for them. There were people I would have done anything to avoid, and from whom I used to hide if I saw them in the distance. Sometimes there wasn't time, and I would have to affect nonchalance in the face of whatever casual or more serious verbal abuse that came my way. I often wonder if anybody has any true friends in their teens; so much time do we spend attempting to project what we imagine to be cool and likeable images of ourselves that we become completely disassociated from what we are actually like. Even if two people *appear* to be getting on with each other at that age, are they *actually* doing so if neither of them is being who they really are, and only find attractive in each other those personality traits that are actually nothing other than a pretence? What an incredibly bleak thought. Best move on. The fact of the matter is that I just never felt as if I was anything like the other boys. And even when I initially tried to project a different version of myself, that never ended up being anything like them either.

So I gave up trying to pretend pretty early on. There just didn't seem any point in it. The only satisfaction I could draw from the whole process was to know that, if nothing else, at least I was being true to myself. To compensate for my lack of a real social life I threw myself into my studies and hobbies. The teaching standard was actually very high, and we were set work and exercises that I found to be genuinely stretching. Science, for instance, was a subject that I had up until that point never really got my head around. But at Willesden Grammar the teaching was rigorous, and I soon realised that by committing vast swathes of information to memory, I could understand things more easily. I learned the entire periodic table one afternoon (partly, it must be said, with the aid of Tom Lehrer's humorous pastiche) and I have never forgotten it. I can remember it even now, and if called upon can perform it as a party trick, although usually only if an evening has become absolutely desperate.

I was once asked to babysit my dear friend Marion Duffett's small baby, and was having real trouble getting (it)off to sleep. Eventually, and at my wit's end, I began to recite the periodic table to it. It was asleep by the time I got to Tungsten (atomic number 74). Marion said that the effect had been remarkable, and the child was actually drowsy for days. Good old science.

'It'?

Simply can't remember the gender, I'm afraid.

Could you perhaps ask?

Bit embarrassing. Much best left vague, I feel.

As you wish.

I opted to study Latin, which I absolutely loved. I have always found it incredibly useful, and I still derive a great deal of pleasure from being able to translate what is inscribed on gravestones and memorial plaques whenever Anthony and I visit an old church. Recently we visited Hereford Cathedral and I was simply unable to shut up as we pored over the Mappa Mundi and then took in some of the inscriptions in the crypt. Anthony was, I think, rather impressed and decided that as a treat I needed to be taken immediately to their (rather nice) café the moment I first paused for breath.

I also sang in the school choir. I was lucky, from a musical point of view, that my voice didn't break until I was quite mature. For quite a few years I had a very decent soprano voice and people who know anything about these things will tell you that there is no sound in the world quite like that of a boy soprano. We didn't get all that many chances to perform, but we practised once a week and I relished it. I used to take the music home with me between rehearsals so that I could do extra work when I was at home. We had an upright piano, but it was regrettably in the sitting room and Angela and Ralph (when he was around) always insisted that the television should take precedence over the piano, and relied heavily on violence to ensure that this state of affairs remained unchallenged – a completely scandalous view from an arts perspective, but one that I bore with considerable fortitude. I rehearsed my singing in my bedroom and if I ever wanted to make sure that I was starting on the right note I would come downstairs and nip into the sitting room, play the note a couple of times on the piano, run out again before I started to have cushions thrown at me, and then hum it to myself on the stairs until I got back to my room and broke into song. If I was distracted on this journey – by one of my parents saying 'hello', for instance, or 'why do you always have to keep humming?' – I'd have to go back downstairs again and get the note a second time, whereupon I would be treated to a further shower of cushions. I love cushions these days – indeed I have a vast collection of cushion covers that we use in rotation according to the seasons – but as a child I saw them only as missiles.

As I say, having a soprano voice was useful from a musical point of view as it meant that I always got to sing the melody and – because of the scarcity of boy sopranos

– was regularly chosen to sing solos that I might otherwise not have had the chance to in a more competitive environment. But from a social point of view being a soprano until the age of fifteen had, for reasons I am incapable of understanding, a severely detrimental effect on my ability to earn the respect of my peers.

'Here she comes!' someone would shout as I entered the classroom or the dining hall, and then people would begin high-pitched screeching *en masse*. To this day a sudden high-pitched noise – a child in pain or a bus driver hurriedly applying the brake – can have an extremely deleterious effect on my otherwise quite robust mental health. In addition to this I was given the nickname 'Bianca', after the opera singer Bianca Castafiore in the Tintin books. This I found to be extremely hurtful, not least because her character in those books, entertaining as she doubtless is to the reader, is extremely lacking in self-awareness and always presents herself as being rather needy. Also, as I took great pains to explain to the other boys, I am not a woman.

I was incredibly relieved when my voice finally broke, although the timing could not have been worse, happening as it did during a concert which we were part of alongside a number of other school choirs from north-west London. It was a charitable performance of Verdi's *Requiem* at a large church in Mill Hill. Given that a number of girls were taking part in the concert, the fact that I had been given the soprano solo was generally held to be a rather controversial act, and through the many evening rehearsals leading up to the concert I had been on the receiving end of a large number of covetous glances whenever I stood up to sing. Sometimes, such as when we were putting away the chairs afterwards, I was treated with open hostility. One girl, who I was quite convinced that I had come up against during my brief spell studying judo, attempted to trip me, which I felt to be a deeply unchristian act. But I held my head high, and persevered knowing that I had been given the role on merit, and that in the future this girl would undoubtedly be deeply ashamed of her behaviour, and may well have gone on to spend much of her adult life regretting it. I have never had any truck with the jealous.

Sad to relate, perhaps it would have been far better for all concerned if she *had* been given the role, for on the night in question, facing an audience of 450 people and standing in front of a choir of 120 people and an orchestra of sixty I stood up and began to sing the famous 'Libera Me' solo. I had been feeling fairly strange all day, but was fairly certain that this was just down to nerves. It is a particularly unserendipitous fact of life that when one is nervous the very first thing that it affects is one's voice. Actors and singers, therefore, have to work harder than most to counteract the symptoms of nerves and anxiety. Anthony and I often agree that a closed throat is no use to man or beast. It's something that affects him these days in the world of amateur dramatics which he, regrettably, still pursues as a hobby. Anthony's everyday voice is fairly sonorous and relaxed. He's got lovely big lungs and so rarely has to force it; it's like trapped air being released from under the cushion of a leather sofa when one sits heavily upon it, only deeper. In day-to-day life when I shut my eyes I can often feel like I live with Willard White or Don Warrington, yet watch him on stage during the nervous opening moments of the first night of an Agatha Christie or Gilbert and Sullivan and he suddenly becomes a panicked Truman Capote or even a giant Owen Meany. That said he usually manages to get his nerves under control and I am, of course, extremely proud of him, and I hope that goes without saying. In the last couple of years I have seen him play both Mistress Quickly and Nanki-Poo extremely effectively and movingly. (He, modestly, insisted that in both instances the moustache was doing all the work, but honestly he was *so* realistically Japanese. In both roles, actually. Which I thought was an interesting character choice.)

But the nerves I felt all that morning were concealing other more sinister rumblings within; completely unbeknownst to me, puberty was finally approaching. And it was anxious to make up for lost time. I don't know if you know the Verdi *Requiem* – perhaps you caught a snippet during the televised funeral of Diana, Princess of Wales? – but emotionally it's an absolute maelstrom. There's anger, there's sadness, there's fear. And there's a lot of drumming. During the 'Dies Irae' the member of the orchestra responsible for playing the bass drum absolutely hammers the thing relentlessly on the off-beat and the effect is beautiful but devastating. I was seated pretty much directly in front of the bass drum that night, and it was being played by a rather fabulous girl with big arms and exceptional vigour and rhythm. I think of her often when I am dicing aubergine. Every time that she struck the drum's taut skin with her mallet an astonishing 'BOOM' resonated throughout the whole church in an instant, but not before it had passed clean through me. Each time I felt something inside of me lurch wildly, and come loose. It was as if I was being used as a vessel in which to crush ice. Had I been pregnant I would almost certainly have gone into labour.

By the time it got to the 'Libera Me' I was absolutely in bits, not just because of my nerves about singing the great solo in front of such a big crowd, and the anxiety caused by the noise of the bass drum tearing through me, but also by the sheer emotionality of the piece. Honestly, it's heart-rending. I was absolutely wrung out. And I was *in* the ruddy thing. Goodness only knows what it must have been like for the audience. Nevertheless, I stood up out of my chair on the platform in good time, made sure that I stood with as good a posture as I could manage, took a few long slow breaths so that I was sure that my breathing could be as regulated as it could be, and waited for the conductor's eye.

I struck the first note, if I may say, beautifully. That particular church – St Paul's it is called, founded by William Wilberforce – has marvellous acoustics, and the more people within the building the richer the acoustics become. But even though the noise I was making was as it should have been, I suspect I may not have been making the visual impression that I might have wished to. The conductor was wearing a most worried expression, clearly able to interpret from my own look that I was a young man possessed of a strong sense that some sort of disaster was about to strike. The colours around me stopped appearing distinct, but began instead to bleed into one another and to blur. Everything become brown eventually, like old fruit. Things suddenly seemed to slow down, which is actually extremely unhelpful when you are trying to sing in time. I could feel in my shaken-up bones that something bad was about to happen that I was powerless to prevent. I didn't even know what it was. Would there be an explosion outside? A power cut? Perhaps there might be some sort of structural disaster, and lumps of masonry might start raining down upon the audience or even us? Maybe somebody was about to have a heart attack, or faint, or give birth to lizards?

'Libera me, Domine,' I sang, 'de morte aeterna in die illa tremenda; quando coeli movendi sunt et terra: dum veneris judicare saeclum per ignem.'

The conductor was wild-eyed now, as if he too could sense whatever omens I could detect. I felt something like a shelf of rock crack within me, and gulped. The conductor gulped too. He was still beating time with his baton, but the rest of his attentions were focused on me.

'Are you all right?' he mouthed at me.

I stared back at him, and tried to nod gently, but must have somehow come across as demented, as he took a step back as if I were about to lunge at him, teeth bared. He continued to beat out the rhythm and I continued to sing.

'Tremens factus sum ego et timeo,' I warbled, and a couple of lights flickered.

'Dum discussio venerit atque ventura irae quando coeli movendi sunt et terra,' I continued, and outside the church you could hear something – possibly a car's windscreen – shatter.

The moment had arrived. 'Dies irae,' I began, 'dies illa calamitatis ...'

My voice was climbing higher and higher. I was taking leaps up the register with every note I uttered, going up by thirds and fourths every time. The conductor looked ashen, and I doubt I looked too clever either.

'... Et miseriae ...' I am convinced that somewhere in the middle of that word I hit the highest note that I had ever reached in my life. Several members of the orchestra had stopped playing by now. A few members of the choir were giggling, sadly. I tried to carry on, but it was hopeless.

'... Dies magna ...' I attempted, but at that moment my throat made a noise like a ruler snapping. Nothing came out of me other than dry wind. Then a sort of baked rasping. And then everything stopped. The conductor was no longer looking in my direction but just sort of gazing into the middle distance, with misty-looking eyes. The hand that clasped the baton was still beating but no longer marking out a rhythm. Rather it seemed as if he were signalling for help, exhorting everyone else to sing or play as loudly as possible so as to drown out whatever sounds I could or couldn't make.

I made one last attempt, and a noise did come through. '… Et amara valde …' I sang. Incredibly deeply. Tom Waits would have been proud of the sound I was now making, but the conductor it seemed, was not. 'Please sit down,' he mouthed, and followed this up with a few gestures, to make sure that I was absolutely certain what he meant.

I sat out the rest of the concert in a daze. I understood what had happened to me but cursed the wretchedness of the timing. This had been a great opportunity for me, and I had stood up and made a series of extremely unpleasant noises in front of a huge audience. Still, at least puberty was finally underway. That ought to make the changing rooms at school a slightly less miserable place to be, I thought. Wrongly, as it turned out.[1]

There were meant to be refreshments served after the concert, but I begged my parents to take me straight home.

'That was interesting,' my mother said.

'Did you have a bit of a tickle in the throat at one point?' asked my father.

'The day of wrath,' I replied in a deep voice. 'That day of calamity and misery; a great and bitter day indeed.'

---

1 I would dearly love to describe what it was like for me in the school changing rooms, but I simply can't. I tried to write it out in longhand one afternoon and broke several pencils. It is too painful, simply, for me to recollect. I can probably leave it up to your imagination. Wet towels were often involved though.

'Right,' said my father. 'And how was the rest of your day?'

His question went unanswered.

Ginger Tea with Strawberry

I've always loved making my own teas. I was only at university for a term but in that time I shared a set of rooms with a Sri Lankan gentleman, Marvin, who taught me pretty much everything I know on the subject. We were at a rather strict college, alas, and he got into the most frightful brouhaha with the authorities about window boxes that rather soured things on the tea-making front. He also taught me some rudimentary yoga moves. I think of him often.

Now then, making tea – if you wish to make your own from scratch – is a rather long process. So if you're looking for a 'quick fix' – not the sort of thing that *I* tend to look for, it must be said – please, with all due respect, look elsewhere. You will need to start with a garden already full of roots and berries and flowers of the sort that appeal, or you'll need to plant one. Once you've achieved this, the very best time for you to go out and pick, pluck or harvest them is mid-morning, or depending on how much direct sunlight your garden receives, when the dew has all gone. Pick a huge amount. Far more than seems sensible.

You then need to dry it, somewhere warm, perhaps

even dark (an attic perhaps? That's certainly what I use. But then I'm lucky enough to have one and I am all too aware of the painful fact that not everybody does. Perhaps you have somewhere else appropriate, such as a panic room), for anything up to two weeks. Lay your herbs or flowers or whatever it might be down on top of some baking parchment, or rather a lot of kitchen towel, or even a tea towel (perhaps one with a humorous slogan on it that has long ceased to tickle you) and spread them out as thinly as you can. You then need another protective layer of parchment, paper or tea towel on top so as to avoid dirt landing on your herbs or flowers or whatever. After nine or ten days check them regularly, and the first instant you realise that all moisture has gone, scoop them up and lock them in something airtight, such as a Kilner jar or even Tupperware if you can bear it.

You are now only a little under a fortnight away from actually being able to make a cup of tea. In this instance, as I mentioned above, ginger tea with straw-berry. I know it seems odd to call this 'ginger tea with strawberry' when it actually contains, as you shall see, more strawberry than anything else, but the simple fact of the matter is that ginger has a far more powerful taste than strawberry does. It could cut through almost anything, could ginger. If this tea were a sofa, then the strawberry would be artfully arranged cushions and the ginger would be an iron spike right through the ruddy middle of it. (This sounds, I'm sure you'll agree, like rather an unusual sofa. But I hope the point I make is a clear one.)

For this you will need …
   Strawberry leaves, 9 oz of
   Mint leaves, 4½ oz of
   Crushed, dried ginger, 1 or 2 tsp of

Place them all together in a jar, pop the lid on and give them a shake. Then put it to one side for ten days, to give all the aromas and flavours a chance to blend. Then when ten days have passed – enough time, frankly, for you to go on a residential driving course or to start getting to grips with Venice – boil a kettle and warm your teapot. Then empty the water from the pot that you have used to warm it and add as many teaspoons of your tea as you are going to make cups and, of course, one for the pot. Let it brew for seven minutes – longer if you can wait – and then pour it through a strainer. If you feel it's a little tart then add a little honey. But please not sugar. And certainly not 'sweetener'.

Worth the wait? I very much think so. Do raise a cup to Marvin, as I always do. When I remember to.

Chapter 13

RELIVING MY TEENS

I know that my teens fall into the remit of a childhood memoir, but I have to say there's only so much of it I can bear to relate. It was, as I'm sure you can guess, a deeply unhappy time for me. Willesden Grammar was not a place that ever made me comfortable or welcome. You must know a little bit about me and what I am like (otherwise you couldn't possibly have felt compelled to pick this thing up and read it), and so I would like you to take a few moments to yourself and imagine, vividly, what it must have been like for me at an all-boys' school as a teenager. Have you done it yet? Well, let me tell you, it was worse than that. Far worse. When I think about my time spent at that school it causes shivers to run down my spine not dissimilar to those that run down it when I recall the electric carving knife that my father always insisted on using when I was little, and that first moment shortly after turning the thing on and started to carve a roast that he inevitably hit bone. An appalling sound, barely softened by being recollected rather than just experienced. That too is how I feel about my teenage schooldays. So if it's all the same with you, I would rather like to gloss over much of them.

I would rather not write in any great detail about the way that I was treated in the school changing rooms, or the utter humiliation that befell me whenever I stepped on to the sporting field. About the way that the harder I tried to run the slower I always got, or the way that people hurled balls at me hard as I struggled in vain to protect my face.

I will not dwell on the habits of those boys who found it amusing to pull down one's games shorts whenever teachers weren't looking, or sometimes when even I wasn't looking so that I promptly tripped and fell when I attempted to move. I do not wish to describe the dreadful ritual whereby older pupils would patrol the corridors looking for a younger boy and then, having found them, grab the waistband of their underpants and then lift them higher and higher, all the while inexplicably chanting the word 'Melvin' and putting an unbearable strain on one's genitals and perineum until they (the underpants) ultimately snapped.

I do not wish to expand upon the tricks that were played on me in school assembly. About the way that people would pinch me so that I cried out at deeply inopportune moments – perhaps when a death in the school was being announced – and I would then get into terrible trouble. I do not wish to describe my attempts to get into the school play that were always thwarted by a teacher who took against me mercilessly and who always described the standard of that year's auditionees as 'unusually high'.

I don't wish to dwell upon the fact that by a considerable margin my best friend at the age of sixteen was one of the school dinner ladies. Nor can I bear to tell you the details of the time that I tried to 'get in' with some of the naughtier boys in my year and met in a park to get drunk, only to be brutally mocked for bringing a picnic blanket. (It was a lined one. I didn't wish for my bottom to get wet.)

Neither do I wish to tell you about a piano teacher to whom I became far too close. And vice versa. I just don't want to think about any of that at all. I wonder if, instead, you might permit me to go off at a rare tangent and describe a rather more recent experience? Thank you. That is very decent of you.*

For some weeks now, a leaflet has been coming through our door. The letterbox of the door, I should say. In fact, now that I really think about it – and at this juncture I would like to make it extremely clear – as clear as clear can be in point of fact – that I do *really* think about what I write. 'So does it all just sort of *tumble* out of you?' people occasionally say to me at parties, be they drinks parties, dinner parties or even semi-formal après-christening gatherings. 'I'm afraid not,' I generally reply. And then I briefly explain to them, in layman's terms, all about that pesky little necessity that is commonly referred to by my brethren and I in the writing community as 'graft'. People generally enjoy being put straight, I find. You see, the whole of the first sentence of this paragraph is in rather severe danger of leaving my readers completely in the dark and quite possibly in a panic. When I say that a leaflet has been coming through the letterbox of our door (need I point out that it's the *front* door that I'm referring to? Perhaps so. I am all too aware – and indeed more than a little flattered

Damien, I'm not sure that is all right. It's a great big chunk of your childhood.

I would appreciate your support here actually. It's a very sensitive issue, basically a panic attack waiting to happen.

Well, could you try? Perhaps, if it's too painful to put pen to paper, we could send a typist round to yours and you could dictate. Would that be simpler?

It would not. Force me to write about those days in any great detail and I would soon be found wandering drunk and naked around Queen's Park. Or is that the sort of thing that your publicity department would welcome? If so, they are IMMORAL.

I can see that you feel strongly about this. Let's talk about it at a later date.

250

– that my readers come from a wide variety of backgrounds and so who's to say with which customs they are familiar? Not me, I'm quite sure. Wouldn't dream of it. And don't.), what I mean by this is that multiple copies of the *same* leaflet have been descending on to our camelback beige high cotton doormat. In so doing, these leaflets, and indeed the intrepid leafleteers for whose conveyance and despatch we owe so great a debt, have been attempting to convey to us that 'a festival of food' was soon to be held in a well-sized venue not at all far from our place of abode, and that the organisers of the festival and indeed prospective stall holders would be extremely grateful if members of the public such as ourselves wouldn't mind awfully seriously considering thinking about popping along and then seeing what the whole thing was all about. I hope that's clear.[*]

* I have read the above paragraph five times now, Damien, and I'm still not at all sure that it makes any sense at all.

Read it again.

I am always anxious to do my bit to support those who produce, promote, sell and indeed eat food, not just as a food writer but also as a citizen. That said, if one has a reputation or profile within food circles, then that can make attending these sorts of events rather more of an ordeal than one might otherwise like. Please forgive me if you think that that is an arrogant thing of me to say, I beg of you. I am not suggesting – even for a moment – that I am recognisable in the same way as, say, Tom Cruise or Margaret Atwood are. I do not have as regular a television presence as some members of my profession, but I do appear on the thing occasionally and – flattering as it doubtless is to be asked if I actually am who I appear to be – that doesn't always make visiting such events as easy as it otherwise might be.

I raised the matter of risking a visit to the food festival with Anthony as we neared the end of breakfast, outlining – as briefly as the circumstances permitted – a small selection of my fears. Anthony didn't reply at first, but I wasn't sure whether this was because he was thinking deeply about the issue, or because he was concentrating too hard on the newspaper that he always claims to be reading on his iPad. I did what I consider to be the sensible thing in situations like this, and calmly repeated exactly what I had said to him word for word at a very slightly higher volume.

'I heard you the first time,' he said, and not for the first time. 'It'll be fine. Let's just go.'

I reminded him of the occasion when the two of us had been returning from a weekend with friends on the north Norfolk coast, and on our journey homeward had glimpsed some hoardings advertising a food festival as we pootled our way through Swaffham.

'Ooh,' I said. 'Do you think that a food festival might be a worthwhile diversion?'

'If they have a lavatory we can use,' replied Anthony and the matter was settled.

So we parked up, paid in, I embarked on a bit of a gander and off went Anthony to make use of the lavatory facilities. No sooner was I in the place than I fell into an absolutely fascinating discussion with a cheese-making gentleman all about the effects that different properties of muslin cloth could have on the length of time it takes various of his cheese to mature. Twenty-five minutes later Anthony returned muttering darkly about razor clams, which rather brought things to an end as far as cheese chat was concerned. Anthony said something about eating something as long as it was reasonably dry, and so we stopped off at a stall that was offering a rather diverse range of oat cakes. This was where things began to go a little wrong.

'Are you Damien Trench?' said the lady operating the stall.

Now what on earth can one possibly say to that? It is not, after all, a question that leaves an awful lot of room for nuance. It is also a question I was once asked on the upper deck of a bus by some teenagers a few days after the transmission of an episode of a television panel show called *I Beg Your Pardon* that I had ill-advisedly taken part in. On that occasion I had answered in the affirmative and for my troubles been rewarded with a rather graphic list of reasons why I could never really be considered one of life's winners. I also had to put with some rather uncharitable remarks about my chinos. Ever since then, I have been rather on my guard in such situations, and so I attempted to blend directness with a hint of mystique.

'I might be,' I said to the lady.

'You are though, aren't you?' she asked.

'Well … yes,' I agreed. And that was that.

She seized me by both hands, pulled me towards her, and launched into a passionate monologue that covered a selection of dessert recipes that I had once offered up in print, her difficult relationship with soft cheeses and her husband's irritable skin. So intense was her manner that it was extremely difficult to tell if she was scolding or praising me. All I knew was that she was staring so intently at me that I became worried that parts of me would dry up and just drop off like smoked chipotles. Also, her eyes were so extremely wide open that I began to worry that it might be dangerous to let so much light into your head. As soon as she stopped speaking, I thanked her for being willing to share, broke free from her grasp, panic-bought three punnets of raspberries on the way out and then sprinted back to the Uno as fast as fast can be. I looked at my wrists once I was in the passenger seat and discovered that she'd left marks.

'Remember that?' I asked Anthony.

'Well, if you don't want to go, then we won't,' he said, rather unhelpfully in my opinion.

'Of course, the other issue to consider,' I said, 'is provenance.'

He sighed, put down his iPad and said simply, 'What?'

'Where the food comes from. Sometimes at events like this, the net does seem to have been thrown fairly wide. We all used to think – didn't we? – that the point of a farmers' market was to give people a chance to buy directly from local producers. But the definition of the term "local producer" is perhaps somewhat baggier than it used to be. Personally – and I don't like to judge: it's absolutely not my place and I never think it will be – I think that if you're going to be making sausages at the other end of Kent and then driving them all the way up to north-west London to sell them, then you're not just deceiving yourself if you have the words "local produce" painted on to the side of your van. As I say, not my place to judge.'

By this point Anthony was absolutely gripped. I could tell. He was doing that thing where he pretends to be completely uninterested in what I'm saying, as a way of making me speak more.

'Now there is a thought, actually. You don't think that these people are rivals of the farmers' market, do you? The last thing I would want is to being seen as having taken a side. My dream is that both endeavours should be able to live side by side, and together in perfect harmony. Just so long as they happen on different days of the month.'

Anthony, rather gallantly I thought, insisted that the decision on whether or not we should go to 'the bloody food festival' lay completely in my hands, and so off he went to shower (I like to shower prior to breakfast, Anthony prefers to do so after. But we can't all be alike, can we, or what sort of world would that be?) and left me to mull things over further over a second and then indeed third cup of espresso. There really was much to consider. But the local politics of visiting the thing aside, absolutely my biggest fear was being recognised, made a fuss over and then quite possibly ranted at by a big-eyed somebody with a loud voice but very little in the way of clarity of thought.

Anyway, by lunchtime I'd made up my mind and decided to brave it. If it all turned out to be too much we could very easily leave again, and I'd have a Bach Remedy with me just in case. And it was rather fun in the end. No one recognised me at all, which really was the most blessed of reliefs, and they had some rather fun hot food on. I was content with a slice of quiche and had the pleasure of watching Anthony eat an entire paella intended for two with only the aid of a plastic teaspoon. If I have a message here (and I never intend to use these pages to preach from; that would be, to my way of thinking, absolutely and completely unforgiveable) it is simply this: don't ever be afraid to try things, and never overthink anything if you can at all help it.

Paella: A Seafood One

I am not Spanish. But I often think it would be awfully fun if I were. Not least because my national dish would be paella. Actually, it must be awfully nice to come from a country where everybody can agree on what the national dish *is*. What is ours? Fish and chips? Sandwiches? Curry? Pulled pork? Hawaiian pizza? I suspect our own uncertainty is simply symptomatic of the very confused state that Britain currently finds itself in in terms of identity. Let's face it, the place is an absolute ruddy mess, isn't it? Dear oh dear. Post-Brexit, we've all, sad to say, been forced to reflect very seriously upon the nature of selfness, sameness and belonging and I'm not at all sure that I like where it's left us. What a gloomy thought. Let's crack on before we all get too glum. You'll feel a lot better after you've been to see your fishmonger. I know do. (Unless Paul who used to just do Saturdays but now does some days during the week is working there. An appallingly sarcastic young man, who finds it amusing to mimic the voices and mannerisms of the regular customers, and who I personally suspect has issues.)

For this you will need ...

   Olive oil, extra virgin, lots of

   Onion, 1, an absolutely massive one, peeled and chopped ever so finely

   Garlic, a pair of cloves, crushed

   Tomatoes, big and juicy, pair of, chopped and the skin removed

   Some salt

   Sugar, 1 tsp of

   Saffron

   Sweet paprika, 1 tsp of

   Squid, 4 – they don't have to be big ones

   Arborio rice, 14 oz of

   Fish stock, just over 1 pint of

   Dry white wine, 1 large glass of – little bit for you, most of it for the dish

   Shrimps, as big as you can find, at least a dozen but no need to stop at that (never skimp on shrimp. That's my motto. Well, one of them)

   Clams, two and a half dozen

Gosh, I'm excited about this. Get down your paella dish. (Please tell me you have one. Otherwise, stop what you're doing, jog down to your local cook shop and buy one or you'll be absolutely stymied. Go on. Run!) Put it on some heat, add some oil and then throw the onion in. Keep pushing it about the paella dish with your wooden spatula of choice until it is nice and soft, then put the garlic in and follow it immediately with the tomato. Keep stirring. Don't ever stop stirring, or you will *regret* it. Put some salt in and the teaspoon of sugar. (If I'm perfectly honest you *can* do without the sugar if you are of a mind to avoid the stuff, but it really does make a lovely difference to the whole dish. Go on. It's only a little bit.)

Now you can add the saffron – just a pinch I reckon, but you may absolutely love the stuff in which case you can fling a little more in – and also the sweet paprika. The oil will be jolly hot by now, so do please be careful. Once the tomatoes are no longer instantly recognisable as tomatoes you can add the squid – leave the tentacles exactly as they are but chop the body into rings – and let them really hit the hot oil for a minute or so. Then add the Arborio rice, and give it a fierce stir so that every single ruddy grain of the stuff has oil all over it. Put that all to one side for the moment, or at least on a very low heat and turn your attention to the stock.

Get a separate pan out, put the stock in it, take a slurp of the wine and then add most of what remains of it along with a little salt and then let it all come to the boil. Then pour most of it over the rice. Hopefully it will give off a brief, almost deafening, sizzle that will make you feel tremendously *alive*.

Give it all another big stir and then don't touch a grain for another twenty minutes or so, just so long as the pan is right over the top of the gas burner (or equivalent) and is capable of cooking evenly. If not, turn the pan about from time to time, and think seriously about getting a new cooker.

When the rice and squid etc. have been cooking in this way for about eight minutes of their allotted twenty, spread the shrimp out on top of the rice and steam them, adding a little extra stock at this point if you think it's required. It's very easy to see when the shrimps need to be turned because the underside will have turned pink.

While that's all going on, get your clams in a pan with a little bit of water, really not all that deep – a centimetre or so – and a splash of white wine. When a clam opens, it is ready. If it is being stubborn, leave it *well alone*. Remove them from the pan, and place them delicately on top of the rest of the paella. And there you have it. Put the big thing right in the middle of the table and let your guests tuck straight in. If you've invited any. Anthony and I can polish off a whole one to ourselves. In fact he would do it all by himself if I let him. He seriously has to be watched sometimes.

Chapter 14

SEVENTEEN

In this crazy old world, people often assume that certain things are the case, don't they? The way that we should all live our lives has been decided upon – or deemed[1] – by some frankly sinister and unseen group. Please don't make the mistake that I am about to embark on some sort of conspiracy theory; that is absolutely not the case. I am not about to suggest that various members of our royal

---

1 I do like the word *deemed*, it has ever such a lovely ring to it, don't you think? It's a gentle sounding, slow-vowelled word, like *unguent* or *bellow*, those sorts of words that you can somehow never rush, even if you're trying to spit them out in a fury. And yet at the same time, it's a word that you can use with real emphasis, or sarcasm even. 'Who has *deemed* this to be the case?' you might ask at a public meeting of council representatives when one of them makes one of those absolutely ludicrous claims that they seem to think people will just blindly go along with, such as, 'Nobody uses libraries any more,' or 'Gun crime is under control,' or 'Food allergy labelling legislation does not come under the remit of your borough council, sir.' 'And just who has *deemed* this to be the case?' you can reply, safe in the knowledge that even though your questioning will have a frustratingly negligible impact on the frankly arbitrary decision-making process, you have at least had the opportunity to unleash some satisfying vowel sounds, which can sometimes be almost enough to take the edge off.

family (beloved or otherwise) or high-ranking politicians are actually lizards who have taken on a human form, for example, or make the (I think we can all agree frankly far-fetched) claim that huge numbers of people who work for public planning departments are susceptible to bribery from property developers. This is not the place for such theories, attractive as they may be to various camps.

No, the sinister, unseen group that I refer to are those people who have decided that, for instance, absolutely everybody must carry a 'smart phone', and be continually prepared to 'download apps' in order to get anything done. Or that everybody has a working printer and scanner in their home-office, and consequently, rather than ever sending anybody some paperwork for them to fill in and return, they simply send you something that you yourself have to print out, before you can fill it in and return it. Or that if people want directions for how to get somewhere, then all they actually need is a postcode that they can tap into their 'sat nav', and the machine will just magically guide them there.

Well, I'm sorry to have to be the one to pour a bucket of cold stock over these beliefs, but actually, NO. We do not all choose to live our lives like that. Some of us do not want to own 'smart phones'. We've got a mobile phone that we're used to, we know how to work it, and that will do very nicely, if it's all the same with you. If I approach the gentleman, or lady, manning, or whatever the female equivalent of manning is (mansplaining?) the information desk in a busy London train terminal and ask her what time the next train for Bicester North will be leaving (an incredibly unlikely scenario, I grant you. There is, apparently, a 'fashion village' there, but whatever a 'fashion village' either is or – rather more likely – imagines itself to be, it is not something that I feel a need or wish to broaden my horizons so far as to experience. (UPDATE: I've just shouted downstairs to my partner Anthony to ask if he has ever found himself visiting Bicester Fashion Village, and if so, what's it like. He says that there's a branch of Pret A Manger there. No further questions, your honour)), then what I am really hoping that they will do is to tell me, in a nice clear voice – doesn't have to be RP, that's not what I think *at all* – what time the next train to Bicester North will be leaving. That is all. I make no further demands of them. Obviously I'd prefer that they aren't wearing ill-fitting clothes, or chewing on gum, but I appreciate the age we're living in makes no assurances on such matters. I don't even require them to wish me a good trip, or a cheerful day. I'm delighted if they do, but I don't throw tantrums if they don't; they're busy people after all, and there may well be a queue of people behind me who are also in need of having vital travel information relayed to them and would prefer, on balance, not to be held up from receiving such information by the likes of me being showered with kind thoughts and wishes. That's just life, isn't it? And if you can't deal with it, you're in for a pretty bumpy ride. I certainly do not wish to be furnished with the very information that I have sought, only for the exchange to be suffixed with the suggestion that it might be worth my while 'downloading an app' so that I do not have to queue up for such information again. (On one occasion I asked someone sitting at a so-called information desk a question about departure times and received the retort, 'Have you tried looking at the departure board?' 'Yes,' I said, 'and the moments I spent struggling to comprehend its meaning triggered a migraine that your attitude is doing very little indeed to alleviate.' I don't think she got the reference, but then perhaps there wasn't one.)

I do not wish to download an app, and have to stare at a screen, and use my perfectly conventionally proportioned thumbs to type in questions on buttons that aren't real buttons but instead just images of buttons that are of a size only suitable for people with extremely unconventionally proportioned thumbs, which is to say absolutely bloody tiny. In the words of Peter Kosminsky, 'No. No. No.' I want to use my mouth to form actual words, which in turn shall form actual questions posed to an actual flesh and blood person and I want them to reply to me, using their actual mouth to form words which shall in turn form sentences. I can put it in no simpler terms.

As for people who send forms for you to print out yourself, such as lawyers and people who work for the council and so forth, I really think this is not on. It is presumptive *in the extreme* to posit that everybody is possessed of their own printer in full working order. As it happens, I do possess my own printer in full working order, but that is absolutely not the ruddy point. Because though the printer may itself be in full working order, I myself am not capable of using the – and I'm sorry for swearing, really I am – bloody thing. Were it a matter simply of pressing PRINT and the printed pages emerging from the printer moments after, then that would be all well and good. I'd go so far as to say I'd welcome it. That would be a perfectly reasonable outcome. But that isn't what happens. You click on the thing that says PRINT and then the wretched machine starts using words like DEFAULT and CURRENTLY OFFLINE and I find myself SCREAMING. My partner Anthony bought me a printer for my study. He installed it for me. He showed me how to operate it. He talked me through it. He wrote additional notes to help me understand. It worked. But I absolutely swear to you that if I try to use the thing when I am alone in the house it simply refuses to work, and I become unusually distressed. Once – and I am no one's idea of a violent man – I punched my printer so hard that the plastic casing cracked, and the little flap concealing the printer ink cartridges flipped open, never to be fully functioning again. I would quite honestly – and this will sound like hyperbole but really isn't – rather die in battle than attempt to use my printer unsupervised.

My feelings in regards to such matters are, I am sure, completely reasonable. But what about my aversion to people who offer postcodes as if they are meaningful directions? 'Is this not a misplaced resentment, Damien?' I can hear you begging. No. It is not. Because – and I am not deliberately trying be shocking – I. DO. NOT. DRIVE.

There, I've said it. I know. People always think I'm joking. But I'm not. I don't. I can't. My partner Anthony and I own a car – a Fiat Uno if this sort of thing interests you. It certainly doesn't interest me – and Anthony holds a UK driving licence (Automatic), but that is as far as it goes. Damien Trench, cookery writer and diarist, drives not. And nor shall I. Not in this life or the next, if it's up to me (and who's to say if it is, quite frankly? It could be up to ANYONE or NO ONE, and I am simply not well positioned enough to say. I am an agnostic, not an atheist.)

My antipathy towards driving can be traced – all rather too easily, it is my sad duty to relate – back to my teenage years.

There is a terrible pressure in turning seventeen. It's turning sixteen or eighteen that society, the mainstream media and so forth make all kinds of fuss about, because those milestones bring with them more obvious entitlements – being able to smoke, to drink, to join the army, to vote (all things I have done in my time, though none of them to excess I think. Not that there's any pride to be had in not voting to excess. It's hard to think of a way in which it would be *possible* to vote to excess without actively engaging in electoral fraud, which sounds like the most appalling bother. Clearly the postal vote system is open to abuse – but then *what isn't*? Rather than taking any rightful pride in not being part of such behaviour, my personal feeling is that one should instead feel shame in not voting when you have the opportunity. I am not about to take the chance to leap astride one of my political hobby horses (of which I have seven) and gallop rantingly back and forth across the keyboard in one of my typing *frenzies*, but at the same time I am not in any way ashamed to state that I am a great believer in democracy, even if it's sometimes extremely hard to keep faith in its results).

[NOTE: I have just read that paragraph back to myself, and feel that I should add that in addition to never voting to excess, I wish to make it extremely clear that I never joined the army either, to excess or otherwise. I have, it almost but not quite goes without saying, the most *enormous* respect for those who serve in Her Majesty's – or indeed, for that matter, anyone else's – armed forces (with the obvious exceptions of any dictators – Alexander Lukashenko, to name but one) but I have never joined their number. The fact that wars, even despite everything that's gone on previously, still happen is, to my mind, something of a shame, and it is extremely difficult for us civilians to even begin to understand what it must be like to be engaged in warfare. It is probably – and I don't say this lightly – pretty ruddy stressful at times, and these people deserve our respect and indeed sometimes gratitude (whatever our opinions of the people who have made the actual decision for them to go to war; really rather low at times). Such is the political fallout from war, that all too often the efforts of those actually on the ground are overlooked. The catering corps, for example, must have an incredibly difficult job on their hands. Cooking for large numbers is never easy. We had twelve people over for supper last Saturday, with three vegetarians, a coeliac and two lactose-intolerants among their number, and it was most certainly not a walk in the park, by anyone's standards. I had to offer a choice of three desserts, and anyone who wanted to have cheese and oatcakes needed to have it in another room. The thought of preparing food for hundreds of (presumably) tired men and women in a war zone, the imminent threat of coming under fire constantly looming over one, would absolutely bring me out in hives. And to attempt any kind of slow cooking when you're on the move like that is near impossible. Amazing people, the catering corps. I have nothing but respect and admiration for them.]

But when I was at school it was turning seventeen that people found the most exciting. Smoking and drinking could be done illicitly from a much younger age, which took some of the excitement away from turning sixteen or eighteen. But driving (unless one really did come from an extremely difficult background – and trust me I have every sympathy for those who do) is something that most teenagers would be rather afeared of doing outside the law. People would count down to their seventeenth birthday because that was when you could acquire – with to my mind a bafflingly small amount of admin (no psychological profiling, for instance, or a short survey to answer on attitudes) – a provisional driving licence.

At Willesden Grammar, when one was studying for A-levels, in addition to the eight or so lessons one had timetabled for one's chosen subjects, one was also left with a number of 'free periods'. As far as the staff were concerned, these free periods represented an opportunity for further study, for additional reading and for essay writing. I generally welcomed this opportunity to try to get ahead with my school work, but for many other pupils the lack of supervision was all too much of a temptation, and they were unable to prevent themselves from larking about and being lairy. Some people would stroll out of the school gates to find somewhere to smoke, or even meet up with members of the opposite sex. (Perhaps they met up with members of the same sex too, but this was never really talked about.) Others nipped into pubs for a cheeky half. Perhaps even a game of pool or darts. At that age I always found these sorts of places rather terrifying, and so never joined such a party.

(This was long before the smoking ban and the rise of the so-called 'gastropub', of course, both of which have changed public houses for the better, as far as I am concerned. (With some caveats, it must be said; if a public house is going to be selling hot food on the premises, then really it ought to be freshly cooked on the premises, rather than just a load of ready meals delivered by a truck from a catering suppliers and then simply heated up. Heating up is not cooking; any more than just stuffing things in drawers is tidying. Or being dragged back to the shore by a lifeguard is swimming. (Another word on the subject of catering suppliers. Do the drivers and delivery people they employ make a habit of obeying parking and loading regulations? I rather fancy that they don't. One sees a Brake Brothers lorry (and others too, it must be said) parked with half of its wheels upon the pavement in a no-loading zone so often, that one rather wonders if it is in fact company policy to always behave in this manner. (I might not drive, but I certainly know the rules of the road, and I stick to them. I once had a taxi driver who told me that he could speed things up a little by nipping down a one-way street. I told him in no uncertain terms that I was not prepared to be a passenger in a vehicle driven so recklessly and demanded that I be dropped off there and then. I paid the exact amount on the meter, not a penny more, and left the driver to think about his conduct. 'Only trying to help you out, mate,' he said, in mitigation. 'Road criminal,' I countered, and just kept walking.))))[*]

This is an astonishing number of parentheses. Well done.

Many thanks.

As well as doing schoolwork, the use of free periods for 'improving activities' was also officially sanctioned. For some this involved reading newspapers or practising musical instruments. For others, working out in the gym. If I ever fancied a break from my studies, I tended to wander over to the dining hall and go and chat to one of the dinner ladies, who were always a most approachable bunch. Officially, students were forbidden from entering the kitchen area on grounds of, I think, health and safety. There were a couple of (male) kitchen supervisors who sometimes used to sneer at my presence, but the dinner ladies always gave them short thrift. Besides, I always made a point of putting on an apron, disposable gloves and a hairnet, so they could hardly claim I was doing any harm. We'd chat about this and that and exchange culinary tips.

Now, the problem with these free periods was that in the eyes of the school, taking driving lessons was also considered an improving activity. This meant that lessons could be booked and billed through the school office, and thus driving instructors could drive on to school grounds to collect pupils for lessons. My parents thought that this sounded extremely practical, and as my seventeenth birthday approached they offered me a course of driving lessons as a gift. This was, it must be said, an extremely generous offer on their part. Angela had had the same gift, and been absolutely thrilled with it.

(Not that I have ever been happy sharing a vehicle with her since. I'm quite sure that she won't mind my saying that she is an incredibly aggressive driver, not just in terms of lane positioning, manoeuvring and speed, but also in terms of language. She needs to change the horn almost as often as the tyres, in fact. I'm sad to relate that as a passenger she is, if anything, even worse, treating the driver with the same lack of respect as that of all other road users. Not all that long ago, on the way between a funeral and the reception (where the food was, I'm sorry to say, memorably unpalatable. Possibly the worst sausage rolls I have either seen or tasted. Such a shame when they really are not that difficult to make yourself. Honestly, I could weep tears of frustration sometimes. Can't remember who the deceased was) I found myself sharing the back seat of a car with my sister. My father was driving, and my mother was occupying the front passenger seat. It was like being a child again. My poor father took a wrong turn before we had even left the grounds of the cremato-rium, and all hell broke loose. My father realised what he'd done immediately and apologised, but it was too late. My mother started ranting about a lack of respect for the dead and my father's inability to perform a rather wide variety of tasks that my mother considered well within the capabilities of most males of the species. I appealed for calm, but with little effect. Angela leant forward, pulled the hand brake on, and ordered my father out of the car. Barely had my father climbed into the back and put his seat belt on than my sister completed a manoeuvre the complexity of which could only be matched by the savagery with which it was accomplished. 'The gear box!' my father said, pleadingly. 'My eyes!' my mother said. (She had recently undergone laser eye surgery, and was *convinced* that her eyeballs were not as secure in their sockets as they ought or used to be.) 'Shut them,' my sister said. Then she got out, ordered my father back into the driver's seat and returned to the back with me. 'Why are you looking so sickly?' she asked me as my father slowly recommenced his driving. I declined to answer, and instead lowered the window next to me in the hope of feeling some cold air on my face. 'Do shut the window,' my sister said. 'This place stinks of ash or something.' (Perhaps, on reflection, my recollection of the food is coloured by the memory of the journey to it.))

But whilst my sister was absolutely delighted to be given driving lessons – in fact she passed, first time, after just six lessons, although she was also the recipient of a six-month ban not long afterwards for the combined offence of speeding and being obstreperous in conversation with a police officer (this is not how the police described her behaviour, by the way, merely my interpretation of it) – I was altogether rather less excited by the prospect of learning to drive. Partly, it must be said, because from my vantage point in the back seat, driving had always looked rather complicated and stressful, especially the way my father had done it. It looked absolutely impossible to me to operate all those buttons and levers and things that clicked on and off, not to mention keeping control of the big circular device, and to work out where one was going, and avoiding colliding with all the other road users, and all the while having your nearest passenger engaged in a programme of quite ceaseless tutting. I just couldn't understand how my father ever managed it, quite frankly. In fact, now that I think about it, he couldn't always cope with this sort of pressure, especially once Angela's propensity for sudden rage began to manifest itself. Sometimes in the midst of some fraught journey (a return from Broadstairs sticks in the mind for some reason, although it is just one example of many) my father would turn off a main road and head down some winding country lanes.

'Oh, what have you gone and gone down here for, you demented old fool?' my mother would ask.

'Because he's an imbecile,' my sister would answer helpfully from the back.

'I just need to stop for a pee,' my father would say

through pursed lips. And then he'd park the car, get out and disappear into some woods.

'Go and find where your father's got to, Damien,' my mother would say after a few minutes, and I'd obediently potter off and look for him. I'd always follow him into the woods and find him not peeing, but kicking a tree over and over again and repeating the phrase 'this bloody family'.

'Everything OK?' I'd ask.

'Just having a quick pee,' he'd say, before launching one final and often frenzied assault on the poor tree. Then we'd walk back to the car together.

'Better?' my mother would say as my father settled into the driver's seat.

'Oh, much better thanks,' he'd reply as he buckled up.

I never told anyone about my father kicking trees. It was our little secret, I suppose.

But it was not just the prospect of potentially finding myself having to chauffeur my mother and sister that I found so intensely stressful. Rather it was the thought of being one of those boys who was picked up by a driving instructor in a free period and who then had to drive out of the school gates. This may sound nothing short of splendid, but actually to me it represented some sort of hell.

Willesden Grammar School no longer exists. While I have no objection whatsoever to the closure of any sort of selective school, I do still believe that in purely archi-tectural terms it was a crime to completely demolish the thing. Far be it for me to say that corruption must surely play a part in some of the decisions made by the planning departments of any number of local councils, but clearly something rum was up when the decision was made to send in the demolition experts and bring the whole pile – still doubtless echoing with the sounds of laughter, fighting, sneering, crying and the occasional bit of teaching – crashing to the floor.

I am not suggesting that it was in any way beautiful, but it was a perfectly good example of the sort of thing that it was: one of those vast, tall, flat-fronted – broad-shouldered one might almost say – brick Victorian school buildings that loomed over the street of brick Victorian terraces that it found itself, not unreasonably, slap bang in the middle of. It was set back from the road, so that there was space for a sizeable playground in front of it. This was the spot in which driving instructors would park their cars and then stand and wait for their instructees to arrive. There must have been thirty enormous windows overlooking that playground, and as soon as any pupil who happened to be looking out of one of them spotted a driving instructor's car pull up and manoeuvre itself back into position, word would spread like wildfire.

Within moments, hundreds (it seemed like thousands sometimes) of schoolboys would be squeezing themselves into position at these windows trying to get a glimpse of whoever was about to emerge from the main building into the playground for their first driving lesson. Then, as the poor pupil climbed into the passenger seat, the banging and whistling and cat-calling would start. Woe betide anyone who happened to stall the car inside school grounds. The jeering and the laughter seemed to echo around the building for hours. This always seemed to me like the most intolerable pressure for people to be put under, and yet the school seemed powerless to prevent it. Perhaps the headmaster, and I'm afraid I wouldn't put it past him, thought this sort of ritualistic abuse to be in some way character building.

My sister never had to endure this sort of thing at her school, and frankly I doubt very much if she would have put up with it for a moment. But this was the way of things at Willesden Grammar, and so when my parents suggested that I too might like to have driving lessons, I tried to fudge the issue.

'Oh, that's certainly a very kind offer,' I told my parents when the issue was first raised. 'But I don't really think that driving is particularly … *me*.'

'What on earth are you talking about?' my mother said. 'Driving isn't particularly anyone. It's a verb.'

'It's a gerund, actually,' I countered and then instantly regretted it.

'You try and talk some sense into him,' my mother ordered my father. 'He's gone off on one.'

My mother left the table and then went and stood, as she often did during these sorts of discussions, directly behind me. It was thoughtful of her, actually, as although I could still hear her rolling her eyes, I couldn't see her doing it.

'Driving is a jolly useful thing to be able to do, Damien,' my father said.

'We live in London,' I said. 'I don't need to be able to drive. There's the underground. There are buses. I love buses, you know I do.'

'Public transport is a wonderful thing, Damien. Your commitment to publicly funded infrastructure is admirable,' said my father.

'Don't allow yourself to get distracted, Samuel,' my mother muttered from behind me. She never called my father 'Samuel' unless she was becoming agitated by him. (Although now that I think about it, she called him 'Samuel' about seven or eight times a day.)

'I'm trying to talk here,' said my father. 'If you want to be part of this conversation, come and sit at the table. It's no use just standing there rolling your eyes.'

'I'm not *rolling* my eyes,' my mother snapped. 'I have weak superior oblique muscles. All my family do.'

'Oh God,' said my father and then put his head in his hands.

Fifteen seconds of silence followed, at the end of which my father said, 'Please have driving lessons, Damien.'

'I don't feel that this is the right time,' I said.

'Of course it's the right time,' my mother said. 'Seventeen *is* the right time.'

'Can't I have lessons in the school holidays?' I said.

'If you have lessons now, you'll be able to drive in time for the school holidays. Just think: you'd be able to drive us all to Broadstairs.'

My father grimaced slightly, but said nothing.

'I'm not sure I'd be able to take the pressure,' I said. 'If you have driving lessons at school everybody watches you get in and start the car. They bang on the windows. They shout. It's like the Colosseum.'

'The Colosseum doesn't *have* windows,' my mother said, missing the point by a considerable margin.

'They whistle. They holler.'

'If that's what people do, then they do it to encourage each other,' she said.

'I really don't think they do,' I said.

'It does sound a little bit unlikely,' my father said.

'What was that, Samuel?' my mother asked.

'Nothing,' said my father quietly.

'Anyway, you love performing in front of a crowd,' my mother said. 'Think of those concerts where you play the piano.'

'The audience is a little more self-selecting,' I said.

My mother emitted a sigh that caused several of the kitchen unit doors to rattle.

'Being able to drive isn't just useful,' she eventually said, 'it's actually good for you. Think how much it helped your sister deal with her anger.'

I couldn't think of a way of responding to this statement truthfully without bringing up the subject of mental health issues, and so I said nothing.

'Just do it,' said my father quietly, almost pleadingly. 'Just agree with her, and then it's all over.'

'Fine,' I said. 'I'd love to have driving lessons.'

'We should ask that nice man who taught Sheila's daughter, don't you think, Samuel? He was awfully amusing at that barbecue.'

'Why not?' said my father, who didn't sound as if he had been even remotely amused at a recent barbecue.

And so it was that on the day of my seventeenth birthday, at twenty past eleven in the morning, a car drove into the playground at the front of Willesden Grammar. I had told no one that I was about to start driving lessons, and did not linger in the playground waiting for the car's arrival for fear of being spotted by prying eyes and two and two being put – cruelly – together. Instead, I took up position at the fire exit nearest where I thought that the instructor's car was most likely to stop. I was going to wait for the car to come to a complete standstill, then I'd take a quick glance about for spectators, and then all being well, I'd able to break cover, sprint the twenty feet or so to the car, jump in and demand that the instructor drove off school premises as quickly as possible.

I looked through the crack in the door as the car came to a stop. I opened the door and peeped out, only for the car to burst into life again and commence a manoeuvre. I'd seen a hundred driving instructors arrive and simply park before now with a minimum of fuss. So what the hell did this guy think he was *doing*? In order to turn the car around to face back towards the gates it was only necessary to turn a relatively tight circle. But my instructor seemed to think that the entirety of the empty playground represented space that had to be used, and began reversing with only the gentlest of steers back to the far corner of the playground. I tried to duck back into the building but the fire door had slammed shut behind me. I peeked up above me to see if any of the boys had yet come to the windows, but the coast was still mercifully clear. The instructor's car had reversed back as far as it possibly could now, and so I began walking towards it, only for it to start coming towards me at some speed, the engine roaring in a manner that I didn't think (and of course I'm no expert in these regards) sounded all that healthy. I waved at the driver to get his attention, and he acknowledged me by blasting his horn twice.

I hardly dared look over my shoulder now. Surely that would have started to bring people to the windows. He then executed what I later learnt is called an 'emergency stop', the noise and suddenness of which put me instantly on edge. I had wanted the first occasion that I was picked up from school by a driving instructor to be a discreet affair, not a series of loud, attention-grabbing stunts. I was absolutely convinced that my first experience was going to be appallingly nerve-wracking and was desperate to be eased in gently with a minimum of onlookers. But this clown from a ruddy barbecue was attempting to draw as large a crowd as possible.

When I was convinced that the car was absolutely not about to suddenly move off again, I began to tiptoe towards it, but the instructor had other ideas. He opened his door, leapt out and bellowed, 'Are you Damien Trench?'[2]

'Yes,' I said weakly. 'How do you do?'

'I'm Tony. I met your parents at a barbecue. Your dad's a right laugh!'

Tony, it seemed, was not only the owner of a three-door saloon; he also possessed a very thin moustache and rather more confidence than it was possible to find endearing. He leant his left elbow on the roof of his car and then stuck out his right hand for me to come and shake, like those ladies at publishing parties who proffer a cheek, leaving you no option but to advance and give them a peck. (I should clarify that the thought of giving Tony a peck could not have been further from my mind.)

'Nice school, this,' he said as he shook my hand, and looked up at the building. 'Oh, is it just for boys?'

2   Perhaps there is some connection between this incident and the feeling of complete fear that I am momentarily gripped by whenever I am recognised by one of my readers when I am 'out and about' such as the aforementioned incident in Swaffham. I can be approached by the kindest and gentlest-looking of sorts in a completely unthreatening environment such as a delicatessen or farmers' market or even a garden centre, and yet when they utter the words 'Are you Damien Trench?' I am quite often stuck by a sense of total, almost irrational, panic. This is why, on occasion, people who have approached me in this way have, before I've had a chance to calm down and gather myself, been met with a quite bewildering array of responses. 'Who's asking?', 'What of it?' and 'no' are all things that I have heard myself saying before taking a few deep breaths and saying something along the lines of, 'Well hello there. As a matter of fact I am.' Most people, by and large, tend to be delightful. Don't you think?

I followed his gaze, and gulped. Really rather hard. The windows that had been mercifully empty moments ago were, as a direct result of Tony's noisy manoeuvring and equally loud revealing of my identity, now lined with row upon row of expectant faces of boys gathered in anticipation of seeing somebody mess up. They looked, to a boy, absolutely delighted.

'They all there to watch you struggle?' laughed Tony. 'It's like the Colosseum.'

'The Colosseum doesn't have windows,' I said.

'What?' said Tony.

And then the banging began; hundreds of boys banging their fists against the windows and chanting my rather unimaginative nickname.

'Trench the Stench! Trench the Stench! Trench the Stench!'[3]

3 Not only was this nickname unimaginative in the *extreme*, it was also completely unwarranted. I had, and indeed always have had, an extremely conscientious approach to personal hygiene (certainly by that point in my school career) and looking back it seems deeply ironic that of all the boys at Willesden Grammar, I should be burdened with a moniker that suggests that I was anything less than fragrant. I have always been blessed with – I am proud but definitely not gloating to say – excellent olfactory senses, something that I get from my mother's side, I believe (one in the eye for those many, many people one meets who insist that sense of smell jumps a generation) and my taste buds and smell receptors are, dare I say it, really rather nuanced. I have showered or bathed twice a day – fastidiously – all my life and I never intend to stop. Even at a young age I took an active interest in soaps and bath products, placing as much if not more emphasis on their scent than I did their effect on the skin.

'Quite a crowd of admirers you've got there,' said Tony. 'Let's put a little show on for them. You. Driving seat. Now.'

I obeyed, but as I walked towards the car I could feel the blood draining from my face, and instead start to occupy my limbs and extremities, all of which began to throb with discomfort. The banging on the windows grew louder, and so did the chant that accompanied it, the first and third syllable matching the percussive downbeat. It was ugly, for sure, but in their defence it wasn't arrhythmic.

As I reached for the handle of the driver's door, I turned round and attempted to look up at the school building in as nonchalant a fashion as I could manage.[4] I was rather surprised to see that the numbers of the people at the windows had been swelled by the arrival of some of the

---

Not that I was bothered by this nickname, you understand. I was more than capable of laughing it off. But, privately, I found it to be absurd and hypocritical that I could be referred to as 'The Stench' by a group of people whose body odours when combined, after even light exercise, made our changing rooms a place where I found it impossible not to gag and retch. They all knew deep down that I didn't smell. They just gave me the name because – of course – it rhymed. There was also a boy called Kelly who they all called 'Smelly Kelly', which was equally preposterous. He actually smelled rather beautiful. But as I say, it's all in the past now, and does not bother me in the least.

4   Nowadays I absolutely abhor nonchalance in all forms, quite possibly in response to my days at school. Nonchalance is always affected, never actually felt, and is I think one of the main symptoms of the disingenuousness that is slowly killing this country. Twitter is possibly another. That said, it is an understandably valid tool in the armoury of a teenager.

teachers. Clearly they must have been attempting to clamp down on this behaviour, but whatever their efforts, they had been ineffectual. Several of them, perhaps in an attempt to empathise with the students and thus better understand their motives, had actually joined in with the banging and the chanting, but ceased when I saw what they were doing, my icy stare presumably bringing them to their senses. Mrs McKeith, the home economics teacher with whom I had clashed[5] on several occasions on a variety of subjects ranging from dried herbs and shop-bought pastry to the use of fan-assisted ovens, appeared to be smirking. I tried to hold her gaze, but soon realised that try as I might I couldn't actually open the driver's door without turning around. I was, in fact, grasping only at thin air, and a quick peek in the direction of the car showed me that the handle was still a good six inches out of my reach. Clearly my nervous spasms, or perhaps a subconscious determination, were drawing me away from the car. The laughter emanating from the school building rose as I turned to give the handle my full attention, but still I couldn't get the blasted thing to open.

'Oh yes, should have mentioned that,' said Tony. 'She can be a bit stiff sometimes. No luck?'

'None so far.'

'You stay there and keep trying, I'll get in and open her up from the inside.'

I did not like the way that Tony talked about his car.

5   Verbally.

In fact I already felt very keenly indeed that I wouldn't like the way that Tony talked about *anything*. I was suddenly desperate, though, to be inside that car. Not so that I could share a confined space with Tony and his doubtless ill-chosen aftershave, but just so that I could shut the door and muffle the sounds of my fellow pupils and several of the staff, who were now laughing even harder as I tugged vainly at the door handle. I shut my eyes and pulled at the door with all my might, but at that moment Tony must have leant across and released it from the inside, and the next thing I knew the thing opened and connected with me with considerable force.

The very next thing I knew was that I was now on the floor of the playground writhing around, winded and clutching my knees to my chest in agony. The noise now emanating from the school building was just animalistic, and the thought of the looks on the faces of those making the noise was too unbearable to even contemplate. The door had hit me in the – I'm sorry to use the word, but it's hard to paint the picture without it – testicles very, very hard. Harder, in fact, than I had ever been hit in the testicles before, and I had been hit in the testicles *a lot*. Mainly by Angela, who was going through a period in her life when she felt that this made for a sensible denouement to a wide range of discussions. The crunch of footsteps near my side alerted me to the presence of Tony, who had got out of the car and was now standing over me.

'Are you all right, Damien?' he asked. 'It rather looks to me as if you've caught one in the gonads.'

Tony's sneering use of the word 'gonads', and the drawling manner in which he rolled the word around mouth, lengthening and stressing each syllable, made me feel even sicker. *GOWE-NAAADS.* Ghastly.

'I … can't … breathe,' I said. I opened my eyes to see Tony staring down at me, his face a mixture of faux-concern and ill-concealed amusement. 'Gets more painful as time goes on, doesn't it?'

The fool was right, of course. The pain did get worse.

'I'll be fine,' I said. But then I was sick. And then I blacked out.

Someone arrived with a glass of water, and Tony and a teacher helped me up, and dusted me down. It was agreed, sensibly, I think, that perhaps there was no need to go any further with today's driving lesson. I'd got as far as opening the door, after all, and it's generally best not to rush these things. Tony slapped me hard on the back, said 'I'll be in touch with your parents' before getting in the car, still chuckling to himself, and driving off. The teacher led me gingerly back to the school building so that I could be taken to the nurse's room. I looked back up at the school building, but the windows were now deserted. All apart from one, in which stood Mrs McKeith, who had a blank expression on her face but was slowly and silently hand-clapping me. She knew nothing about cookery, that woman. Nothing.

I tried driving lessons again in the school holidays, but it wasn't a success. And although I can remember my first driving lesson in excruciating detail, the others I received and how it all ended remain a blur. I can only very vaguely remember a light going from amber to green, a mis-step on a pedal, a stalling engine, the sound of Tony's rueful laughter, and a cacophony of honks from behind. Then a callow, regretful, haunted seventeen-year-old, flinging open the driver's door and sprinting off, deaf to the pleas of his instructor. 'Damien! Damien! Come back! There's twenty minutes left! We've still got to do some work on your reversing around corners! You've left your scarf!' But on ran the teenager, never to see that scarf or sit in the driver's seat ever again.

That being the case, however, I do like to think of myself as being rather a good passenger. When I am at home in London I make a point of using public transport whenever possible. (In fact, I make a point of using public transport *wherever* possible too – Berlin, Paris, Manchester, Hull, Oxford, Andover, Abergavenny, Inverness, Ipswich, Canterbury, Brighton, Budapest, Tokyo, Stockport, Glasgow, Edinburgh, Dundee, Kirkcaldy, Largs. I have had memorable bus journeys in all these places.) That is to say, I use public transport for distances that would be impossible to cover *on foot*. I absolutely love walking, but sometimes one has to say 'enough is enough'. In a city, I tend to think that any journey over about four miles is probably a bit much for the old shoe leather. And if I'm laden down with shopping, then it may well be consid-erably less than that.

Years and years of pounding away in the kitchen has left me with reasonably strong upper body and core strength, but even so, anything more than a full Bag for Life in each hand, and I'll probably begin to tire after about a mile and a half. I once popped into, entirely on the off-chance, a grocer's shop in Paddington. The man behind the counter had, as a result of some sort of brain malfunction (something I can certainly empathise with. Heaven knows I've had the odd temporary short circuit of the mental wiring: I once signed up for a twelve-week spin class), ordered in a quantity of quinces that defied belief or reason. The whole place was absolutely fit to bursting with the things, and the poor man seemed to me to be at his wit's end about it.

'I'm just going to have to throw them all away,' he said. 'I don't think I've sold one, and I've got so many it looks like that's all I sell.'

Now, in defence of the people of Paddington, the quince is by no means the most versatile of fruits. And whatever the cultural make-up of the area is, and I'm no expert, it didn't seem to be one that was conducive to large-scale preserve making. Which is, not to put too fine a point on it, a damn shame. Quince preserve is utterly heavenly. Especially with manchego.

'You can't just throw them away. That's practically criminal. It would be an unforgiveable act of waste,' I said. (I hate, and have always hated, waste. It's one of the things that makes me most ashamed to be from the western world.) 'I'll take the lot. Fifty pounds?'

'Forty,' said the man, and we shook on it.

But in fact 'the lot' proved to be far, far too many. After we'd filled every single one of the Bags for Life that I tend to keep carefully folded about my person at all times (seven), it began to dawn on me that there was simply no possible way that I could take any more. I'd done a few rough mental calculations as we were loading the bags, and had already come to the shocking realisation that my larder was already forty jars short for the job in hand. Obviously the Kilner Company was going to be benefiting from my incorrigible impulsiveness.

'Actually, I don't think I could possibly take any more than this,' I said. 'I simply won't cope.'

'But what shall I do with the others?' the man said.

'Oh, just throw them away,' I said. 'Nobody will mind.'

'I'm going to compost them,' he said.

'Quite right,' I said. 'That would be my suggestion.'

I staggered out into the street with four bags in my left hand, and four in my right (I was already carrying a large bag of brown rice, did I say?) and immediately began to list wildly. I am not blessed with enviable balance at the best of times (possibly to do with one of the several inner-ear infections I suffered as a child), and four large Bags for Life filled to the brim with quinces is very slightly less heavy than three large Bags for Life filled to the brim with quinces and one filled with brown rice, and I found myself unable to compensate for the difference. I took three slow and tentative steps forward, then put the bags down and swapped them over to see if I had any luck carrying each bag in the opposite hand, which meant that I was now facing in the opposite direction to that which I intended to travel. So having picked the bags up again, I tried to demi-pirouette but the weight was too much and I fell forward on to the bags, knocking two of them over.

The man from the shop came out and helped me reload the bags. I gave as best assistance as I could from my position on all fours, but then more customers arrived and the man went back into the shop to serve them. I stayed on my haunches for a period of no longer than four or five minutes to get my breath and nerve back, until a policeman squatted down in front of me, accused me of drinking and asked if there was someone he could call. I told him that it wasn't sobriety I was lacking in, but upper body strength and sufficient jars.

Twenty-five minutes later my partner Anthony opened the front door to a policeman explaining to him in a solemn voice that I had been found drunk and slumped in the Paddington area, and needed looking after. Anthony looked, understandably, aghast at this idea.

'He's not really a daytime drinker,' Anthony said.

'I'm really not,' I said.

'Explain this, then,' said the policeman. And went to the car to retrieve my Bags for Life.

'Would a sober man buy this much fruit?' he said, placing the bags down on the doorstep.

'No,' said Anthony.

'I'll leave him with you, sir,' said the officer, and headed back to his car.

'I've just over-reached myself,' I told Anthony. 'I haven't been drinking.'

'I know,' he said. 'But I thought it was just easier to admit that you were, rather than trying to explain to him what you're actually like.'

I have no idea what he was talking about, but he says these maddening things from time to time. Anyway, rare instances like these aside, I prefer to walk.

But when walking or public transport aren't options (thank you, by the way, Dr Beeching; thank you *very much*) then Anthony and I will travel in our pastel blue Fiat Uno. Given that Anthony is six foot seven, it might seem a somewhat extraordinary choice for us to choose a car that is so very small. The Fiat Uno is often termed a 'super-mini', and certainly it is not the most spacious vehicle on the road. But as with everything, an awful lot of thought went into our purchase of the vehicle. It is extremely rare for us to carry more than one passenger in the back, and so Anthony is able to put his seat back as far as is possible without fear of crushing any occupant immediately to his rear. The height of the steering wheel is also adjustable, so that he is able to position it higher than his still very high knees. It's refreshing, actually, to see a steering wheel so high these days. It looks rather old-fashioned, as if Anthony is Spencer Tracy or the like. Which makes me Katharine Hepburn, I suppose. I certainly agree with much of what she had to say about discipline and rules. 'Without discipline, there's no life at all,' she once said. And I completely agree. I mean you've got to force yourself out of bed in the morning and get on with the day, haven't you? More pertinent is her remark that 'if you obey all the rules, you miss all the fun', which I have framed in our kitchen. It's become something of a maxim for me in the kitchen, actually. A lot of cookery writers can be incredibly prescriptive, but I don't think that's fair to people. You've got to leave room for people's instincts and tastes. There are a lot of people who say that you should only cook your meringues in the oven, and never use a blowtorch on them. Well, I'm sorry but I simply cannot agree. If you're lucky enough to have a blowtorch – and if you're the sort of person who enjoys a brûlée you'd be mad not to save up for one, by the way – then you should jolly well make sure that you take the chance to use it. If you don't like using a blowtorch on your meringues, fine. Don't. But don't deny others the right to. The kitchen is not a dictatorship. Mine isn't anyway. If it were I wouldn't ever allow Anthony to do paperwork in ours, but as it is I simply cannot stop him.

We have never been the sort of people to look enviably upon those who drive 'gas-guzzlers'. Our planet, may I remind you, is dying. Running a car that is bigger than you actually need is an act of brutal irresponsibility, and such people should probably be taxed more heavily. And not just at the pumps. These sorts of large vehicles are also, by and large, most unaesthetic. I'm not suggesting that we should always value beauty over sustainability, but it must be a consideration. If you choose to have beautiful things, you make the world a better place for people whose gaze falls upon them. Likewise, if you buy ugly things, then you cause others distress, and such people should probably be taxed more heavily. This is why the arts deserve to be subsidised. The joy they bring actually improves the health of the nation. Apart, notably, from the frankly disastrous period when Mary something-or-other was chief executive of the Royal Opera House. And the Uno, originally an Italian design, of course, but now Brazilian made, is a lovely looking thing. Certainly for a car. If you're prepared to ignore the straightness of the edges for a moment, it has something of the Aga about it, and that I find incredibly comforting. (Although the Uno, it must be said, warms up and cools down rather quicker!)

'But don't you struggle for boot space?' we're often asked. Well, the quick answer, as it happens, is, 'No. We don't, actually.' Whenever we go anywhere, we bring nothing with us that isn't absolutely essential. Anthony is in charge of loading the car, and I am in charge of the actual packing. We have two small, and indeed matching, suitcases. Montblanc is our current preferred brand. I cannot pretend that these are inexpensive, but they really are worth it for their winning blend of beauty and inde-structibility. As a younger man I was – and I'm rather embarrassed to think of myself being like this – very much of the opinion that one could get by with cheap luggage. But actually one cannot, as eventually I found to my cost somewhere on a bumpy train ride between Milan and Genoa, when my suitcase was thrown from the luggage rack, split open on impact and its contents (including, inevitably, a number of Parma hams) went *everywhere*. It was a life-changing incident in many ways, and I've not skimped on luggage since. Nor would I wish you to. Small suitcases are always big enough if you pack carefully. (Have you read Marie Kondo on folding? Oh, but you must. You'll see your underwear in a completely new light.)

Anthony, when we were first courting, was the sort of person who would just blindly bung any old thing that came to hand into an astonishingly and needlessly capacious suitcase, and think that he'd probably be covered for all eventualities. This was an area of his life in which I could see I was going to have to make efforts to mould him somewhat. Because he would invariably be wrong. I once took him away for the weekend to stay with some friends of mine in Sussex, and after they had shown us into their guest bedroom (beautifully appointed, actually. I don't think you can ever go wrong with a bit of tongue and groove in an *ensuite*) and told us to make ourselves comfortable before aiming to come downstairs again for pre-dinner drinks at approximately quarter to seven, Anthony hauled his enormous *impedimenta* on to the bed, opened it up and its contents made me instantly stagger. I shall never forget what I saw before me: six pairs of socks (black), three pairs of 'basketball shorts' (lurid), four T-shirts (emblazoned with the names of various breweries), a single plaid shirt (rather nice actually) and a pair of trousers I couldn't even bring myself to garden in unless for some reason I wanted to leave my neighbours under the impression that I was in the grip of a psychotic episode. There was also a toothbrush, a tube of toothpaste and a travel-sized deodorant (roll-on), that he'd packed loose. He'd brought no shoes with him other than the black Oxfords he wore for work. I don't think I have ever felt so panicked. Anthony, still standing in his business suit, seemed incapable of sharing my terror.

'What's wrong?' he said. 'It's all comfortable stuff.'

'Comfortable?' I said. *'Comfortable?* I can't parade you in front of my friends dressed in any of this stuff!'

'I don't want to be paraded,' he said. 'I'm not a horse.'

'A horse', I said, 'would probably have put rather more thought into its packing.'

'Well, perhaps you should have invited a horse instead?' he said, sitting heavily on the bed. 'You told me that this was just going to be a relaxed weekend.'

'"Relaxed" doesn't mean "dress as if you hold the rest of the world in contempt".'

Still, there's no point making a big deal of things, and we did the best we could. I steamed Anthony's trousers in the bathroom, mended a few tears, borrowed an iron and told a slight fib about his having taken his weekend shoes to be resoled and the cobbler having to suddenly shut unexpectedly early owing to the high pollen count. I made him wear one of my V-necks over his shoulders as an accessory and told Anthony to stand, where possible, in shadow and we *just about* got away with it, but my goodness it was nerve-wracking. Anthony, for reasons beyond me, struggled to relax so I didn't, alas, pass the most restful of weekends. But we learnt a valuable lesson. Anthony was going to have to change. And in future, Anthony was not allowed to zip shut any item of luggage without me having first inspected its contents. Such compromises are an essential part of all relationships, I told him. He agreed only grudgingly at first, but in time he has become completely reconciled to the idea and I have often noticed that while I am doing all of the tidying and packing in advance of one of our trips he is actually relaxed enough about it to just put his feet up in front of the television or doze on one of the sofas, which I think represents real progress.

Besides our clothing, and spongebags, we actually bring very little with us when we travel. I don't like to bring food with us, for instance, unless it's in the form of a gift for a host (such as nice things from Fortnum's or – if we've had the chance to get north – Betty's). I do not like to build up too many food miles, and prefer to always shop locally. We have, however, been burnt one too many times by inadequate kitchen utensils when staying in self-catering properties, and so we will travel with a few essentials: a cafetière, two sizes of stove-top espresso maker, napkins (with rings), carving knives, cheese knives, preparation knives, a set of chopping boards (colour coded, from Joseph), wine glasses, a corkscrew, a casserole dish, a tagine, a pestle and mortar, tongs and a cutlery canteen. These can all fit very happily in the boot along-side the suitcases, or across the backseat or even behind my chair. It does not, alas, leave space for hitchhikers, but we always give them a cheery wave, or roll down the window (actually the windows are electric, but it's a phrase I love too much to just let it die) and offer them the best of British. I cannot guarantee that people always understand exactly what it is that I'm shouting in these instances, and I have occasionally been accused of sarcasm (or worse), but such is life.

I can normally get all the packing done in a shade under three hours, and I actually find it a very soothing experience. I then leave it by the front door and Anthony places it in the car extremely quickly (too quickly for my liking, sometimes. 'Place it don't plonk it,' I often implore him. 'We just need to *go*,' he usually says) and then starts up the engine.

The other reason why we prefer a car that size is for ease of parking. Anthony, despite all the incredibly helpful assistance I offer him in a loud and clear voice, has never been at his most relaxed when attempting to manoeuvre into a tight parking space. The Uno can be steered into a tight spot more easily than most, and also comes with parking sensors. These are a bit of a godsend, actually, because Anthony doesn't have the most flexible of necks, and thus struggles to twist around to the extent that most drivers can when reversing. Anthony says that the incessant beeping of the sensors puts him on edge, and 'only makes things worse'. They have saved us, I like to tell him, absolutely thousands on insurance payouts and premiums.

It is, by the way, an automatic car. Anthony is only licensed to drive automatics owing, he says, to an administrative error. I'm not entirely sure that I believe him, but I never see the point in just starting rows for the sake of it. But even though I cannot drive, I do like to think that I am an extremely good passenger. I enjoy, for instance, shouting out whenever I spot a potential hazard ahead or to either side that I think Anthony may have missed, and I'm more than happy to be in charge of the navigation. Anthony did actually buy a rather flash 'sat nav' to 'save me the bother', but to be perfectly honest I'm not entirely sure I trust it, so I always keep the AA map open on my lap, and check that we're absolutely taking the best course there is. As a child, roads and routes bored me to tears, but as an adult I am positively brimming with enthusiasm for discussing them to an extent that Anthony sometimes describes, jokingly, as 'grotesque'. I am often having to compete with the voice of the 'sat nav' which Anthony likes to turn up to maximum. There is a range of voices you can choose from, my favourite being a lady called Jennifer with whom I generally agree, even if she could afford to speak more quietly. We once selected an Irish voice called Sean thinking that this too would be soothing, but then he once took us on a route around Bracknell that was so circuitous that Anthony made some rather unacceptable remarks about the Irish. As a result we had to give Sean the old heave-ho.

In addition to us hanging on Jennifer's every word, we listen to Radio 4 or Radio 3. There are commercial stations with playlists that I can tolerate, but I have to turn them off whenever any adverts begin, and Anthony finds this unsettling. Radio 3 we listen to not just for the wonderful music, but also for the marvellous presenters and continuity announcers, every single one of whom is possessed of a voice that one can positively luxuriate in. Listening to Tom Service talking about opera is, in pure sensory terms, not an altogether different experience to having a hot, scented and foamy bath and a loved one bringing you in a mug of tea mid-soak.

Radio 4 is for when one really wishes to engage the brain that little bit more, and perhaps listen to a first-person documentary about goat-herding or women's issues, most of which I can personally empathise with. In fact I never miss *Woman's Hour* if I can at all help it. Anthony is less keen, it must be said, and so I sometimes have to listen on catch up, but speaking from my own point of view, there is very little that I wouldn't happily listen to coming out of the mouths of Jenni Murray or Jane Garvey. The continuity announcer department of Radio 4 is probably the greatest team this country has, and one of its most undersung. I'm not an expert on sports, but I'm not sure that any of our national football teams set the world ablaze with any regularity, and yet they seem to be the ones who occupy the front and back pages of our press. If I had things my way, people would wander about in shirts with the names of Neil Sleat, Susan Rae or Zeb Soanes on and not ????. The biggest downside to Radio 4 is its comedy output which is, without exception, awful. The people on

Please could somebody insert the names of some footballers here?

it are either smug mutterers or sound like dissolute university lecturers struggling to remember *bons mots* they once
overheard in the 1980s, and being rewarded by applause
from the audience when they eventually do so. Sad.

This is one of the many reasons I feel quite sure that
Anthony absolutely loves having me as his passenger.
Anthony needs someone not just to offer alternative navi-
gational ideas, to point out hazards and to fiddle about
with the air conditioning,[6] but also to be in charge of the
radio. Being able to change the radio station is a real skill
for a passenger. It is simply far too much of a complicated
procedure for a driver to manage all by themselves while
keeping both eyes on the road and both hands on the
wheel. Or one hand on the wheel and the other on the
gearstick. Also, the buttons on the thing, in keeping with
the Uno as a whole, are absolutely tiny and represent
something of a challenge for somebody of Anthony's
dimensions. He has very big fingers, and what's more
they barely seem to taper at the ends and thus consequently he needs help coping with all small buttons that
he faces in life. So I am in charge of the radio and can
control it to Anthony's whim. Certain things always put
him on edge – If he hears *The Archers'* theme tune, John

6 Anthony doesn't like to be too hot when he's driving. Nor
   does he like to be too cold. He prefers it, if I'm being
   completely blunt about it, somewhere in the middle. Probably
   on the colder side of the middle though. Not the warmer. It
   can depend though. Whatever: I'm ready to leap into action
   whenever the call to turn the air con up or down or on or
   off comes, and Anthony finds this a great comfort. Bless him.

Humphreys being needlessly aggressive about something he probably doesn't know anything much about anyway or the man on the Saturday morning show that Anthony calls 'that half-arsed vicar', then he'll scream 'CHANGE IT!', and I will jolly well jump to it.[7]

So as a passenger, I have much to offer. But get behind the wheel of a car again? You have to be ruddy joking.

Chocolate Biscuit Cake

Sometimes, as my partner Anthony tells me, all you need is a very naughty, very sticky treat. I used to cook this when I was a very callow youth indeed, and it would give me the most astonishing sugar rush, after which I would feel rather teary and then take to my bed for some hours. I take a thinner slice these days.

For this you will need ...
  Golden syrup, 8 oz of
  Butter, salted, 12 oz of

---

7 I somehow seem to have not made it clear that we also listen to audiobooks. Anthony likes crime novels. I do not. But of course so much actually depends on the narrator. David Sibley is wonderful. Imogen Stubbs is a dream. And as for Martin Jarvis, well ... it's all just marvellous. I could probably very happily listen to Martin Jarvis reading *Mein Kampf*. (Don't check for it, it doesn't exist. It's not been commercially released at any rate. If Martin Jarvis has made an audio recording of *Mein Kampf* then I can only assume it's for personal use.)

Dark chocolate, 4 oz of, that has been broken into chunks

Cocoa powder, 2 oz of

Vanilla essence, a few shakes

Digestives, 1 lb of, jumped up and down on whilst in a sturdy bag

Nuts of your choice, 2 oz of. Walnuts are a bit sour, pistachios too salty, hazelnuts are rather fun – but it's a good idea to roast them a little first. Makes them sweeter and crumblier.

You will also need some more chocolate (about another 14 oz or so) for the topping of whatever type you most enjoy – it could all be dark chocolate, or you could mix it up with some white chocolate. I don't ever use white chocolate though because it is disgusting.

And get a bag of Revels

Get down a big heavy pan with a lovely thick bottom and put the syrup and butter in it and slowly melt them together with a medium heat. When they've melted, take them off the heat and add the broken-up dark chocolate and the cocoa powder and some generous drops of vanilla essence and stir it all together until you have a mightily smooth oneness to which you can now add the bashed-up biscuits and the nuts. Stir again until everything is well combined.

Then line a deep enough seven-inch circular tin

with some baking parchment and pour the mixture into it, spreading it around the tin if it hasn't poured evenly. Set it to one side until it's room temperature and then cover it with cling film and refrigerate. It will need a few hours in there to really harden, so don't panic. Go out and watch a foreign-language film at your local independent cinema or something. Or lie on the sofa with your eyes closed.

All you need to do once the cake has set is melt your (hopefully) dark chocolate, pour it slowly over the cake, and spread it flat with a knife. Then place the Revels into the soft chocolate before it can harden. (Revels are one of my guiltiest pleasures.) It is done. All you need to do is store it in the fridge, ideally in something airtight. If I ever make one of these I also put it in a box so that it's disguised, then if Anthony asks what it is I tell him that it's fish. If I don't he will eat the whole ruddy lot.

Chapter 15

WELL, WHATEVER NEXT?

I left Willesden Grammar unable to drive but with four A-levels and a place at the University of Oxford to study P.P.E. I was incredibly excited about the prospect of going up to Oxford, due in no small part to my great love of Evelyn Waugh's *Brideshead Revisted* and indeed the Granada Television adaptation of the early 1980s. People who don't really know about these things often seem to have the impression that the whole thing is about Oxford, but it really is not. It is on an epic scale. Personally my favourite scenes from the series weren't those that featured Oxford at all but later ones on a cruise liner when Jeremy Irons keeps going to bed with Diana Quick and Jane Asher won't stop being sick. But the Oxford sequences, though rather glib and a little 'anyone for tennis', do have a certain charm. I think the fact that Sebastian Flyte loves quails' eggs is a point very much in his favour. The fact that Anthony Blanche loves *The Waste Land* counts very much against him.

But Oxford, to which I went up immediately – so desperate was I to move on from school – was not at all how I imagined it would be. My college was rather drab, and the sort of people who studied P.P.E. were impossible to get along with, awfully ambitious and deeply venal. I see many of them on the television these days working in various government jobs and I do not miss their company at all.

I came home from Oxford after the first term, and told my parents something that they were absolutely not expecting.

'Mother? Father? I have something to tell you. I am going to catering college.'

Well, I'm sure you can imagine how that went down.*

But that's another story. And a story for another time. The rather splendid bells of the rather splendid church spire that I can see from my study window (admittedly if I put my face right up against the glass and then crane hard and left) are soon to be chiming six, and the working day is nearly done. I put a tagine that I made yesterday afternoon in the warming oven some three hours ago, and it will soon be nearing perfection. Down two flights of thickly carpeted stairs I can hear my partner Anthony pouring gin and tonics, having just opened the French windows to let in a little air. All I have to do is prepare a little green salad, cook some couscous and slice some fabulously crusty bread. It may even be mild enough to eat on the terrace. Anthony went out to the delicatessen earlier today and came back laden with cheeses so the board will be absolutely groaning. He's had his eye on a pair of bottles of Haut-Médoc all week and it may well be their night. Sky Arts are screening a documentary about Isabelle Huppert later, plus I recorded one about Dame

*Bit of an abrupt ending, I fancy.

Yes, do you like it? I recently read Every Day by David Levithan.

I see. You're not deliberately holding something back for Volume Two, are you?

What an appallingly cynical thought. Absolutely not. That said, I've heaps to tell.

Judi Dench earlier in the week, so we shan't be short of entertainment.

I've left myself a few moments to reflect on the journey that we've all just been on together. Nearly 300 or so pages ago I was but a baby, and look at me now; I have somehow entered adulthood. It's not always been a straightforward venture writing this memoir for you, but my goodness it's made me think. I've also had to spend a lot of time chatting to my family about my childhood, and I think we've all rather enjoyed the opportunity to have a bit of a natter and indulge in some no-holds-barred nostalgia. Apart from my sister Angela, who told me she had no interest in it whatsoever. I've left several messages on her phone asking if she might help corroborate a few of the claims made within these pages, but she has not come back to me. Ralph was a little more forthcoming. He sent me a text message saying simply: 'WRITE WHATEVER YOU LIKE, CHEF!'

I hope you've managed to enjoy it. My family is by no means an 'ordinary' one, and on reflection our dynamic seems positively perverse at times. But at the same time I also feel quite convinced that many of our traits are universal. And I do hope that the way that I felt as a younger man strikes a chord with the experiences of others. We are all, I hope, never as alone as we imagine.

Sometimes reflecting on my past has been a source of joy and excitement. Other times it has made feel anxious and a little put out. It has also, it must be said, made me feel a little sad at times. But not, it may surprise you to know, about those episodes of my life that you might expect; the thing that I am saddest about when I look back is how often – until I turned my back on university (something I hope that we'll look at in more detail in Volume Two)[*] – is how often I allowed life to be something that just happened to me, rather than something that I seized by the horns and made a ruddy good go of. I would wonder and worry about how things would turn out, without attempting to control them. This is something that I have changed about myself, and I hope it is something that you feel that you could change about yourself, should you so choose. I believe in the existence of destiny, but I believe that it exists in our own hands. If there is something that you want to do, or see or feel, then you should just go for it. And hopefully these desires will fall within the law and accord to societal norms. Or you might just have to ignore these desires. Still, thanks for your company on this ride. That is all the story I have to tell for now. What a lovely evening it looks like being.

Had a re-think?

No. Merely keeping, as ever, an open mind

ACKNOWLEDGEMENTS

Damien Trench:

This book simply would not exist were it not for the Herculean efforts of my literary agent Ian Frobisher. As loyal and hard-working a literary agent could not be conceived of even in fiction.

My partner Anthony has been a source of great encouragement too, making innumerable pots of tea and trying to keep my spirits up whenever they very occasionally flagged.

I would also like to thank my editor, whose name briefly escapes me.

Miles Jupp:

I would like to thank the many cookery writers whose work I enjoy so much that I began to consider the possibility of inventing one of my own. People sometimes ask me if Damien is based on Nigel Slater or Simon Hopkinson and the fact of the matter is that he isn't. But he is very definitely someone that does the job they do, and who I wouldn't have tried to invent if they didn't exist. I like their work enormously. It is sometimes said that Eric Idle wrote *The Rutles* not because he wanted take the piss out of the Beatles, but because he wished that he'd been one. This is the spirit, I hope, in which I have written about the world of Damien Trench. I can't read Slater or Hopkinson on food without wishing that I could be and write like them. Thank you, gentlemen.

My mother is appalled by/delights in the idea that Damien's mother is based on her. If there is any overlap at all it is extremely minimal, although not coincidental. I would like to thank my mother for – for the most part – not being like Mrs Trench.

I am indebted to the efforts of Richard Roper and Lindsay Davies for their editing and copy-editing respectively. Good people.

My agent Molly Wansell is just marvellous.

I also want to thank many people who worked on *In and Out of the Kitchen* on the radio and on television including Justin Edwards, Selina Cadell, Brendan Dempsey, Philip Fox, Lesley Vickerage, Chris Brand, James Kettle, Nick Revell, Ade Oyefeso, Mandie Fletcher, Margaret Cabourn Smith, Graeme Rooney, Shaquille Ali-Yebuah, Sam Michell, Gareth Edwards, Maggie Service, Georgina Rich, Sarah Tansey, Mark Wood, Rachel Stubbings, Geoff Slack and Chris Morris and everyone at Guilt Free Studios, as well as many members of the BBC Radio Drama Company who did such amazing work.